and its Ene

MRS. MARY RIGHTEOUS EXPLAINS HER POSITION TO THE POPE

The Permissive Society and its Enemies

Sixties British Culture

Edited by Marcus Collins

R O
Rivers Oram Press
London, Chicago, Sydney

Published in 2007
by Rivers Oram Press, an imprint of Rivers Oram Publishers Ltd
144 Hemingford Road, London, N1 1DE

Distributed in the USA by
Independent Publishers Group, Franklin Street, Chicago, IL 60610
Distributed in Australia and New Zealand by
UNIReps, University of New South Wales, Sydney, NSW 2052

Set in Baskerville by NJ Design
and printed in Great Britain by T.J. International Ltd, Padstow

Frontispiece reproduced by courtesy of Gerald Scarfe

British Library Cataloguing in Publication Data
A CIP catalogue record for this publication is available from the British Library

ISBN 978 185489 147 1 (paperback)
ISBN 978 185489 146 4 (hardback)

Contents

Notes on the Contributors

Colin Campbell is Professor of Sociology at the University of York. He has published widely in the fields of the sociology of religion, the sociology of consumption, sociological theory, and culture and cultural change, and is probably best known for *The Romantic Ethic and the Spirit of Modern Consumerism* (Oxford, 1987) and *The Myth of Social Action* (Cambridge, 1996). His research on cultural change in the modern era has recently been published under the title of *The Easternisation of The West.*

Gerry Carlin lectures in English at the University of Wolverhampton and has published in the areas of modernism and twentieth-century culture.

Rychard Carrington hangs moderately loosely in Cambridge, England. In 2002 he completed a doctoral thesis entitled 'Cultural and Ideological Challenges of the London Underground Movement, 1965–1971' at Anglia Polytechnic University. He does a little teaching at Anglia and at The Open University. He also performs poetry and reviews folk and old rock music.

Marcus Collins is Research Lecturer at Bangor University and Assistant Professor of Modern British History at Emory University in Atlanta. He is author of *Modern Love: An Intimate History of Men and Women in Twentieth-Century Britain* (London, 2003) as well as a number of articles on gender, sexuality, popular culture and national identity. He is researching the Beatles, and the experience of postmodernity in late twentieth-century Britain.

Matt Houlbrook is Senior Lecturer in History at the University of Liverpool where he teaches in the social and cultural history of twentieth-century Britain. His book, *Queer London: Pleasures and Perils in the Sexual Metropolis, 1918–57*, was published by the University of Chicago Press in 2005. With Harry Cocks, he's edited the collection of essays, *The Palgrave Guide to the History of Sexuality* (Basingstoke, 2005).

Julian Jackson is Professor of Modern French History at Queen Mary College, University of London. He has written widely on the history of twentieth-century France from the 1930s to the 1960s. His most recent book, *The Fall of France* (Oxford, 2003), was one of the winners of the Wolfson history prize in 2003. He is working on the politics of French homosexuality after 1945 with particular reference to the French homophile movement 'Arcadie'.

Mark Jones is a Senior Lecturer in English at the University of Wolverhampton, where he teaches contemporary literature and culture, and also contributes to the Film Studies courses. He has written on science fiction, pornography and popular music.

Arthur Marwick was Emeritus Professor of History at The Open University, UK, where he set up the History Department in 1969 and founded the Sixties Research Group in 1992. He held visiting professorships at Buffalo, New York; Stanford; Paris, France; Memphis, Tennessee; and Perugia, Italy. His most important recent publications are *Beauty in History: Society, Politics and Personal Appearance* (London, 1988); *The Deluge: British Society and the First World War* (2nd edn, London, 1991); *The Sixties: Cultural Revolution in Britain, France, Italy and the United States,* c. *1958–74* (Oxford, 1998); *A Modern History of the British Isles, 1914–1999: Circumstances, Events and Outcomes* (Oxford, 2000); *The New Nature of History: Knowledge, Evidence, Language* (London and Chicago, 2001); *The Arts in the West since 1945* (Oxford, 2002); *British Society since 1945* (4th edn, London, 2003); and *It: A History of Human Beauty* (London, 2004).

Alison Oram is Professor of Cultural History at Leeds Metropolitan University. She has published widely on gender and lesbian history, including *The Lesbian History Sourcebook: Love and Sex between Women in Britain from 1780 to 1970* (London, 2001), co-authored with Annmarie Turnbull, and *'Her Husband was a Woman!': Women's Gender Crossing in Modern British Popular Culture* (London, 2007). She is currently working on the politics of sexuality and gender in public and private history making.

Willie Thompson comes from a peasant background in Shetland and was educated there and at Scottish universities. He was an activist in the Communist Party from 1962 until its disbandment in 1991. Latterly he was Professor of Contemporary History at Glasgow Caledonian University and is the author of several books on the history of the left. He is currently secretary of the Socialist History Society and lives in Sunderland.

Acronyms

BSSSP	British Society for the Study of Sex Psychology
CCCS	Centre for Contemporary Cultural Studies, University of Birmingham
CHE	Campaign for Homosexual Equality
CND	Campaign for Nuclear Disarmament
COC	Cultuur en Ontspanningscentrum (Culture and Leisure Centre, Netherlands)
CP	Communist Party
CUARH	Comité d'Urgence Anti-Répression Homosexuelle (Emergency Committee against Homosexual Repression, France)
FHAR	Front Homosexuel d'Action Révolutionnaire (Homosexual Revolutionary Action Front, France)
GLF	Gay Liberation Front
GLH	Groupes de Libération Homosexuel (Homosexual Liberation Groups, France)
HLRS	Homosexual Law Reform Society
ICSE	International Committee for Sexual Equality
MRG	Minorities Research Group
NSM	New Social Movement
NWHLRS	North Western Homosexual Law Reform Society
PACS	Pacte Civil de Solidarité (Civil Solidarity Pact, France)
PIE	Paedophile Information Exchange
RSSF	Revolutionary Socialist Students Federation
SDS	Students for a Democratic Society, USA

USASLL Socialist Labour League
SWP Socialist Workers' Party
WLM Women's Liberation Movement
YCL Young Communist League

Acknowledgements

Most of the chapters in this volume were first presented at the XVth Summer Conference of the Institute (now Centre) for Contemporary British History. Heartfelt thanks go all those who participated in the conference and especially to its organisers, Harriet Jones, Michael Kandiah, Virginia Preston and David Cannadine. The Rivers Oram team of Liz Fidlon, Linda Etchart and Caroline Lazar provided invaluable support and guidance throughout, as (in a different manner) did my partner, Leonie Welberg. The University of Newcastle generously gave me the time and resources to start a project that was to be finished at Emory University with the assistance of an exceptional graduate student, Joe Renouard. However, the biggest thank you goes to the contributors, whose perseverance brought to completion a project that proved to be harder and larger than any of us had originally imagined.

Marcus Collins
Atlanta, 2005

Dedication

As this volume went to press, one of its contributors died. It is dedicated to the memory of Arthur Marwick (1936–2006): an inimitable product of, and expert on, the 1960s.

1. Introduction
The Permissive Society and its Enemies

Marcus Collins

How might we write the history of *The History Man*? Malcolm Bradbury's 1975 novel of that name is set in 1972, at the fag-end of an incendiary era. The action takes place in Watermouth, an English university town with its due complement of drop-outs and tenured radicals. Its protagonist is the trendy sociologist Howard Kirk, who has jettisoned his parents' 'code of ethical constraint' in pursuit of power and pleasure.[1] The plot revolves around his quest to impose his will upon all those he encounters at work and play, bedding women and baiting liberals along the way.

There are several ways to read a text of this kind.[2] One is to treat it as fiction rather than fact and, as such, the province of cultural criticism: one reason for the dearth of historical scholarship on the 'Swinging Sixties' and its close cousin, the permissive society. Another is to view it as a period piece testifying to the singularity of the era, a line customarily taken by popular histories and celebrity memoirs.[3] Conservative moralists portray the monomaniacal and megalomaniacal behaviour of Howard Kirk's contemporaries as revealing the paradoxically coercive nature of permissiveness.[4] It might alternatively be argued that Howard's delusions of grandeur blind him to his own marginality. From this perspective, his ambitions appear vainglorious, his actions contradictory, his victories petty and his ivory tower existence detached from everyday life.

This volume takes a different tack. Far from being resistant to historical analysis, texts such as *The History Man* raise issues of periodisation and agency of class, gender and generation that are central to the history of post-war Britain. That the inherently interdisciplinary subject of permissiveness requires historians to integrate the political, social and cultural strands of their discipline—and to relate them to parallel work in cultural studies and the social sciences—should be welcomed. So should the manner in which the subject attracts popular interest, since it gives historians the opportunity both to widen their audience and to scotch myths. But demythologisation need not entail the demonisation of permissiveness practised by the right. Nor need scholars place the term within inverted commas, as if questioning its very existence.[5] Permissiveness was neither a catastrophe nor a canard, but a significant if contested liberalisation of behaviours and beliefs that began well before the 1960s and continues to this day. In this introduction, I'll use *The History Man* as an entry point into examining what permissiveness was, when it appeared, who supported it, who opposed it and why it deserves re-examination.

The Nature of Permissiveness

Unlike many Americans, the British used permissiveness to mean much more than Dr Spock's easy-going childrearing techniques before the sixties or moral anarchy thereafter.[6] One of the most illuminating definitions of the word came in 1967 from Tom McGrath, the editor of the underground newspaper *IT*. He characterised it as one 'manifestation' of a whole 'new attitude': 'Permissiveness—the individual should be free from hindrances by external Law or internal guilt in his pursuit of pleasure so long as he does not impinge on others.'[7]

The legal restraints to which McGrath referred concerned issues of morality. They had been undergoing wholesale reform since the late 1950s, transforming the relationship between state, society and individual. Print censorship was relaxed in 1959 and that of drama in 1968. Citizens won the right to take their own lives in 1961 and murderers got to keep theirs after 1965. Off-course betting became legal in 1960, as did abortion and male homosexuality in limited fashion in 1967. The National Health Service (Family Planning) Act of the same year extended access to contraception regardless of marital status, while the Divorce Reform Act of 1969 dissolved marriages that had undergone 'irretrievable breakdown' after two years in consensual cases and five years in contested ones.

The liberalisation of the law was only one facet of permissiveness. McGrath's disavowal of 'internal guilt' indicates that those affected by legal change were no passive recipients of civil liberties.[8] Radical theologian Douglas Rhymes duly urged his readers to overcome both their guilt and any deference to 'priest, Church, politician or parent' when making moral choices.[9] Advocates of permissiveness equated individualism with iconoclasm, described by McGrath as a rejection of leaders and by cultural commentator George Melly as a 'cool refusal to pay homage to traditional bogeymen and shibboleths'.[10] Disdain for convention sat uneasily with the pluralistic dimensions of permissiveness. McGrath commended the 'international, inter-racial, equisexual' dimensions of the 'alternative society', while the anarchist Mick Farren stated that 'each and every individual has unique needs and desires that are entirely his own.'[11]

Permissiveness encouraged people to express and satisfy these desires. McGrath urged everyone to follow their 'inner voice in the most honest way possible', the Bishop of Woolwich advised Christians to be 'Honest to God', gays 'came out' and the future politician and perjurer Jonathan Aitken incongruously applauded his generation's 'remarkable frankness'.[12] Self-expression often took creative forms such as the 'wild new clothes' and 'strange new music sounds' that caught McGrath's attention in 1967. The previous decade or so had witnessed a cultural efflorescence in Britain that encompassed everything from painting to hairdressing. Sixties' culture emphasised what McGrath termed 'the individual's right to pleasure (orgasm)', one of many links between permissiveness and the concurrent sexual revolution.[13] Hence magazine editor Richard Neville championed hedonism and theatre director Charles Marowitz characterised the 1960s as being less permissive than 'passionate'.[14]

The primacy given to freedom, pleasure and sexuality necessitated a rethink of morality and religion, leading McGrath to write of a 'new spiritual movement'.[15] Some defined the 'New Morality' in terms of the abolition of prohibitions: '[a] change from Don'ts to Dos'.[16] Others toyed with moral relativism, the anthropologist Edmund Leach declaring societal strictures to be entirely 'arbitrary'.[17] Liberal theologians preferred to restructure Christianity around a situational ethic in which 'nothing can of itself always be labelled as "wrong"'.[18] But for humanists, permissiveness was inseparable from a process of secularisation that replaced the

Christian 'morality of conformity' with a new 'morality of freedom'.[19]

Freedom, individualism, iconoclasm, pluralism, openness, pleasure, creativity and a new morality: all these characteristics of permissiveness are on display in *The History Man*. Howard and his wife Barbara liberate themselves from the 'high ethical standards and low social expectations' of their upbringing and experiment with all manner of transgressive behaviours: 'making love in parks, smoking pot at parties...rubbing margarine on each other in bed, going on demos'.[20] Individualism and iconoclasm fuel their rejection of anything suggestive of tradition and convention. They throw parties that mix 'heteros with homos, painters with advanced theologians', indulge in 'extreme bouts of frankness' and seek 'high erotic satisfactions' in their sex lives.[21] Their creativity finds expression in their funky clothes and in Howard's fashionable writings, which exhibit a 'frank sense of participation in the permissive scene'.[22] And the contrast between the 'puritanical' morality of their parents' generation and their own libertarian attitudes forms a recurring theme in the book. 'Nothing in consenting sex is perverse', states Barbara.[23]

The History Man does not simply outline permissive mores. It scrutinises and satirises them. Howard maintains his freedom of action by denying it to others: the right-wing student drummed out of the university, the sociobiologist denied a platform for his opinions, the babysitter whom he beds then dumps. His individualism is undermined by both his modishness and his Marxism, while his anti-establishment posturing belies his status as an 'institutional man' with a 'stuffy job' and a 'stuffy academic manner' to match. He 'talks about liberation, openness, all the time', but exploits his position to crush diversity and to conceal his wrongdoing.[24] His pleasures frequently entail another's suffering and his writings are faddish and fatuous. Though he has dispensed with traditional morality, Barbara disputes whether he offers any viable alternative. She chides him for having 'substituted trends for morals and commitments' and derides him for representing 'what we have instead of faith'.[25] This contrast between rhetoric and reality, while providing much of the novel's comedy and dramatic tension, helps to explain why scholars have queried whether permissiveness led to the 'positive changes' trumpeted by McGrath and, for that matter, whether it was something of an optical illusion.[26]

Origins

Howard Kirk is conventional in his periodisation of permissiveness. He follows Philip Larkin's lead in dating its beginnings to 'that year of social movement', 1963. It was then that he and his wife changed their appearance (Howard sprouting one of that year's 'many new beards'), their attitudes (as they start 'transcending reality') and their actions ('running with their clothes off through the wind').[27] If 1963 was the dawn, 1968 represented the high noon for their ambitions, a year of exhilaration and confrontation in which 'the new world waited to be born.' Howard regrets that his hopes went 'undelivered' then and remain so in the early 1970s, but he has still not given up on creating 'a world of expanded minds, equal dealings, erotic satisfactions'.[28] However, there are signs that the dream has palled in the intervening years. By 1972, the forces of permissiveness have splintered into their constituent factions as women embrace feminism and liberals retreat into 'evasive quietism'. Meanwhile, the gap between Howard's permissive verbiage and bullyboy tactics grows ever wider.[29]

So did the 1960s witness the heyday of permissiveness and, if so, what preceded and succeeded it? The question of antecedents is neatly posed by Jonathon Green's observation that that 'most of the cultural "revolutions"' of the 1960s had been 'carried out long before'.[30] The cause of sexual pleasure and cohabitation (misleadingly named 'free love') had become something more than mere libertinism thanks to such utopian socialists as Richard Carlile and Robert Owen in the first half of the nineteenth century and George Drysdale and Havelock Ellis in the second.[31] And though revisionist historians strain credulity when describing Victorians as being generally 'permissive', a fully-fledged libertarian agenda emerged within avant-garde circles at the *fin de siècle*. The anarchist George Bedborough's assertion of 'the paramount right of the individual to self-realisation in all non-invasive directions' in 1897 was reiterated by many writers over the following half-century.[32] Noel Annan has noted the tolerant attitudes of most mid-century intellectuals and Virginia Nicholson has examined how bohemians tried to mould their lifestyles around such ideals. In 1933, an overlapping group of thirties' radicals endorsed the Federation of Progressive Societies and Individuals' call for 'the release of personal conduct from all taboos and restrictions except those imposed in the interest of the weak and the young'.[33]

There is, in short, abundant evidence of permissiveness among intellectuals many decades before the 1960s. What had yet to emerge was anything resembling a permissive society. Permissives in the first half of the twentieth century were a self-conscious minority who perceived themselves to be battling against the combined forces of public ignorance and institutional opposition. The institutional roadblocks erected by the churches, the censors and the government were indeed formidable. The churches were perhaps the most flexible of the three inasmuch as influential Protestants developed what I have termed a 'Christian mutualist' programme between the wars.[34] Christian mutualists acknowledged that 'our immediate ancestors seem to have carried reticence on sexual subjects too far' and sought to make amends by sanctioning contraception within marriage in support of gender equality and spousal harmony.[35] At the same time, gambling, divorce, homosexuality and abortion continued to be deemed sinful by most devout Christians and the Anglican hierarchy felt it their duty to hold the British to a uniform moral code. The Church of England's submission to the Royal Commission on Marriage and Divorce in 1952 stated that 'It must be the desire of all responsible people that by the deliberate will of its citizens and by the operation of the Nation's laws, the national standards and habits should approximate as far as possible to the Christian standard.'[36]

Censorship formed another bulwark against permissiveness. Ross McKibbin has demonstrated that controls on film and radio managed to suppress not only obscenity, but anything smacking of controversy.[37] Censorship of the written word was less successful in stopping debate (of which there was plenty), but confined it to just that. For example, it was safer to write about homosexuals in abstract terms than to discuss their specific sexual habits. Some indication of the effectiveness of censorship comes from the records of the Public Morality Council, which had assisted London's authorities in policing indecency since 1899. While forever on alert for signs of turpitude, the organisation saw it as a containable problem in the 1940s. At the beginning of the decade, it reported concerns about a number of films, two theatres and under a dozen night clubs (all of which were promptly raided by the police).[38] And at its end, though upset by stage nudity and 'rife' homosexuality, it found little in broadcasting to 'give offence on moral grounds' and objected to only one film.[39]

Governments were in no hurry to reform the laws concerning personal morality before the late 1950s, whether out of conviction, inertia, a prioritisation of economic issues or deference to perceived popular sentiment. 'The [obscenity] law is founded on public morality', declared Tory Home Secretary William Joynson-Hicks in 1929, and fears of a public backlash influenced the post-war Labour government's decision not to endorse divorce reform or the abolition of capital punishment.[40] Rab Butler used the same rationale when Home Secretary in 1957 to shelve the Wolfenden Report's proposal to decriminalise male homosexuality. 'My dear boy, this is all very fine', John Wolfenden recalled him saying, 'but you are way out in front of public opinion.'[41] Politicians may have overstated public opposition to permissiveness. Mass Observation's 'Little Kinsey' survey of 1949 revealed a surprising lack of inhibition among its sample of two thousand men and women, a majority of whom supported sex education, birth control and divorce.[42] But ordinary people did not frame their opinions in the laissez-faire terms favoured by permissive intellectuals, who were in turn all too inclined to dismiss 'herd morality' as utterly hidebound. Anti-permissives' claims to represent the general public therefore went largely unquestioned.[43]

These three institutions ceded little ground to permissiveness in the 1950s. The Church stood firm, censorship lessened only at the end of the decade and the government seemed keener on establishing royal commissions than introducing legislation upon controversial issues. The ethos which they upheld nonetheless came under increasing challenge, as Colin Campbell argues in his chapter in this volume. The significance of the 'Angry Young Men' writers was that they rescued permissiveness from its association with an ageing intelligentsia by modernising and democratising bohemianism. Their characters' trademark irreverence, frankness, impetuosity and pursuit of personal fulfilment created the rudiments of a philosophy for youthful rebellion.[44] The anti-gentlemanly broadsides appearing from the mid-1950s onwards likewise championed expression over repression and honesty over hypocrisy. As I have written about elsewhere, those who blamed Britain's decline on a gentlemanly elite poured scorn on superannuated 'Establishment canons' of morality.[45]

Traditional values appeared discredited to their defenders and detractors alike at the turn of the decade. Conservative moralists warned of a 'long, apathetic slide into national decadence', with post-imperial Britain going the same way as imperial Rome.[46] More startling was the extent to which their critics shared these misgivings. Philosopher Colin Wilson valued 'self-control' above 'desire for comfort', journalist Kenneth Allsop deplored the 'new permissiveness' in schlocky literature and playwright John Osborne resembled his most famous character in being 'an old Puritan at heart'.[47] Accompanying this hostility to the affluent society was what Allsop described as 'a panicky feeling that the old points of reference have been lost'. State-of-the-nation writers likened early 1960s Britain to a 'wasteland' that had abandoned old standards without adopting new ones.[48]

The 1960s

Permissiveness was therefore widely associated with anomie, anarchy and decline at the beginning of the 1960s. Though pessimism endured throughout the decade, it was countered by the notion that the permissive society brought national renewal. The sudden relaxation of church teachings, government policies and censorship in the 1960s represented a triumph for liberal progressivism. The Church of England simultaneously reconciled itself to the New Morality and to its waning authority over matters of personal conduct.[49] The key text in this regard was *Putting Asunder* (1966), a policy paper on divorce commissioned by the Archbishop of Canterbury. The report not only lifted the church's opposition to no-fault divorces; it also conceded that, because practising Christians were no longer in the majority, it was 'unjust' and 'socially disruptive' for them to lay down the law for others.[50]

However half-hearted in their intentions and cack-handed in their implementation, legislative reforms registered much the same shift towards respecting individual rights. Whereas governments had once equated permissiveness with anti-social behaviour, reformers accepted that individual deviance was often a lesser evil than social intolerance. Consider the contrast between two official reports on marriage commissioned 20 years apart. In 1947, the Denning Commission operated on the assumption that the preservation of marriage was in the 'interest of society'. In 1967, however, the Scottish Law Commission suggested that the 'interest of individuals' trumped that of the collective in determining whether or not couples should divorce.[51]

Liberal censors liberalised censorship. Sir John Trevelyan, who served as Secretary to the British Board of Film Censors from 1958 to 1971, disarmingly confessed to being 'opposed to censorship in principle' and advised studios how to make their racy films pass muster as art.[52] Similarly highbrow motives inspired Hugh Carleton Greene, the BBC's Director-General from 1960 to 1969. He saw it as the duty of artists to engage in 'provocation' and that of broadcasters to provide them with a platform to do so in the interests of 'widening the limits of discussion and challenging old taboos'.[53]

Trevelyan and Greene found it easier to justify their actions due to Britain's cultural pre-eminence in this period, a phenomenon as extraordinary as it was unanticipated. The symbiosis that formed between music, fashion, cinema and the visual arts in mid-1960s London rid Britain of its frumpy image. A city containing the Beatles and the Rolling Stones, Mary Quant and Vidal Sassoon, David Bailey and Terence Donovan and Biba and Habitat soon lost its inferiority complex. Equally significant was the manner in which British culture challenged existing aesthetic standards. Alex Seago argues persuasively that the Royal College of Art pioneered a postmodern 'erosion of traditional distinctions between high culture and the market-place' in the 1950s.[54] By the following decade, it was no longer self-evident that high culture was superior to popular culture or, indeed, how each term should be defined. British icons likewise redefined female beauty (Twiggy), male beauty (Mick Jagger), artistry (Lennon and McCartney) and heroism (James Bond).

Britain overcame its reputation for prudery by conducting a carnivalesque breaking of taboos in the 1960s. The first C-word in a paperback (1960), the first F-word on air (1965), the first drug reference in a Beatles song (1964) and the first full-frontal centrefold in a soft-core magazine (1971) could be taken to signify liberation or decay, but either way they indicated a weakening of controls. While this process was furthered by the relaxation of censorship, contrary attempts to restore public decency often achieved the same effect. The prosecution of *Lady Chatterley's Lover* in

1960 made it a bestseller, Christine Keeler's nude body became the defining image of the Profumo Affair of 1963 and Marianne Faithfull served the same role in the 1967 Redlands drugs trial.

British culture also exhibited what Richard Neville called an 'intense, spontaneous internationalism' in the late 1950s and 1960s. It embraced American music, Italian fashion, French existentialism and Asian mysticism as well as the hedonism imputed to black immigrants. 'Thank goodness they've come into our midst', remarks a white character in Colin MacInnes' *City of Spades* (1957): 'they bring an element of joy and violence into our cautious, ordered lives.'[55] MacInnes used cosmopolitanism to rebel against British conservatism, as did *The History Man*'s Howard Kirk when parroting 'the latest slogans from Paris' and Barbara when bedding an Egyptian as an act of post-colonial transgression.[56] Others created a hybrid culture incorporating native and indigenous influences: the foundation of rock music and pop art. Insodoing, they revamped Britishness and turned it into an exportable commodity. No longer considered puritanical, parochial and philistinic, Britain suddenly, improbably, became cool.

Boundless cultural innovation created the notion of 'Swinging London' in 1966, and the subsequent enactment of major legislative reforms earned Britain the reputation of being a full-blown 'permissive society'. Both labels smacked of media hype in their exaggeration, generalisation and thirst for sensation, wilfully ignoring as they did the workaday lives that most people lived most of the time. They nevertheless served a real need: that of giving a name to a cultural upheaval perceived by many contemporaries to be unprecedented in its speed and scale. The future Tory minister John Gummer noted that mid-1960s treatises on New Morality appeared 'so old-fashioned' by 1971, while that same year John Wolfenden marvelled that his 1957 proposals concerning homosexuality and prostitution sounded 'Victorian' fourteen years on.[57] The fierce pace of change, which proved so unsettling to Gummer and Wolfenden, was experienced by trendsetters in much more positive terms. Artists relished the innovation and experimentation possible within this fluid milieu, photographer David Bailey reportedly considering the 'bright, brittle quality' of his subjects all the more alluring because 'it tarnishes so soon.'[58] And consumers like the teenage Twiggy were captivated by the wealth of 'up to date, up to the minute, brand new and streamlined and contemporary' products appearing in the high street. 'Anything modern was wonderful, and anything old was terrible' in her eyes.[59]

This infatuation with modernity allayed fears that permissiveness spelt national decline. Fashion designer Mary Quant declared Britain's youth 'the most forward-moving set of people in the world in all fields' and actor Michael Caine equated 'decadence' with an 'effeteness' rudely contradicted by 'the average Englishman's' newfound sexual vigour.[60] A touch more sophisticated was journalist Peter Evans's argument that babyboomers did not care that England was a 'spent power'. Politicians obsessed with 'yesterday's splendours' were in his view ignoring the nation's 'surprisingly fine record of achievement, of breakthrough, of expansion and influence in all the arts and on all the world'. To misquote Dean Acheson, Great Britain had lost an empire but had found a role—that of the world's trendsetter.[61]

The 1970s and Beyond

Towards the end of the decade, there appeared a slew of instant histories-cum-obituaries of the 1960s that declared the revolution to be over. In 1969, the erstwhile satirist Christopher Booker announced the implosion of the 'libertarian dream' and Heather Cremonesi claimed that London's 'Permissive Paradise' had turned into 'a vision of hell'.[62] In 1970, George Melly lamented that pop culture's 'Revolt' had been commodified into 'Style' and journalist Bernard Levin looked back on the 1960s as 'the years in which things could happen that could not happen now'.[63] This 'death of the sixties' narrative has dominated subsequent writing.[64] Some writers, including Arthur Marwick, David Alan Mellor and Laurent Gervereau, date the decade's end to the oil crisis of 1973–4, thereby underscoring the centrality of affluence to their models of cultural change.[65] Others, particularly countercultural memoirists, focus on the demise of the Underground in the 1970s and the 'the revenge of the grey men' in the anti-permissive 1980s.[66] The 'Days of Hope' were gone, claimed David Widgery in 1989. Fellow counterculturalist Jeff Nuttall confessed himself eager to die in 1991 since he would 'never know such optimism again'.[67]

It might help here to distinguish between permissiveness and the 1960s. Decades have to come to an end and, as we have seen, the turn of the decade encouraged contemporaries to memorialise the 1960s and then move on. The sense of disjuncture was compounded by the concurrent splintering of the Underground into multifarious New Social Movements, which brought down the curtains on a cohesive, self-confident and culturally dominant London scene. But neither the end of the 1960s nor that of the Underground betokened the end of permissiveness *per se*. Rychard Carrington's and Gerry Carlin's chapters in this volume suggest that London's counterculture was as much a victim of its own contradictions as of government persecution. And, when we examine broader cultural and social trends, the 1970s and 1980s present a confused picture of countervailing permissive and anti-permissive developments.

The greatest changes in the 1970s and 1980s were cultural in nature. High culture became more pluralistic thanks to the rise of identity politics. As Patricia Waugh writes in her survey of literature since the 1960s, this encouraged 'more and more social groups…to speak for themselves, within their own terms and with their own distinctive voices'.[68] Low culture failed to 'notic[e] that the 1960s were over', according to Leon Hunt. He uses case studies to show how sit-coms, pulp fiction and sexploitation films popularised a permissive culture of transgression previously considered too outrageous for mass consumption. Joseph McAleer identifies parallel developments in Mills and Boon romance novels, which cagily introduced premarital sex in the 1970s before depicting oral sex in 1982 and masturbation in 1983.[69]

The counterculture underwent fragmentation rather than extinction. The gay and women's liberation movements that emerged from it were more closely linked to permissiveness than either cared to admit, while successive editions of Nicholas Saunders's *Alternative London* detail how countercultural communities grew beyond Chelsea and into far-flung suburbs during the early 1970s.[70] Still further afield were the bucolic music festivals and New Age communities studied by George McKay. He sees them as forming part of a whole battery of 'cultures of resistance' that perpetuated—indeed, expanded—the counterculture's quest for liberty and ecstasy over the following decades.[71]

Permissiveness provoked mixed reactions among the wider population in the 1970s and 1980s. A good guide to mid-1970s attitudes is provided by an NOP poll conducted in April 1975 (Table 1.1). The first thing to note is that permissiveness was not a hot-button issue in 1975. Between 69 and 84 per cent of respondents expressed neutrality, slight agreement or slight disagreement in reaction to permissive statements (the middle three options on a seven-point scale). Furthermore, although most answers produced anti-permissive majorities, not all did so. A clear majority was in favour of unrestricted access to abortion, and an overwhelming majority said the same about birth control, suggesting that family planning was considered differently from other permissive causes.

Table 1.1. Attitudes to permissiveness in 1975

Agree				**Disagree**				**(%)**
+3	**+2**	**+1**	**0**	**–1**	**–2**	**–3**	**Net***	**Mid****
Abortion should be made legally available for all who want it								
5	9	38	14	25	5	4	+18	77
Divorce should be made easier								
3	5	27	17	40	5	3	–13	84
Birth control should be provided free to all who ask for it								
12	14	44	10	15	3	2	+50	69
Homosexual couples should be able to live together openly								
1	2	13	31	28	10	15	–37	72
Homosexuals should be allowed to marry each other								
2	4	24	22	27	11	10	–18	73
Censorship laws should be made stricter								
3	3	29	16	32	11	6	–14	77

Source: NOP (1975), in *World Political Opinion and Social Surveys: Series One—British Opinion Polls*, part i, Reading, 1990, vol.150, p.16. * The 'net' score equals the percentage of positive answers minus the percentage of negative ones. ** The 'mid' score equals the percentage of respondents choosing the middle three options on the seven-point scale (i.e. the sum total of +1, 0 and –1 responses).

Longitudinal surveys of public opinion provide further evidence that there was no concerted anti-permissive backlash in the 1970s, though they suggest that something of the sort may have emerged in the 1980s. Table 1.2 indicates increasing apprehension about permissive activities in the late 1960s followed by diminishing concern from then till 1981, after which the figures rose rapidly. The trend is the same for every question. Support for the legalisation of male homosexuality repeats this pattern (Table 1.3), gaining acceptance in the 1970s before AIDS played its part in reversing the trend. In 1988, a third of respondents admitted that the disease had reduced their tolerance of gays.[72]

Table 1.2. Q. Do you think any of these are very serious social problems in Britain today?

	1965	1967	1968	1973	1976	1977	1981*	1983	1985	1988
Drug-taking	56	85	83	73	61	67	63	67	90	95
Pornography**	–	–	–	–	–	–	38	51	52	95
Gambling	31	36	47	30	32	35	25	34	34	48
Homosexuality	26	31	31	20	22	18	17	32	35	48
Prostitution	29	28	30	28	20	20	20	23	29	42

Source: Gallup, 1965–88, in *World Political Opinion*, ser.1, pt.1. * Gallup conducted the poll twice in 1981—these are the figures for May. ** The pornography question was asked for the first time in 1981.

Table 1.3. Percentage thinking that homosexuality between consenting adults should be legal

1957*	1966	1970**	1977	1979	1981	1986
38	39	39	58	62	63	55

Sources: Gallup, 1966–1986, in *World Political Opinion*, ser.1, pt.1; * Robert J. Wybrow, *Britain Speaks Out*, 1937–87: *A Social History as Seen Through the Gallup Data*, Basingstoke, 1989, p.52; ** NOP, 1970, in *World Political Opinion*, ser.1, pt.1, vol.129, p.68. The NOP question was comparable to that asked by Gallup.

A number of one-off polls, while providing no information on the direction in which attitudes were heading, also demonstrate the strength of anti-permissive sentiments in the 1980s. For example, in 1984 respondents were five times more likely to consider divorce laws too lax than too stringent, while in 1988 those who thought homosexual sex was morally wrong outnumbered their opponents by a ratio of four to one.[73] Reproductive issues may once again have bucked the trend. Table 1.4

shows that support for providing contraceptive information to the young and unmarried grew with each successive poll, and studies conducted in 1967 and 1983 showed no change in attitudes towards abortion in the case of the mother's health being in danger or the possibility of the child being born with a physical handicap. Even so, the balance of statistical evidence appears to indicate that the tide turned against permissiveness in the 1980s.

Table 1.4. Percentage agreeing that contraceptive advice should be available to unmarried young people

1963	1966*	1973	1975	1985
41	52	64	74	86

Source: Gallup, 1963–85. * The 1966 poll specified that the advice be dispensed in a public clinic.

The reverse was true in the 1990s. The government-funded British Social Attitudes Survey registered a striking liberalisation of attitudes concerning personal relationships during the decade, with the young leading the charge.[74] Behaviour also changed rapidly, so that by the end of the century seven out of ten first partnerships were cohabiting and nearly four out of ten babies were born outside of marriage.[75] Institutions such as the monarchy, the Church of England and the Conservative Party that had difficulty dealing with women's autonomy or homosexuality endured schism and ridicule as a result.[76] Although alternative lifestyles continued to be criticised by the right-wing press, they became ratings grabbers for media outlets targeting a youth market. Channel 4, which promoted itself as 'the channel for people who value freedom, permissiveness, hedonism, discernment, experimentation, ambition and individuality', became something of a freak show.[77] In sum, Britain was a much more permissive society at the turn of the millennium than had ever been the case in the 1960s.

Popular and Elite Permissiveness

Bradbury explores the class, gender, generational and political dimensions of the permissive society by including most of its stock characters in

The History Man: Barbara as the feminist, Howard as the would-be revolutionary, his colleague Henry Beamish as the liberal progressive, his student George Carmody as the right-wing critic and other Watermouth undergraduates representing radical youth. His view of the social dynamics of permissiveness is a complex one. He portrays 1960s Britain as having provided opportunities for social mobility to such people as the Kirks. Ambition propelled them from their modest backgrounds into elite circles even as they maintained a contempt for established social hierarchies. Howard is a great class warrior, styling himself a 'terror to the selfish bourgeoisie' and gleefully proclaiming their 'death' in one of his books. But he is also a hypocrite in that he launches the book at chi-chi Hampstead gatherings, indulges in lavish 'inconspicuous unconsumption' and finds no room for common-or-garden townspeople in his purportedly inclusive parties.[78] The gulf between town and gown is further exposed in the fractious days of '68, when the burghers of Watermouth 'poked students on the buses with umbrellas'.[79]

This raises the question of how exclusive was permissiveness. Did it transcend social boundaries or reinscribe them? The foremost believer in popular permissiveness is Arthur Marwick, who contends that the 'the liberation of the 1960s affected, and was participated in, by majorities.' He questions the validity of such terms as subculture or counterculture on the grounds that their ideals 'permeated' wider society, a claim bolstered by Steve Humphries and Miriam Akhtar's oral history of the 'unseen and unheard majority' in 1950s and 1960s Britain.[80] The opposite case is made by writers who identify an antagonistic relationship between permissiveness and the mainstream. Conservative moralists claim that a 'Lilac Establishment' foisted permissive reforms upon the proverbial 'blue-collar worker and his wife', whereas socialist theorists portray subcultures as being in conflict with the hegemonic forces of capitalism.[81] Many celebrity memoirs reinforce this notion of an embattled permissive minority. Charles Marowitz believes the 'vast majority' of the population had little in common with the 'small but dynamic' counterculture of which he was a part, rock critic Nik Cohn estimates Swinging London to have consisted of no more than 5,000 people and the ubiquitous Jim Haynes seems determined to list every one of them in his autobiography's twenty pages of acknowledgements.[82]

One way to reconcile these viewpoints is to acknowledge the love-hate relationship that existed between elite and popular forms of permissiveness. Youth subcultures were by definition exclusive and oppositional, as illustrated by sociologist Sarah Thornton in her revealing study of clubbing in the 1990s. Though classless in one sense, clubbers imposed their own forms of classification and stratification akin to Pierre Bourdieu's hierarchies of taste.[83] The same went for Swinging London and its Underground successor which, according to one of its members, 'put a lot of the emphasis on being just that bit more hip than the masses'.[84] Membership of this elite significantly required neither birth nor breeding. Jonathan Aitken wrote of a 'talent class' and Christopher Booker of a 'New Aristocracy' drawn from 'a complete gamut of the social scale'.[85] One of the barons of this New Aristocracy, Paul McCartney, noted with satisfaction that an eruption of working-class creativity had finally made it 'okay to be common'. In this, if in nothing else, he and Howard Kirk were cut from the same cloth.[86]

Permissiveness was not confined to this tight-knit avant garde. The outer reaches of London sustained a mod culture unknown to the 'chic people in central London' as well as a network of libraries, evening classes and small-time venues that 'defined the scene of the punters, rather than the stars', in the words of music writer Fred Vermorel.[87] Richard Hoggart noted that all large cities contained their own gambling clubs and strip joints by the end of the 1960s and local histories describe thriving youth cultures in the likes of Surrey and Birmingham.[88] Art colleges and universities also served as provincial outposts of permissive culture and radical politics: hence the Kirks patronise Watermouth's 'radical bookshop…family planning clinic [and] macrobiotic food store'.[89] Permissiveness was also not a solely English affair. New research by Angela Bartie shows that the Edinburgh Festival generated its own share of cultural controversy in the 1960s and even the otherwise puritanical Northern Ireland spawned a student movement that at its inception resembled those in Continental Europe and the United States.[90]

Market mechanisms yoked together the popular and elite strands of permissiveness. The relationship between the permissive society and the affluent society deserves further study, but we can at least say that young consumers at once fed and fed off the output of the fashion designers, artists, photographers, musicians and filmmakers at the hub of the London scene.[91] Some members of London's bohemia were happy to bottle the *Zeitgeist* for mass consumption, prompting Mary Quant to remark that 'Snobbery has gone out of fashion' (and to provide the gowns for Watermouth University's congregation).[92] Others resented the erosion of their 'much-valued exclusiveness'. Jeff Nuttall mocked the 'ironic sight' of counterculturalists disowning their own creations as soon as they became too popular.[93]

Quantitative measures allow us to distinguish between those who experienced permissiveness and those who actually approved of it. Tables 1.5 to 1.7 present the findings of an invaluable NOP poll conducted in January 1970. They bear out Marwick's contention that the general population was affected by the 'cultural revolution' going on around them.[94] Four-fifths of all categories of respondent—men and women, young and old, middle class and working class—acknowledged that 'People's attitudes towards sex in the last ten years have changed a lot.' But that did not mean that most people favoured most aspects of permissiveness. The NOP sample overwhelmingly welcomed some of its more eye-catching manifestations, with mini-skirts and bikinis topping the list. Smaller majorities backed the liberalisation of the divorce and abortion laws, but most recoiled from anything hinting at licentiousness. Nude women, dirty books, free love and drugs all attracted widespread opprobrium. People were correspondingly unlikely to view themselves as participants in the permissive society. Only one-third of those polled by NOP in 1970 identified with the changing sexual attitudes of the 1960s. A similar proportion told Gallup in 1985 that they broadly approved of the sexual revolution and a mere 13 per cent considered that they had taken some part in it.[95]

Class differences in the 1970 poll were less pronounced than gender differences, let alone generational ones. The higher-class ABC1s were a few percentage points more permissive than C2DEs on most questions, but only in the case of the Pill, homosexuality and the state of sexual morality did double-digit gaps emerge (Table 1.6). Though later polls also found working-class respondents to be less accepting of divorce, prostitution and abortion, recent behavioural studies caution against considering permissiveness a middle-class cause.[96] For example, women from poor families were more likely to have babies when teenagers and to raise them alone. The American sociologist Judith Stacey notes that such disadvantaged women are simultaneously 'genuine postmodern family pioneers' and the ones who 'suffer most' from today's more fluid household structures.[97]

Table 1.5. Attitudes to sex in the media in 1970

% disapproving of ('There is too much sex in...')	N=984	Age		Sex		Class	
	Y	16–34	35+	M	F	ABC1	C2DE
Television	57	39	68	47	68	55	58
Films	54	46	58	48	59	55	53
Books and magazines	63	54	67	59	66	60	64
Newspapers	48	37	55	42	55	43	51

Source: NOP, *Report on Attitudes Towards Crime, Violence and Permissiveness in Society* (1970), in *World Political Opinion*, ser.1, pt.1, vol.129, p.49.

Table 1.6. Attitudes to sexual and familial issues in 1970

% approving of	N=984	Age		Sex		Class	
	Y (N)	16–34	35+	M	F	ABC1	C2DE
New divorce law	66 (25)	71	62	71	60	66	65
Changing sexual attitudes in 1960s	32 (48)	51	22	39	26	39	29
The Pill as morally right for any woman	43 (54*)	60	33	50	37	50	40
Legalisation of male homosexuality	39 (NA**)	50	35	40	39	50	34

Source: NOP, *Report on Attitudes Towards Crime, Violence and Permissiveness in Society* (1970), in *World Political Opinion*, ser.1, pt.1, vol.129, pp.44, 54, 56, 68. * The disapproval figure is calculated by combining the scores of those who thought the Pill morally wrong in any circumstances and those who thought only married women should take it. ** This question offered respondents more options than a simple yes or no answer, making it impossible to calculate the proportion opposed to the decriminalisation of homosexuality.

Table 1.7. Attitudes to the permissive society in 1970

% approving of	N=984	Age		Sex		Class		Party		
	Y (N)	16–34	35+	M	F	ABC1	C2DE	Tory	Lab	Lib
Mini-skirts	83 (9)	92	79	83	85	83	85	84	83	85
Bikinis	83 (8)	94	77	85	81	87	82	83	84	84
Coffee bars	80 (11)	88	76	81	80	82	79	79	81	85
Teenage parties	75 (12)	83	70	79	70	77	74	74	75	66
Discos	67 (14)	85	57	67	67	69	66	64	68	72
Gambling	44 (43)	44	44	52	35	40	45	42	45	47
Female imp-ersonators	29 (54)	37	25	29	29	26	30	30	30	28
Unisex clothes	27 (47)	37	22	26	29	30	26	26	28	24
Cohabitation	25 (47)	38	18	32	19	27	24	22	29	31
Strip-clubs	22 (61)	36	14	30	14	25	21	21	23	26
See-through dresses	16 (70)	29	9	24	8	19	15	13	18	17
John and Yoko	13 (75)	23	7	15	10	15	11	8	15	15
Hippies	8 (81)	16	4	11	6	11	7	6	9	10
Young staying out all night	8 (85)	19	3	11	5	10	8	7	8	9
Pep pills	2 (94)	5	1	4	1	4	2	1	3	4
Marijuana	2 (92)	3	<1	4	<1	3	2	1	3	–

Source: NOP, *Report on Attitudes Towards Crime, Violence and Permissiveness in Society* (1970), in *World Political Opinion*, ser.1, pt.1, vol.129, pp.42–3.

Gender

Feminist scholars might baulk at Bradbury's lampooning of consciousness-raising (he mentions a 'Women's Lib Nude Encounter Group') and political lesbianism ('that was *last term*'), while nonetheless concurring with his attack on the chauvinistic aspects of permissiveness.[98] Howard preaches androgyny but acts like an Alpha Male, clashing horns with any man who crosses his path and treating women as either sex-objects or child-minders. Towards the end of the novel, Barbara and Felicity (Howard's student, lover and dogsbody) become conscious of their exploitation under the guise of liberation. They inform Howard that he's benefited at their expense, leading Felicity to leave and Barbara to thrust her hand through a window pane.

Their sense of betrayal placed them in the mainstream of 1970s feminist thought. Juliet Mitchell condemned the 'cult of libertarianism' for having promised freedom but created 'further alienation'. Suzie Fleming complained that permissiveness reduced people to the level of 'sexual objects', and Germaine Greer joined Herbert Marcuse in claiming that 'the permissive society has done much to neutralise sexual drives by containing them.'[99] Such views informed early research on the subject, which conceived of 'the oppressiveness of "permissiveness"' in primarily sexual terms.[100] Feminists criticised the exclusion of women from the permissive society as well as their exploitation in it. Bea Campbell described permissiveness as 'primarily a revolt of young *men*', a charge that receives corroboration from 1970s survey data. Twice as many men as women in higher education supported the counterculture and, predictably enough, young men were three times more likely to approve of see-through dresses.[101] Pioneering research on youth culture also emphasised girls' marginality. In their 1978 article on 'Rock and Sexuality', Simon Frith and Angela McRobbie contrasted the 'collective male activity' of musicianship and sexual expression with an 'individual female passivity' exemplified in the idol-worship of male stars.[102]

Yet permissiveness did not altogether bypass teenage girls and second-wave feminists. Simon Frith subsequently disowned the distinction he had once made between 'male activity and female passivity'. He noted that girls' consumption of music was a creative and fulfilling activity in its own right, a point amply illustrated by American work on Beatlemania and Angela McRobbie's subsequent research on dance.[103] Moreover, many women's liberationists, though appalled at how licence had masqueraded as liberty in the counterculture, remained attracted to alternative lifestyles. Indeed, they hoped that feminism would enable them to achieve the absolute freedom in their private lives that had been denied to them by the male-dominated Underground. The 1971 manifesto of the women's liberation movement accordingly called for free and unrestricted access to contraception, abortion and childcare.[104]

In the 1970s feminists were much more permissive in this respect than women as a whole, whom polls showed to be relatively conservative in their attitudes towards personal morality.[105] Men gave more permissive answers than women to nearly every question asked in the 1970 NOP survey. One telling contrast emerged over whether changing sexual attitudes in the 1960s had been a positive or negative development. Male respondents split down the middle on the question, while women disapproved by a ratio of over two to one.[106] The more controversial the issue, the greater the difference between the sexes, so that whereas the great majority of each sex condoned discos and teenage parties, much larger minorities of men supported drug use, female nudity, cohabitation and hippiedom. Stronger male support for permissiveness was still discernible in the large-scale National Survey of Sexual Attitudes and Lifestyles undertaken in 1990 and 1991.[107] But subsequent polling by the authoritative British Social Attitudes Survey suggests that the gender gap is disappearing in this respect as in so many others. 'Since women and men inhabit the same social world, they share similar views', comment Kerstin Hinds and Lindsey Jarvis in the 2000 edition of *British Social Attitudes*, adding that 'where attitudes have been changing over time, the trend has been towards convergence.'[108]

Generation

Permissiveness's greatest champions in the novel are the young and the young at heart ('Don't trust anyone over 30' being an article of faith to the thirtysomething Kirks). Watermouth students adopt 'new modes of being' at will, and support Howard's campaign to 'Preserve academic freedom' by censoring unfashionable opinions.[109] As such, they are representative examples of a babyboom generation defined by its participation in the permissive society. Most babyboomers consumed its products, as record buying and cinema going became largely their domain and half of sexually active teenage girls took the Pill by 1975.[110] Some of the young lobbied to transform society along permissive lines through student organisations, the counterculture and the gay and women's liberation movements. And, as we can see from the NOP data, they outscored their elders on every measure of permissiveness in 1970. This gave rise to much talk of a 'generation gap' between the permissive young and the anti-permissive old. 'We are not old men. We are not worried about petty morals', declared the Rolling Stones' Keith Richards. '[W]e must seek to re-establish...the superior status of adults', was the contrasting opinion of religious scholar Bryan Wilson, a man determined to win 'The War of the Generations'.[111]

The generation gap was real enough in the 1960s and 1970s and remains so today, but needs to be nuanced in several respects. First of all, the new terminology of 'teenager' and 'subculture' obscured the manner in which young people had long been viewed as dangerously autonomous and licentious.[112] What distinguished babyboomers was not only their greater independence but also their refusal to be marginalised by tribal elders. This was the import of students' demands for a greater say over their education, of the Underground's advocacy of children's rights and of mods' appropriation of the Union Jack and the RAF roundel. As Richard Weight argues, the young's obsession with national symbolism at once represented their claim to be included within a broadened conception of Britishness and to represent the nation to the rest of the world, an ambition triumphantly achieved in 1967 by the Beatles' telecast of 'All You Need Is Love'.[113]

Another reason the generation gap did not become a chasm was that, although the young were more permissive than their parents, few were stridently so. Surveys conducted in the late 1950s and 1950s revealed them to harbour conventional ambitions for families and careers, while the 1970 NOP poll reveals much overlap between those aged over and under thirty-five. Majorities of older and younger respondents condoned coffee bars and divorce reform and condemned narcotics and the counterculture.

Only some sexual matters—male homosexuality, sex in the media, unrestricted use of the Pill and the merits of the sexual revolution—found majorities of each age group on opposite sides of the debate.[114]

Moreover, the young were not implacably opposed to adults and authority figures. One mid-1960s study reported that Scottish teenagers considered adults a 'dull lot' deserving of pity rather than animosity, while another found that their London equivalents felt most resentment towards the older generation's 'distorted stereotypes about their behaviour and moral standards'. Though most of this sample expressed anger towards adults, their belief that generational conflict largely stemmed from misunderstanding suggests that they thought it neither desirable nor inevitable.[115] The limits of youthful alienation were displayed in 1968, when students on mainland Britain found themselves with less to rebel against than their counterparts overseas (Northern Ireland included).[116]

From the other side of the generational divide, adult commentators disagreed over the youth question every bit as much as they disagreed over permissiveness. As Mark Jones argues in his contribution to this volume, anti-permissives espoused a paternalism that applied most directly to the young. They opposed giving children 'what they fancy rather than…what they ought to have' and dismissed adolescent claims for autonomy as evidence of immaturity, criminologist John Barron Mays likening teen culture to a 'toddler's repudiation of parental support and authority'.[117] Liberal progressives conversely conceived of permissiveness in terms of a personal responsibility expected of mature individuals and societies, prohibitions being necessary only 'in childhood and in the infancy of the race'.[118] While children had to be sheltered, teenagers and young adults were encouraged to make decisions and take the consequences. The Latey Commission duly recommended to the government in 1967 that the age of majority be reduced to eighteen years. It considered that any 'withholding of responsibility' was more likely to make teenagers anti-social than well behaved. Paternalism seemed counterproductive.[119]

Yet liberal progressives felt just as 'divided' as *The History Man*'s Henry Beamish over the upsurge of youthful rebellion in the late 1960s and early 1970s. Much as Beamish denounces Watermouth students as 'fascists' posing as free-thinkers, John Wolfenden despised student 'nihilism' when an 'old man'.[120] Their despair stemmed from the counterculture's calculated puerility, as heard in this chant of the London Street Commune:

> Yes we are
> anti-social, unsure, immature
> won't work always shirking
> our responsibilities.[121]

Abandoning all hope that permissiveness would induce responsibility, Wolfenden expected society to become 'adult and mature…in the next few hundred thousand years'.[122]

Politics

The History Man captures the confused politics of the period by offering different definitions of, and rationales for, permissiveness from characters advocating everything from conservatism to communism. Howard's Marxism often appears to contradict his professed devotion to '"liberation" and "emancipation"'. He denies individual agency, crushes dissent and considers tolerance to be the 'soft liberal underbelly' of his adversaries.[123] This tension between the libertarianism of the counterculture and the authoritarianism of the revolutionary left is explored in this volume by Willie Thompson, and was evident enough to some at the time. 'There's no room for me in communism…as an individual', one longhair explained to the sociologist Paul Willis.[124]

Howard's dual affiliation to Marxism and the counterculture seems less odd once it is recognised that both movements defined themselves in opposition to bourgeois norms. Sociologist Frank Parkin found such 'deviant values' to be common among 1960s radicals engaged in what he called 'expressive politics'. This was a type of activism 'less concerned with specific achievement than with the benefits and satisfactions which the activity itself affords' and, as such, equally applicable to those living in communes as to those hawking radical papers in forlorn shopping centres.[125] An alliance between the two was further facilitated by the New Left's efforts to reorient British Marxism towards a lifestyle politics formerly associated with utopian socialists. Its leading ideologues, E.P. Thompson and Stuart Hall, wrote of reframing socialism in 'spiritual' and 'humanistic' terms, while its principal journal, the *New Left Review*, carried prefigurative articles on homosexuality, feminism and youth culture in the 1960s.[126] It was therefore unsurprising that the British gay and women's liberation movements, together with what cultural critic Julie Stephens has termed 'anti-disciplinary politics', had strong if strained ties to the far left in their formative years.[127]

Labour's contribution to permissiveness is embodied in *The History Man* by the party member and university vice-chancellor, Millington Harsent. As a radical educationalist and 'serious supporter of pornography', Harsent is evidently one of Labour's intelligentsia determined—according to political commentator David McKie—to overhaul the 'anomalous, archaic, irrational' laws governing personal morality.[128] They largely got their way in Harold Wilson's 1960s administrations, despite the opposition of James Callaghan and the studied indifference of Wilson himself, who omitted to mention any permissive legislation save the abolition of hanging in his *A Personal Record* of 1971. But permissiveness in the 1980s had the misfortune of becoming associated with the two poles of the party—the Bennite left and the Jenkinsite right—and it encountered ambivalence in Tony Blair's New Labour a decade later. Whereas Home Secretary Jack Straw thought it a 'hopeless endeavour' for 'the secular state to be judgmental about...adult personal relationships', Blair distanced himself from the 'liberal view of the "permissive society"'. And though the Blair government effectively decriminalised the possession of cannabis and lowered the age of consent for homosexual men, it simultaneously curbed civil liberties in the name of security after 11 September 2001. Blair's attempt to balance 'rights' and 'responsibilities' in this Third Way fashion drew criticism from both flanks.[129] The right perceived both tyranny and anarchy in a 'relentless culture of officially-promoted permissiveness', while the left despaired at illiberal policies ironically enacted by a government 'made up entirely of the generation for whom and by whom "the permissive society" was named'.[130]

The British Conservatives were no less conflicted. They portrayed themselves as champions of freedom in the manner of their mouthpiece in the novel, the young fogy George Carmody. 'I happen to believe in individualism, not collectivism', he declares when protesting against what would later be called political correctness.[131] Some influential right-wing figures, from economist Samuel Brittain in the early 1970s to the new-look Tory leadership contender Michael Portillo a quarter of a century later, urged Tories to embrace this brand of Millite libertarianism.[132] They found little support from Tory voters, however, who were marginally more anti-permissive than Labour voters on almost every issue raised by the 1970 NOP poll (Table 1.7). Furthermore, Tory party leaders detested permissiveness' assault on tradition. Margaret Thatcher pilloried the 'permissive claptrap' emanating from the 1960s, aides spun British prime minister John Major's 'Back to Basics' crusade as a 'war on permissiveness', and Conservative party leader William Hague entered the lists against the 'liberal elite' and its ultra-tolerant ways.[133] The Conservatives for once deserved their name, for their anti-permissive rhetoric revealed a visceral fear of rapid social change. Much as Margaret Thatcher contrasted 'fashionable theories' with 'the old virtues of discipline and restraint', John Major defended 'old certainties' against 'fashionable' social environmentalism.[134]

Such antediluvian attitudes had become a liability by the end of the twentieth century. The 'Back to Basics' campaign exploded in John Major's face once the press published revelations about Tory MPs' dissolute private lives. Conservative shadow minister Ann Widdecombe's 'zero tolerance' policy on soft drugs suffered the same fate in 2000 when eight of her Shadow Cabinet colleagues admitted to having smoked marijuana.[135] But even the Thatcher government—for all its bluster—had refrained from reversing any major pieces of permissive legislation when it had the chance. Censorship measures such as the Indecent Displays (Control) Act (1981) and the homophobic Clause 28 (1988) principally sought to remove offensive material from public view, thereby entrenching the privatisation of morality underlying most earlier permissive reforms. Political scientist Gillian Douglas also observes that Thatcherite family policy swam 'with the current' rather than 'against the tide' of the liberalising measures initiated in the 1960s.[136] In 1993, the arch-Thatcherite former Tory minister Norman Tebbit conceded that politicians were unable to instil 'ethical standards and customs'.[137]

He was right. Public policy proved to be a blunt instrument for regulating personal morality. Though Labour Home Security Roy Jenkins depicted permissive reforms as the unfolding of his master plan for a 'civilised society', such self-congratulation obscured the large gap between intentions and outcomes.[138] Like other reformers, he correctly perceived the existing legislation to be as ineffective as it was iniquitous. Backstreet abortions, homosexual liaisons and *de facto* no-fault divorces occurred regardless of laws to the contrary. It therefore seemed a 'good old typical British compromise' (in the words of one parliamentary advocate of abortion reform) to redraw the line between licit and illicit behaviour, thereby reflecting social realities and preventing the law from falling into still further disrepute.[139]

There was nevertheless something paradoxical about reformers' attempts to temper libertarianism with paternalism. The same social changes that inspired permissive reforms outstripped their limited and ameliorative ambitions. The chapters by Alison Oram and Julian Jackson show how lesbians and gay men increasingly refused to behave discreetly, while feminists demanded that abortion be a woman's right rather than a matter of medical discretion. Sloppy drafting further weakened legislation, as when a loophole in the 1960 Betting and Gaming Act allowed high-stakes casinos to be established under provisions designed for bingo halls. In another case, sponsors of the Obscene Publications Act recognised no contradiction between the 'free expression of opinion and the rights of the individual' and 'suppressing the pornography trade'.[140] Juries often thought otherwise and sanctioned the publication of much explicit material of no discernible literary, artistic or scientific merit. By 1970, A.P. Herbert disowned the law that he had drafted for being 'fundamentally at fault' in opening the floodgates to 'corrupt' smut.[141]

Opposition

The greatest advocate of permissiveness in *The History Man* is arguably also its greatest enemy, for Howard Kirk is a consummate hypocrite. But avowed anti-permissives appear only twice in the novel—each time offstage—once when conducting a campaign against pornography and again when picketing a nude production of *The Importance of Being Ernest* in an attempt to 'Keep Britain Clothed'.[142] So were opponents of permissiveness as marginal and cranky as Bradbury implies and, if not, why were they unable to reverse the changes that they so abhorred?

Opposition to permissiveness came mostly from the right. Its greatest propagandist was that self-proclaimed scourge of 'dogma-riddled lefties', the moral crusader Mary Whitehouse, who founded the National Viewers' and Listeners' Association. Its most celebrated political sympathiser was her sister-in-arms, Margaret Thatcher, and its principal mouthpiece became the *Daily Mail*, which stood firm against 'the gospel of permissiveness and self-indulgence'.[143] Yet puritanism, asceticism, communitarianism and a suspicion of the individualistic and the materialistic also spawned an anti-permissiveness of the left, albeit one more ambivalent than its right-wing counterpart. The cultural critic Richard Hoggart at once defended *Lady Chatterley's Lover* and attacked downmarket titillation as representing the tawdriest aspect of a 'Candy-floss World' that promised working people 'an almost unlimited inner freedom' only to deprive them of their vitality, authenticity and moral bearings.[144] The Catholic Labour politician Lord Longford likewise had no trouble in reconciling sympathy for homosexuals with hostility to pornographers.

Opponents viewed permissiveness as morally bankrupt. For the dominant religious contingent, immorality simply meant impiety. C.S. Lewis placed objections to the 'Same Old Thing' of moral absolutes into the mouth of a demon in his *Screwtape Letters* of 1942.[145] However, those of a less religious bent considered permissive doctrines to be every bit as depraved. The novelist Pamela Hansford Johnson contended that 'total permissiveness' had sanctioned a 'freedom to revel' which, in the case of the Moors Murders, sacrificed innocent lives for sadistic kicks. 'If "anything goes", everything goes', she remarked.[146]

To claim that fun caused pain was one example of how anti-permissives sought to reverse the terms of the debate, another being to dispute the link between permissiveness and freedom. Mary Whitehouse accused permissive intellectuals of being at once conspiratorial and coercive. They 'pressurised the young into a stifling conformity in the name of liberation' and were 'illiberal' in their silencing of dissenters such as herself.[147] Others focused on how the foot-soldiers of permissiveness were unable to exercise free will. Teenagers were too young, for all their 'false maturity'. The uneducated were too ignorant, being 'entirely without instinct for selection'.[148] Consumers of drugs and porn were too addled to make informed choices, the Longford Report of 1972 claiming that '"normal" people can become addicted to pornography'. And 'ordinary people', according to John Gummer, lacked the 'intellectual capacity' to practise the New Morality.[149]

The cause of anti-permissiveness was not doomed from the outset. On the contrary, the statistical evidence examined above suggests that anti-permissives could count on majority support on a whole array of issues well into the 1980s. A form of anti-permissiveness also emerged among some gay liberationists and second-wave feminists in the 1970s. The Festival of Light's Evangelical crusade against sexual explicitness prompted the gay magazine *Come Together* to declare in 1971 that pornography 'exploits us all'. For their part, radical feminists argued that the sexual revolution was a 'con trick' that served to 'disguise the oppressive nature of male sexuality'.[150] Their assault on heterosexism fed into rising anxieties over sexual violence from the mid-1970s onwards. Philip Jenkins notes that an issue such as child sexual abuse 'could be accepted and employed in various ways by activists of all political shades, moralists and feminists, conservatives and socialists'.[151]

Yet neither popular support nor fervent campaigning could compensate for anti-permissives' organisational and conceptual weaknesses. The logistical problems facing them dawned on Lord Longford in 1972, when he complained that opponents of pornography lacked any 'effective means of pressure or articulate voice'.[152] Mary Whitehouse's domination of the National Viewers' and Listeners' Association was at once its making and its undoing in that she repelled more people than she recruited. Downing Street routinely burnt her letters to Harold Wilson, claiming that they had got lost in the post.[153] The Festival of Light briefly enjoyed widespread support when founded in 1971, then shrank back to its Evangelical core. Longford squandered his own chance to create a mass movement by modelling his independent report on pornography on a Royal Commission. Instead of being taken seriously, the authors of the Longford Report were ridiculed as a bunch of self-appointed do-gooders, a charge that was as wounding as it was well-judged.[154]

The forces of anti-permissiveness were also fragmented. Mary

Whitehouse's diatribes against 'atheistic humanists and communists' precluded any alliance with disillusioned liberal progressives, while her conviction that 'the woman is essentially the mate, the home-maker and the mother' did not endear her to feminist critics of the sexual revolution.[155] A contributor to *Spare Rib*, Ruth Wallsgrove, explained how Whitehouse's objections to pornography were 'precisely the opposite' of her own. Wallsgrove accused Whitehouse of seeking to censor images showing 'sex as it actually happens' and of doing so 'in the name of the nuclear family and the sanctity of marriage—institutions that oppress women.'[156] *Come Together* drew a similar distinction when urging gay liberationists to protest against the Festival of Light in 1971. Although demonstrators and counter-demonstrators 'should have been unified in one common cause...to see the end of pornography', they disagreed over the nature of sexuality:

> Pornography to [Festival of Light campaigners] represents the idea that sex can exist outside the narrow confines of the strait-jacket called marriage. And so they fear it. They are unable to distinguish between an open and liberating sexuality and the use of sexuality to exploit and oppress...[157]

Gays' worst suspicions of conservative moralists were confirmed when Mary Whitehouse prosecuted *Gay News* for blasphemy in 1977. By this point, however, anti-permissiveness divided gays and feminists among themselves. The idealism of Gay Liberation lost ground to a porn-friendly commercial scene and revisionist feminists questioned separatists' insistence that women spurn men. 'Don't fucking tell me or another woman what to do', declared the unashamedly heterosexual Debby Gregory when putting the case for pluralism within the women's movement.[158]

Conservative moralists' problems were as much conceptual as organisational, for theirs was an unattractive creed unattractively expressed. Their denial of free will to all but highly educated adults, when paired to a desire to protect those who demonstrably did not care to be protected, produced a paternalism verging on authoritarianism. Teds had to be 'made to become boys again', stated the cultural commentator T.R. Fyvel in 1961; a 'lost generation' of youths required 'rules and...punishment' to save them from a 'horrific maelstrom of permissiveness', claimed journalist Lynda Lee-Potter forty years on.[159] More ambitious theorists subordinated 'universal rights' to 'duty' and characterised 'common morality' as a form of 'bondage' necessary for the maintenance of social order. No wonder that protestors brought a 'Coffin of Liberty' to one Festival of Light demonstration.[160]

Equally counterproductive were the melodramatic tendencies of anti-permissive writers. Most adopted a doom-laden tone: hence Christopher Booker's excoriation of the 1960s' 'Death Wish' and economist E.J. Mishan's assertion that 'the unrelenting search for the uttermost in orgiastic experience' was in danger of 'impelling humanity into regions beyond barbarism.'[161] Less pessimistic, if no less histrionic, was journalist Paul Johnson's analysis of September 11. Blaming liberals for their mollycoddling of terrorists, he predicted that the World Trade Center atrocities would 'pull down the curtain on a century of liberalism and permissiveness' and usher in a new 'Age of Reaction, when the clock was put firmly back to severity [and] discipline'.[162]

The problem with such reactionary sentiments was that anti-permissives had no usable past to which to return. So successfully had permissive culture debunked tradition that Mary Whitehouse felt obliged to disavow any 'reactionary' intent and Norman Tebbit cautioned against trying to 'put back the clock'.[163] Victorianism's stock had fallen so low by the 1960s that believers in the 'old morality' rejected 'rigid Victorian rules'. *Lady Chatterley* prosecutor Mervyn Griffith-Jones accordingly distanced himself from 'priggish, high-minded, super-correct, mid-Victorian' attitudes even as he quaintly sought to protect 'wives and servants' from four-letter words.[164] John Gummer preferred to characterise the Victorian age as one of prostitution and pornography and had little better to say about the first half of the twentieth century. In his view, the rot had set in well before 'the break-up of our society' occurred.[165]

Anti-permissives' thwarted nostalgia related to their difficulty in producing constructive proposals. Pamela Hansford Johnson confessed that she had no solutions to the problems she identified and those who claimed to do so found themselves in a bind. When unyielding, anti-permissives appeared unrealistic, as in theologian William Barclay's call for 'uncompromising purity' and that of Sir Arnold Lunn and Garth Lean to stop the 'perversion' and start the 'conversion' of England.[166] But when more flexible, they came across as contradictory by accepting fundamental tenets of permissiveness. The Christian author John Capon commended a 'much more open and uninhibited attitude to sexuality' while supporting the Festival of Light's efforts to censor its every manifestation.[167] The Longford Report bafflingly declared consumption of pornography to be at once an addiction and an 'expression of human choice'. Though hankering after censorship, it nonetheless decried any infringement of 'essential liberties'.[168]

Approaches

> Documented, imitated, derided, psychoanalysed, and frequently condemned in its own time, the Sixties promises to be the most confusing and misunderstood decade of the twentieth century. A conspiracy of moralists will woefully and quite wrongly attack, and therefore perpetuate, the image of the town as a kind of upstart Sodom. The ageing swingers, bearing their once-proud *Time* epithets like leg-irons, will watch their hour slip away… a generation sinking into the muddy clam of history, to be examined in kneeling awe in the tangled dredging-nets of nostalgia.[169]

Peter Evans accurately predicted in 1969 how his era would be remembered. Polemicism and romanticism continue unabated, due in part to the apparent reluctance of British scholars to translate the 1960s 'From Memory to History'.[170] Historians prefer to wait for the dust to settle, but the modest number of academic histories of permissiveness or 1960s culture may also testify to the methodological challenges that they pose. Because historians are primarily trained to handle written sources, they may have difficulty in interpreting music, fashion or television with the same degree of analytical precision. Permissive organisations' iconoclasm, pluralism and consequent tendency towards fragmentation make it harder to conduct institutional histories or to track down sources. As well as examining officials and intellectuals not unlike themselves, historians of permissiveness must do their best to understand bobbysoxers and drug addicts. To cap it all, they may expect to join Jonathon Green in receiving brickbats from 1960s 'survivors...scrapping like mangy mongrels, each determined to impose their own, sometimes self-serving vision upon history'.[171]

These are all good reasons why only two historical books and two articles with titles containing the word 'permissive' or its variants have appeared in the last twenty years. Historians' hesitant approach nevertheless means that the classic models of permissiveness have been produced not by them but by conservative moralists and left-wing cultural critics and social scientists. The conservative model is straightforwardly anti-permissive in identifying an 'enormous and shattering' degeneration of culture and morality.[172] Before the 1960s, they perceive a society built on standards that were grounded in tradition, upheld by law and supported by public opinion. After it, they see little but immorality (described as 'moral relativism'), incivility ('a crisis in manners'), mediocrity ('no artistic or literary masterpieces') and excess ('absolute liberty' tending to 'corrupt absolutely').[173]

Whereas the right portray permissiveness as a calamity, the left view it as something of a false dawn. In his brilliantly counter-intuitive *The History of Sexuality* (1976), Michel Foucault casts doubt on the 'repressive hypothesis' that contrasts a permissive present with an oppressive Victorian past.[174] He sees sexuality as being bound up with power mechanisms that operate through 'incitements to discourse' as well as prohibitions. Expression and repression form different aspects of the same *scientia sexualis* that scrutinises, classifies and contains sexuality.[175] From this perspective, the 'great sexual sermon...[that] chastised the old order, denounced hypocrisy and praised the rights of the immediate and the real'—the rhetoric of permissiveness—is not as liberating as it first appears. 'Western man has become a confessing animal', he writes, who in expressing what he takes to be his sexual identity simultaneously participates in transforming sex into discourse and exposes himself to the public gaze.[176]

Parallels exist between Foucault's critique of permissiveness and that simultaneously developed in the 1970s by the academics-cum-activists operating within the orbit of Birmingham's Centre for Contemporary

Cultural Studies.[177] CCCS theorists (many of whom were also involved with the National Deviancy Conference) share Foucault's fascination with outcasts and his belief that they were subject to containment through classification. They differ, however, in attributing permissiveness to the contradictions within post-war capitalism. In Stuart Hall's view, the permissive society split the middle class between the young and the old, the secular and the religious, progressivism and traditionalism and consumerism and domesticity. Dick Hebdige outlines how subcultures appropriated aspects of consumer culture for their own subversive ends.[178] Stan Cohen claims that respectable citizens created the 'Folk Devils' of their nightmares through alienating and demonising working-class adolescents. Jock Young relates drug use to the waning of the work ethic in an economy shifting from production to consumption, and contributors to the seminal CCCS volume *Resistance Through Rituals* (1975) argue that the commodification of sexuality instigated by the 'dominant culture' undermined the conservative morality that it otherwise strove to uphold.[179]

CCCS writers contend that this crisis of cultural reproduction allowed the young to contest 'the hegemony of the ruling class'.[180] Unlike Howard Kirk, however, they nurse no illusions that resistance foreshadows revolution. Hall writes of the 'disintegration' of bourgeois support for permissive reforms, and *Resistance Through Rituals* warns of the cooption of its countercultural youth wing by a 'profoundly adaptive' capitalist system.[181] Also prone to takeover are the very symbols of working-class revolt. Much as Foucault sees the 'reverse discourses' created by sexual minorities as operating within the same discursive mechanisms governing sexuality as a whole, Hebdige points to the inbuilt obsolescence of subcultural styles. Drawn from mainstream culture, these protest statements are soon drawn back into it in a cycle 'leading from opposition to defusion, from resistance to incorporation'. Stan Cohen's model is bleaker still in its vision of 'control agents' concocting 'moral panics' that served to marginalise youth subcultures and to consolidate the forces of conservatism.[182] What the right portrays as a 'genuine moral and cultural revolution' sponsored by the left is therefore viewed in opposite terms by the left itself. In Hall's view, the 1970s witnessed a 'return to moral orthodoxy, rectitude and "right-thinking"' after the 'extremely limited' liberalisation of the decade before.[183]

The politicisation of the field has come at a cost. First and foremost, right-wing accounts of permissiveness are works of polemic rather than scholarship. Historical arguments are treated in Gertrude Himmelfarb's words as 'weapons in the arsenal of the "counter-counterculture"', which results in a cavalier attitude to matters of conceptualisation and causation.[184] The fundamental conceptual flaw of these studies lies in their binary definition of morality, according to which things are labelled good or bad according to explicitly Victorian standards.[185] This prevents their authors from crediting permissiveness and its maxims of toleration and individual autonomy with being an alternative moral code to their own, as opposed to sheer 'de-moralisation'. It also leads them to overlook the contradictions in their own arguments. Himmelfarb is sympathetic to Victorians for being 'avowedly, unashamedly, incorrigibly, moralists', but castigates latter-day 'moralists' for their politically correct 'paternalism'.[186] Peter Hitchens likewise celebrates 'Tory individualism' while condemning other sorts and, though deploring 'conformism', wishes that parents would inculcate their 'prejudices, opinions, values, morals and habits' in their children.[187]

All right-wing narratives of permissiveness propose a trickle-down model whereby permissive doctrines confined to the deviant fringes of society before the 1960s came to 'pervade the entire culture' thereafter, but none offers a rationale for this process other than unverified (and often unverifiable) psychologising.[188] Christopher Booker blames the rise of permissiveness on collective 'neurosis', Paul Johnson on the ability of 'strange and highly emotional people' to enact legislative reform and Peter Hitchens on media indoctrination leaving the moral majority 'dumbstruck and powerless'.[189] As the last comment indicates, right-wing writers hesitate to ascribe agency to ordinary people. Gertrude Himmelfarb and Simon Heffer both depict the poor as 'victims' of a liberal intelligentsia. Yet Himmelfarb fails to establish a causal relationship between the rise of the counterculture and the 'rapid acceleration of crime, out-of-wedlock births and welfare dependency', whereas Heffer claims that the 'drug of permissiveness' rendered the populace incapable of exercising reason.[190]

The left's critique of permissiveness deserves much more serious consideration. Foucauldian analyses of 1950s homosexuality by Dan Rebello, of 1960s legislation by Jeffrey Weeks, of 1970s sex manuals by Stephen Heath and of mid-century psychology by Nikolas Rose have provided well-researched and thought-provoking correctives to Whiggish celebrations of the permissive society.[191] Furthermore, whereas right-wing cultural critics remain implacably Victorian in paying homage to Matthew Arnold and treating 'popular "culture"' as a contradiction in terms, the CCCS has introduced indispensable techniques for analysing the production and reception of the mass media.[192]

However, models originally formulated in the 1970s are in some need of reappraisal. Foucault's key insight that Victorians and moderns shared a 'will to knowledge' of sex has helped scholars to recognise similarities between the permissive era and its predecessors, but has been much less useful in explaining salient differences. Though Foucault doubts whether there has ever been an 'age of sexual restriction', his portrait of Victorian society oddly mirrors the 'repressive hypothesis' that he disowns.[193] He describes nineteenth-century science as being 'subordinated…[to] morality', schoolmasters on 'perpetual alert' for masturbators, doctors displaying 'systematic blindness' and a bourgeoisie deploying sexuality against workers 'as a means of social control and political subjugation'.[194]

Foucault nonetheless maintains that Victorian prudery was nothing more than a 'tactical diversion in the great process of transforming sex into discourse', much as he minimises the contrary 'challenging of taboos' undertaken by psychoanalysts in the early twentieth century as a 'tactical shift'.[195] Yet except from this very different type of medic, the readily identifiable forces of 'pedagogy, medicine [and] economics' that dominate his account of the nineteenth century do not appear in his briefer survey of the twentieth century.[196] This begs the question of whether sexual surveillance was a predominantly Victorian affair. He thinks not, believing that 'power is everywhere' and must 'hide its own mechanisms' in order to succeed. However, such a universal and 'invisible' *deus ex machina* lacks specificity and analytical power. Like many great works of revisionism, *The History of Sexuality* substitutes one overarching model for another.[197]

Most CCCS texts are similarly overtheorised and under-researched. Sociologists like Phil Cohen who practise participant observation jeopardise their objectivity, while cultural critics such as Dick Hebdige engage in surprisingly little textual analysis in their reconstruction of subcultural mentalities. Both these writers flesh out their empirical findings with psychoanalytic theory, Cohen relating Oedipal conflict to class conflict and Hebdige attributing Teddy Boys' racism to their 'repressed and inverted identification with blacks'.[198] The drawbacks of such an approach are made manifest in the National Deviancy Conference collection, *Permissiveness and Control* (1980). Following Stuart Hall's injunction to consider more than 'conscious intention and motivation', its contributors advance speculative models of social control.[199] Steven Box does not substantiate his claim that hyperactivity in children was a protest against authoritarian education and neither John Clarke nor Nick Dorn demonstrate that the need for a productive workforce dictated a clampdown against delinquents and drug users.[200]

Agency is also a problem in the CCCS' treatment of social groups. Though careful to disaggregate classes along lines of politics, generation and (to a lesser extent) gender, CCCS writers proceed to assume that members of these subgroups possess essentially uniform ideas and interests.[201] The petite bourgeoisie is invariably portrayed as a cohesive reactionary force, whether spawning the anti-permissive backlash of 'lower middle-class suburban housewives', displaying 'envy and resentment' towards working-class rebels, combating the reformism of their 'progressive middle-class' counterparts or representing a 'residual and traditional...individualism' that sapped the counterculture's revolutionary charge.[202] If the lower middle class is the villain of CCCS narratives, then youth subcultures are the victims. Stan Cohen sees youth culture as being as much imposed on the young as created by them and whereas Dick Hebdige credits subcultures with a good deal more gumption, he still depicts their subversive acts as 'just so much graffiti on a prison wall'. The scholars most responsible for establishing the post-war significance of teenagers are paradoxically reluctant to acknowledge their social impact.[203]

Youth and the petite bourgeoisie are pitted against each other in Stan Cohen's model of moral panics: the most influential and controversial idea to emerge from the CCCS. Historians studying all manner of times and places have found that the concept of moral panics helps them to understand how in-groups and out-groups define themselves against each other and how apparently irrational behaviour serves social and political functions. However, a sceptic might argue that the term owes its widespread applicability to its very imprecision. P.A.J. Waddington considers it 'a polemic rather than an analytic concept' because it provides no criteria to assess whether the societal reaction was as disproportionate as the word 'panic' implies. This holds true for the two classic CCCS accounts of moral panics—the reaction against mods and rockers in the 1960s and the mugging scare in the 1970s—in which there exists a tension between the authors' descriptions of subcultures engaging in genuinely rebellious behaviour and their discounting of public fears to the same effect.[204] The authors encounter further difficulties in tying moral panics to a broader 'escalation in the control culture'. Public concern in both cases focused on coercive violence rather than the consensual behaviour legitimised by permissiveness. Their identification of a militant illiberalism in the mid 1960s or early 1970s also conflicts with the polling evidence examined above. CCCS writers seem too inclined to accentuate the negative and eliminate the positive.[205]

The contributors to *The Permissive Society and its Enemies* adopt no single methodological approach, drawn as they are from the fields of cultural studies and social science as well as history. Most chapters are empirical, some more theoretical and their scope ranges from case study to meta-narrative. They also present no common line on the nature of permissiveness. It is seen as broadly emancipatory by Arthur Marwick, Willie Thompson and Colin Campbell; as riven with contradictions by Matt Houlbrook and Gerry Carlin; and as potentially exploitative in Mark Jones's disturbing account of paedophilia.

The nine chapters are loosely categorised into sections on sexuality, youth and politics. The three chapters in the first section, while all dealing with homosexuality, approach it from different perspectives. Matt Houlbrook demonstrates how the toleration sought by respectable male homosexuals in the mid twentieth-century further stigmatised those of lower status and higher spirits. Without a similar need to avoid criminal prosecution, the 'homophile' lesbians studied by Alison Oram established more independence from medical authorities and came closer to forming a 'New Social Movement' before the advent of Gay Liberation. Julian

Jackson's comparative perspective provides another contrast between homosexuals persecuted and tolerated by the law. He examines how gay organisations developed differently in Britain from France, where homosexuals were less constrained by legal sanctions than by a universalistic model of citizenship.

As we have seen, the young were simultaneously considered to be permissiveness' greatest proponents and those in most need of protection from it. Their role as agents is tackled by Colin Campbell, who outlines how they briefly overcame their class and cultural differences in the heady days of the counterculture. Mark Jones uses cultural representations of paedophilia to explore how adults viewed the question of whether the young were sexual beings and whether they should be treated as such. Related issues surfaced in the 1971 *Oz* trial, which Gerry Carlin uses as a window upon the aesthetics and sexual politics of the counterculture.

The politics of permissiveness are the central concern of the last three chapters. Rychard Carrington's study of *Oz* editor Richard Neville makes the case that the British counterculture was more Millite than Marxist. Willie Thompson finds that it was precisely these liberal aspects of permissive ideology that proved so hard for the revolutionary left to stomach, however eager it was to capitalise upon youthful idealism. Finally, Arthur Marwick draws on his unrivalled comparative knowledge to place British developments within a wider Western perspective.

Howard Kirk's scholarship represents the worst of permissive culture in being 'very empty but…always on the right side'.[206] The following chapters aspire to its finest qualities in their novelty and creativity. Permissiveness revitalised post-war Britain. It would be no bad thing if *The Permissive Society and its Enemies* introduced a little of the same verve into how post-war Britain is studied.

2. *Daring to Speak Whose Name? Queer Cultural Politics, 1920–1967*

Matt Houlbrook

> I have no doubt that we shall win, but the road is long, and red with monstrous martyrdoms. Nothing but the repeal of the Criminal Law Amendment Act would do any good. That is essential (Oscar Wilde, 1898).[1]

In 1967, as the Sexual Offences Bill decriminalising private sexual acts between consenting adult men was passed by the House of Lords, its sponsor Lord Arran marked the moment by looking back to this most famous of 'martyrs'. 'Mr Wilde was right', he observed: 'the road has been long and the martyrdoms many, monstrous and bloody. Today, please God! sees the end of that road'. As he linked the legislative victory of 1967 to the decades of pain Wilde had anticipated in 1898, Arran evoked a teleological narrative of struggle, progress and eventual liberation, crystallised through the metaphor of the 'road' to reform.[2]

For Arran, as for many commentators then and now, the Sexual Offences Act was a key event in a confident and self-congratulatory narrative that portrayed post-war Britain as a 'permissive society.' Here the decriminalisation of 'homosexuality' embodied a wider and more intangible sense of tolerance, liberalism and respect for individual rights and freedoms. Recent obituaries of Labour politician Roy Jenkins represent him as 'the great reforming Home Secretary', an agent of progressive cultural change whose legislative reforms were emblematic of a historical era. In this context, whether viewed as the embodiment of post-war progress or a sign of a nation in terminal moral decline, virtually all writers assume the Sexual Offences Act's powerful symbolic resonance.[3]

If 'homosexual' law reform has assumed a central place in debates surrounding the 'permissive society,' 'permissiveness' itself occupies a similar prominence in all queer political histories, with Arran's linear narrative being aligned to the story of what Jeffrey Weeks terms 'our' collective 'coming out'.[4] Although Weeks, Montgomery Hyde, Stephen Jeffrey-Poulter and Patrick Higgins dispute the importance of particular events, their stories share a familiar plot, chronology and cast of characters. 'We' struggled though a series of 'monstrous martyrdoms' against a repressive state and society to produce the conditions of 'our' own emancipation. The tragedy suffered by Wilde and countless others culminated in the unprecedented 'witch-hunt' of the 1950s that in turn prompted the countervailing Wolfenden Report of 1957, urging law reform. In a more tolerant climate, the sober pressure-group politics of the Homosexual Law Reform Society (HLRS) secured the 'victory' of 1967, but was quickly surpassed by the spectacular 'stunts' of the Gay Liberation Front, and the mature assertiveness of Pride and Stonewall. Here the 'permissive society' and the Sexual Offences Act are, to paraphrase Chris Waters, milestones in 'the forward march of homosexual emancipation'.[5]

Against this Whiggish progressive history, I want to develop an alternative reading of queer politics between the First World War and the late 1960s, one that treats the unifying operations of Wilde's '*we*' and the '*Homosexual* Law Reform Society' as problematic, rather than given. Though the emergence of a reformist queer identity politics appeared unequivocally affirmative, it was consciously underpinned by powerful exclusionary trajectories that encapsulated profound antagonisms *between* queer men. As they challenged the legal prohibition of their right to privacy by publicly articulating a respectable 'homosexual' subject—the deserving beneficiary of reform—queer men contested the meaning of their practices both with representatives of the dominant moral order *and* amongst each other. The meanings of 'we' and the 'homosexual' for whom rights should be secured were neither self-evident nor inclusionary and, like teleological narratives of 'emancipation', effaced—and continue to efface—multiple and inalienable sexual and social differences.

The creation of a respectable 'homosexual' subject was, in this context, a central point of fissure rather than fusion. It was assembled from interwoven legal, scientific and medical discourses and a particular moral politics of space. It was articulated within disparate cultural sites: in the courts, medical journals and the respectable press and, after the Second World War, in novels, autobiographies, sociological investigations, HLRS literature and testimony to the Wolfenden Committee. Never simply denying these differences, nor subsuming them into the singular category 'homosexual', this political project depended upon the recognition *and* rejection of practices positioned beyond the boundaries of respectability. In short, the 'homosexual' was constituted through and within broader matrices of sexual difference, defined by his distance from practices and people repudiated as abject, immoral and dangerous.

If this project succeeded in bringing the discreet and respectable 'homosexual' within the boundaries of social acceptability and formal citizenship, it did so precisely because it deliberately excluded men unable to fulfil the requirements of respectability. Those who inhabited the spaces beyond these parameters—the effeminate 'pansy', the man driven by uncontrollable lust into the city's abject public spaces, the working man moving between male and female partners—were left to face continued social outrage and the ever-increasing threat of arrest. Queer political interventions were about power. They were about elite men's privileged ability to access the sites of cultural and political influence and to create the 'homosexual' in their own image, affirming and liberating a narrowly conceived conception of the self and sexual practice, just as they excluded vibrant alternatives created, primarily, by working-class men. The post-war accommodation between the HLRS, medical and legal 'experts' and the British state—symbolised by the 1967 reform—cemented a growing division between the respectable 'homosexual' and the disreputable queer.[6]

The Contradictions of Queer Politics

In 1933, at the conclusion of a sensational Old Bailey trial, the Recorder of London, Ernest Wild, launched into a characteristically intemperate diatribe:

> The peculiarity of sexual perverts is that not only do they not think they are in the wrong but they think they are right and they regard any kind of interference as an infringement of individual liberty. These people glory in their shame. Sometimes they are blatant with regard to it.[7]

In the dock before Wild were thirty-two 'sexual perverts', on trial for 'corrupting public morals' following their arrest in a Holland Park Avenue ballroom. Arresting officers had described a 'blatant' spectacle of sexual transgression. Men had danced together. They had embraced, kissed and been intimate. They had worn women's clothes and make-up, and called themselves 'Lady Austin's Camp Boys'.[8]

Rather than cower before Wild's wrath, these men—most of whom worked in London's hotels—rejected any moral censure of their actions. Instead, they 'gloried' in who they were. During the raid and subsequent court proceedings, they produced a powerful critique of the laws of which they had fallen foul. As such, they articulated an oppositional politics of sexual difference in which they were moral, rather than immoral; they were citizens who claimed the rights innate to all Englishmen, rather than threatening outsiders. Of one policeman David M. asked:

> Surely in a free country we can do what we like? We know each other and are doing no harm...it is a pity these people don't understand our love. I am afraid a few will have to suffer yet before our ways are made legal.[9]

He was not alone in rejecting the state's right to police 'our ways'. During the raid, Austin S. declared one plainclothes constable to be 'too nice' to be a detective, promising to 'love him and rub his Jimmy for him for hours'. When cautioned, Austin replied that:

> There is nothing wrong in that. You may think so but it is what we call real love man for man. You call us Nancies and bum boys but...before long our cult will be allowed in this country.[10]

Austin and David interwove the language of British liberty, intimate privacy and medical aetiologies of sexual difference to challenge the law's moral foundations. Theirs was a full-frontal attack on a law that was both unjust and—since their desires were innate—incapable of policing them into 'normality'. The ballroom was thus a constitutive site of difference, positioning the Camp Boys in opposition to the 'normal' world beyond. 'We are all of our own class', Albert A. told officers. 'We are a species of our own. You could tell us a mile off', observed the Duchess. If 'our own class' denoted common cultural practices and 'a species of our own' suggested commonalities of physiology and character, their conjunction invoked a queer identity that was essentialised and self-evident. Moreover, as the language of mutual possession suggests, this was shared and unequivocally affirmative.[11]

Such discourses of social, medical and biological classification allowed Albert and David to challenge those power structures that marginalised them. Though denigrated as 'nancies', they celebrated their effeminacy—Austin defining camp as 'beautiful and artistic'.[12] Positioning themselves within a canonical queer history reinforced this process, so that law reform was portrayed as the 'vindication of our patron saint, the glorious Oscar Wilde'.[13] Here the claim to privacy—carried into the courtroom—became equated with the right to be 'gloriously', 'blatantly' and unequivocally different.

These spectacular encounters with the law thus mobilised a powerful articulation of queer citizenship that would never otherwise have entered the public domain. The law exposed queer men in order to contain the threat they posed to British society. Simultaneously, however, it provided an arena in which its power could be critiqued and a queer politics of identity developed. Ironically, the sexual offences laws generated the conditions of their own instability.

Alongside such direct encounters with the law, the pervasive threat of arrest sustained a more generalised critique of the sexual offences laws in the first half of the twentieth century. Like the arguments explored above, this position cohered around the deployment of medical discourse and the assertion of the queer's right to privacy. Yet the relationship between these two positions was profoundly antagonistic. The Camp Boys' assertion of their right to visibly occupy urban space existed in persistent tension with a largely middle-class political culture of discretion that sought to evade the law by becoming invisible to it. What for the former was a claim to the inalienable right to public difference was for the latter the very opposite. Their claim to privacy was predicated upon the refusal of difference and display: the notion that, apart from his sexual object choice, the 'homosexual' was a 'normal' man, and therefore no threat to British society. Privacy was claimed through *both* the promise of social conformity, *and* its valorisation as constraining difference. Once tolerated, the 'homosexual' would be able to live in complete accord with social norms, vanishing into the respectability of domesticity.

The most sophisticated version of this position, drawing on the earlier work of Edward Carpenter, John Addington Symonds and Havelock Ellis, was articulated in George Ives's *The Continued Extension of the Criminal Law* (1922) and Anomaly's *The Invert and His Social Adjustment* (1927).[14] Both, to varying degrees, appropriated contemporary medical discourses and deployed a moral politics of space in order to distinguish the repugnant queer from the respectable 'homosexual'. For both, it was the latter who should be left alone to enjoy his pleasures in private, unmolested by the moral guardians of society.

This claim started from the premise that, as Ives argued, 'homosexuality' had a 'physiological basis…[and] is ever latent in the actual nature of man'. Punitive legislation contradicted 'all the fresh evidence furnished by modern science'.[15] Such arguments were bolstered by a critical engagement with dominant notions of the queer's depravity that illustrated the antagonisms *between* queer men. For Anomaly, cases involving unashamedly effeminate men or those arrested in parks or urinals were 'unpleasantly prominent' in the courts and newspapers. The result was a popular image of 'an abnormally lustful person of more or less insatiable and uncontrollable impulses'. He admitted that 'when one realises the assumptions upon which the laws…are based it is easy to understand their draconian severity'.[16]

Despite endorsing such notions, Anomaly simultaneously distanced the 'homosexual' from these figures, thereby arguing for the continued criminalisation of public 'vice' whilst still claiming his inalienable right to privacy. As such, he articulated a dominant 'homosexuality' that was private and invisible, explicitly repudiating difference: 'the invert in his emotions differs but little from his normal brother…that his sexual reactions are inverted does not necessarily imply other deviations from the normal'. This was at once a statement of present fact and a promise for the future: the respectable 'homosexual' would assume the full responsibilities of citizenship once granted rights. Anomaly reinforced this argument by advising 'the invert' to 'adjust his movements to those of the crowd'. Anticipating Wolfenden, he advanced the 'reasonable hope that co-operation between justice and science will result in the drafting of recommendations which will be acted upon by those whose duty it is to reform our laws.'[17]

This invocation of 'co-operation'—together with such men's involvement in the British Society for the Study of Sex Psychology—indicates that the medical and scientific professions were viewed as potentially crucial allies in generating tolerance and understanding for the 'homosexual'.[18] Anomaly accordingly invited Dr R.H. Thouless to write an introduction to *The Invert*. Citing the 'grounds of science', Thouless endorsed Anomaly's attempt to distance the moral and discreet 'invert'—whose desires were rooted 'partly in hereditary factors'—from the 'perversion' of those arrested in public. For him,

> The mere possession of the 'homosexual' disposition is not a matter for moral condemnation at all. In a society made charitable by scientific knowledge the chaste invert would meet from the normally sexed the pity and sympathy given to the disabled instead of the shocked condemnation which is often his lot at the present time.

'The virtuous love of a homosexual', Thouless concluded, 'is as clean, as decent and as beautiful a thing as the virtuous love of one normally sexed…at the same time homosexual vice is as foul and hideous as heterosexual vice.'[19] The implications were clear: the private 'homosexual' should no longer face retribution from the law.

From the 1920s onwards, the respectable 'homosexual' and the progressive 'expert' thus forged a precarious alliance in questioning the state's right to intervene in men's private lives. The impact of their arguments was initially limited. The writings of Ives or Anomaly never reached beyond elite circles, the BSSSP drew tiny progressive audiences and the continuing persecution of 'homosexuals' discouraged most from publicly identifying with the cause. Despite this, familiarity with their defence of private 'homosexual' acts seems to have grown—paradoxically through the prosecution of 'respectable' men arrested in those very spaces mapped as abject and degenerate.

Unease at the moral condition of London's streets and parks generated a massive increase in prosecutions for queer 'street offences' between the wars. In many of these cases, magistrates expressed growing disquiet with police practices, particularly the use of uncorroborated testimony, agents provocateurs and apparently fabricated evidence.[20] Such criticisms intersected with what J. B. Lopian terms a 'deeper and more serious malaise in the relations between the police…respectable public' and magistracy.[21] Recurrent cases involving 'respectable' men and women arrested for 'street offences' suggested instances of police malpractice. The ensuing outcries generated a series of Home Office and Met inquiries into the gap between working rules and legal conventions, culminating in the Street Offences Committee (1927) and the Royal Commission on Police Powers and Procedures (1928).[22]

This volatile climate sustained a generalised critique of law enforcement, through which queer men exploited the law's procedural morality, challenging individual prosecutions for importuning or gross indecency by exposing the transgressions of individual police officers.[23] As Ives noted with bitter irony,

> So little…seems needed to constitute an offence that an alleged smile or wink, or look may cause an arrest…any young person is at the mercy of any two detectives hunting in couples…[who have] a degree of unchecked authority which places the liberty of citizens entirely in their hands...[24]

These tensions came to a head in 1927 with the prosecution of Frank Champain, a schoolmaster, war hero and Oxford cricket blue who had been arrested for importuning in urinals around the Adelphi. Convicted at Bow Street and sentenced to three months' hard labour, he appealed to the County of London Sessions, where his defence counsel, the prominent barrister Henry Curtis-Bennett, supplemented extensive evidence of

Champain's 'good character' with a ferocious attack on the arresting officer's conduct. The appeal was remarkably successful. The judge quashed Champain's sentence, publicly affirmed his character and took the unprecedented steps of awarding costs and forwarding details of the case to the Home Secretary, William Joynson-Hicks. The public furore was such that Joynson-Hicks referred the case to the Street Offences Committee.[25]

After the case, a Mr J. Chester wrote to the Commissioner of Police, condemning the 'pack of lies' told by the officer involved as 'most damnable to British Justice'. Seeking to prevent the fabrication of evidence, Chester demanded that importuning statutes be made equivalent to those regulating female prostitution. 'I pray that the time will not be far off', he wrote, 'when that Bill is passed making it impossible for an arrest unless a member of the public comes forward to say he or she has been annoyed and also gives evidence.' While he withheld sympathy for blackmailers or the 'degraded young men who live on a kind of prostitution', Chester demanded protection for the 'young innocent men...who do not do these things for a living'. In this, he tentatively began to map the essential site and character of the respectable 'homosexual', locating this figure *outside* the promiscuous public realm and arguing that law reform would reduce the number of importuning cases: 'As I have studied these man-woman characters intimately, I know quite fully that they do not solicit as is said they do, in the streets, but rather in a very much more different, sociable way'.[26]

Chester's critique was further elaborated in London's courts, as defendants paired unease over the operation of the law with medical aetiologies of sexual difference. It was Curtis-Bennett who developed the most consistent version of this position through a series of high-profile cases. His clients tended to be prominent and wealthy men, exploiting their class to secure magisterial sympathy and the best legal representation. In 1932, for example, Curtis-Bennett had a solicitor's six-month sentence for gross indecency waived on the grounds that the 'mental strain and anguish' and collapse of his career was punishment enough.[27] Primarily—as with Champain—Curtis-Bennett combined attacks on police procedure with evidence of 'good character'.[28] From the late 1920s, however, he and his clients began to work out the implications of medical discourses, transforming a generalised critique into a direct courtroom defence. In 1927 he defended a former army officer, Robert M., against charges of gross indecency. His submission, supported by the testimony of two 'Specialists', moved uneasily between environmental and medical aetiologies, yet hinged upon definitions of innate 'homosexuality':

> [My client] served…in India for a considerable period. Whether this has affected his mind or not it was difficult to say but he was undoubtedly a man of abnormal mentality. His condition called for institutional rather than penal treatment.[29]

Though this defence failed, Curtis-Bennett succeeded in 1930 in overturning a clergyman's sentence for importuning by attributing his actions to a 'malady'.[30] By the 1940s, the legal implications of scientific knowledge were clearly established. In 1944, when Frederick Levy argued that the case of a vicar arrested for importuning was 'really one for a doctor's consulting room rather than a prison cell', the judge noted that such arguments were 'getting more and more common'.[31]

The relationship between respectable 'homosexual' politics and the legal authorities was consequently more complex than the simple opposition between a nascent emancipation movement and repressive state. For if magistrates inflicted the full force of the law on the effeminate and many of those arrested in public, their reactions to men who appeared otherwise respectable were as likely to involve sympathy as violent condemnation. The legal establishment was thus never a static or united persecuting force, but engaged in an ongoing dialogue with elite queer men, resulting in conciliatory gestures by progressive magistrates influenced by medical opinion.

In 1932, for example, the Chairman of the London Quarter Sessions, Cecil Whitely, gave a widely reported lecture on 'The Problem of the Moral Pervert' at the Institute of Hygiene. Whitely had come to consider imprisonment 'an altogether futile method of coping with this class of case'. In cases of gross indecency, he noted that:

> It was essential to protect the public but the future of the

> condemned man had to be considered. The tragedy was that many of these men were of good social position and sometimes brilliant intellectually and with a long record of good service to their name.

Whitely recommended treatment at 'an institution suitably equipped with medical staff' for such respectable—if 'unfortunate'—characters. He concluded that 'the subject seemed a matter for medical men rather than lawyers'.[32]

Whitely was not alone in the judiciary in articulating such ideas. The London magistrate Cecil Chapman was a long-standing member of the BSSSP and publicly criticised the logic of punishing people for what he considered a medical condition. The North London magistrate Claud Mullins developed a similar relationship with the Institute for the Scientific Treatment of Delinquency in the 1930s. He regularly sought medical reports prior to sentencing queer offenders and—following a favourable prognosis—made treatment a condition of probation.[33] Such pressures were reinforced by a wider unease at the law's intervention into private space. Judge Atherley Jones regularly acquitted defendants at the Old Bailey. In 1922, he argued that 'although people who tamper with young persons…ought to be punished very severely, cases of gross indecency between adult persons ought not to be brought to court but should be a matter for the men's consciences'.[34] The use of discretionary judicial powers, either in outright acquittals or in substituting probation and medical treatment for a penal sentence, embodied a veiled opposition to the sexual offences laws.[35]

From the mid-1920s, increasing numbers of such cases were reported in criminological and medical journals, respectable broadsheets and mass circulation tabloids. The interactions between progressive medical opinion, respectable 'homosexual' politics and legal practice sustained an emerging public critique of the sexual offences laws. If this focused upon individual cases, it nevertheless established continuities between the reforming positions mapped out by Ellis and Carpenter in the 1890s and those that would be articulated with increasing vociferousness after the Second World War.[36] However tentatively, ambiguously and exclusively, however reliant upon mobilising sympathy for the poor, suffering 'homosexual' and however dependant on reinforcing the stigma attached to particular practices, elite men were probing at the law's margins to construct a legitimate private space.

Permissiveness, Privilege and Privacy

It was in the 1950s and 1960s that these trajectories converged, and the tensions and ambiguities inherent in queer political interventions solidified into a rigid bifurcation between the respectable 'homosexual'—the beneficiary of law reform—and the disreputable queer, who continued to be the subject of social opprobrium and regulatory intervention. The rapid social changes unleashed by the Second World War threatened Britain's demographic stability, generating profound concerns about the integrity of the family, gender roles and the nation's youth. Set against the increasing visibility of London's queer underground during the war, such anxieties coalesced upon the 'social problem' of 'homosexuality'. An increasing number of tabloid exposés, orchestrated by moral entrepreneurs like Douglas Warth at the *Sunday Pictorial*, gave pejorative notions of sexual deviance greater public prominence. Here the queer, a predatory, effeminate and lustful danger to the nation and its manhood, embodied a wider post-war crisis of Britishness.[37]

Set against the growing intensity of policing in this climate, however, critiques of the sexual offences laws formulated before the Second World War acquired a growing public resonance after it. Following high-profile prosecutions of John Gielgud, Lord Montagu and Peter Wildeblood, periodicals like *The Times* and *New Statesman* reacted against the excesses of tabloid sensationalism, drawing upon progressive medical and legal opinion to demand a reasoned discussion of 'homosexuality'.[38] In 1954, responding *both* to moral panic *and* that 'considerable body of opinion which regards the existing law as…out of harmony with modern knowledge', the Home Secretary, David Maxwell-Fyfe, appointed the Departmental Committee on Homosexual Offences and Prostitution, chaired by John Wolfenden.[39]

In mapping 'dangerous sexualities' through the evidence generated by official bureaucracies and 'expert' witnesses, the committee sought to render them visible as a strategy in their effective regulation.[40] Simultaneously, however, it generated the discursive space that allowed elite 'homosexual' men to challenge their association with pejorative notions of sexual difference, prompting a powerful political intervention that coalesced around opposition to the law. As the committee convened, its members were 'approached by a number of homosexuals anxious to discuss their problems'.[41] Captain L.H. Green sent Wolfenden copies of Symonds's *A Problem in Modern Ethics* (1891) and Carpenter's 'sane and reasonable' *The Intermediate Sex* (1908).[42] G.H. Macmillan offered to testify 'as to the point of view of one who had experienced homosexuality'.[43] Anatole James highlighted blackmail cases, arguing that 'the sooner the law is altered the better'.[44]

The committee agreed to listen to such men. 'The idea', noted the secretary, W. Conwy Roberts, 'is to...see what a few [homosexuals] look and behave like.'[45] Yet only elite 'homosexuals' caught the committee's eye. Of the three men who eventually testified, Patrick Trevor-Roper was a Harley Street consultant; Carl Winter, the director of the Fitzwilliam Museum in Cambridge; and Peter Wildeblood, the former diplomatic correspondent for the *Daily Mail*. All approached Wolfenden via Goronwy Rees, a mutual acquaintance and committee member, in an attempt to counter what Winter termed the 'disproportionate emphasis on ['homosexuality's'] more morbid aspects'.[46] For Trevor-Roper,

> Several of us felt...that the homosexuals they would have to give evidence to the committee would be the ones they could lay their hands on...who had been caught or...had been in prison or occasionally exhibitionists...We felt that they might not get a more considered view of people who are in fairly established jobs.[47]

Those who dared to speak the name of 'homosexuality'—those *allowed* to speak—were unequivocally respectable men 'in responsible positions [who] had successfully concealed their inversion'.[48] In providing an enabling space for queer politics, Wolfenden privileged certain voices at the same time as it silenced others.

Though Leslie Moran thus discerns a pervasive distinction between a 'canonical code' of 'homosexuality' deployed by experts and the disruptive language of queer men, it seems instead that both groups shared cultural styles, interpersonal networks and modes of representing the 'homosexual'.[49] Roberts thus thought Winter 'a very decent sort of chap'.[50] This cordial familiarity pervaded the proceedings. Before testifying, Trevor-Roper and Winter lunched with a 'sympathetic' Wolfenden in the University Club. Upon arriving at the Home Office, Trevor-Roper reported that Rees 'gave us a very warm and encouraging entrance, saying that...he is entirely on our side'.[51] While the disreputable queer was beyond acceptability, Wolfenden's encounter with these men eventually led him to criticise 'the assumption we are dealing with "queer people", whereas it seems that many homosexuals are in other respects normal'.[52]

The formal proceedings of a Departmental Committee provided a privileged political space within which to define the 'homosexual' subject and the case for law reform. When isolated to individual court appearances, the 'homosexual's' claims could be easily dismissed as an attempt to evade justice and the implications of medical aetiologies were limited to the *ad hoc* substitution of 'treatment' for imprisonment. When made by the visibly different, such claims were simply untenable. When confined to medical journals, this political position was unable to generate sufficient tangible momentum for reform. Whilst the arguments advanced by Trevor-Roper, Winter and Wildeblood were thus embedded in those developed in the 1920s, the community they addressed and the position from which they spoke the 'homosexual's' name had changed radically. In Wolfenden, the respectable 'homosexual' spoke directly to state appointees granted the authority to recommend legislative change. Since they had come forward willingly, rather than been forced into public scrutiny, they spoke with particular moral authority. Finally, they addressed an interpretative community of men like themselves, sexual orientation excepted.[53]

By narrating a singular 'homosexual' subject through their written and oral testimony—elaborated, in Wildeblood's case, in his autobiography *Against The Law* (1955)—these men developed a case for law reform that was simultaneously liberating and exclusionary. Their position hinged upon reconfiguring an impermeable and ineffable boundary between respectable and disreputable—public and private—with greater rigidity than had been the case between the wars. If all nodded towards existing critiques of policing, the earlier salience of such arguments was effaced.

Any plea on behalf of those arrested in public threatened to destabilise the respectable subject envisaged as the beneficiary of reform, eliding him with the abject realm mapped so assiduously by tabloid commentators. Instead, their arguments combined medical discourses with representations of urban life that characterised 'homosexuality' as both a privatised condition *and* a set of cultural practices. In Frank Mort's terms, they 'dramatised [their] sense of self through a series of confessional statements about the acceptable places in which "homosexuality" could be represented and practiced.'[54]

These arguments pivoted around a common narrative of sexual disclosure: the public confession of identity exemplified by Wildeblood's simple declaration that 'I am homosexual'.[55] Tacitly recognising the respectable 'homosexual's' social invisibility, this narrative mimicked the movement from secrecy to revelation common to tabloid reportage. It did so, however, in order to articulate a particular claim to privacy. For Wildeblood this marked the movement from darkness into light, from silence into a knowledge over which he and men like him claimed authority. Yet this was not the basis for asserting the 'homosexual's' right to a public life, but a necessary tactic to secure the foundations for a discreet *private* life. Rather than that affirmative claim to sexual difference made by men like the Camp Boys, freedom from the threat of exposure would allow the 'homosexual' to retreat once more into silence. These men came out purely so that they could then go back in again, constructing a respectable subject predicated upon the space of the middle-class home.

The notion that 'homosexuality' was an 'inherent biological characteristic' enabled them to define their desires as a privatised condition rather than a social problem.[56] Moreover, medical aetiologies meshed neatly with the careful mapping of the public-private boundary through which they articulated the 'homosexual's' respectable discretion. Drawing upon a middle-class moral politics of space, public queer life was represented through the tropes of promiscuity and abjection. In explicitly coding this as the realm of depravity and disorder, they—like Anomaly before them—partially endorsed tabloid narratives. Wildeblood railed against 'the promiscuous homosexual, who seeks his lover in the street':[57]

> You do not want people behaving badly in public. If you are going

> to have homosexuality...it might just as well be discreet...Soliciting, whether it is homosexual or heterosexual, is obviously a social nuisance and will have to be curbed.[58]

This hostility was echoed by their dislike of the effeminate queen, who was, Wildeblood noted, 'deplored' by 'homosexuals within the strict meaning of the word...of necessity extremely cautious and discreet'.[59] This rigid distinction was mirrored by a careful attempt to disassociate themselves from public images of the predatory queer—the corrupter of otherwise 'normal' men, youths and boys. 'Pedophilia' was, as Winter put it, 'just as revoltingly strange' to men like him as to society in general—'an entirely separate condition'.[60] Moreover, since all three emphatically rejected the argument that a 'normal' man could be corrupted and denied any personal attraction to such men, they effaced the threat of 'homosexuality' suffusing British society.[61] 'Homosexuality' was reassuringly confined to both the private sphere and a tightly-bound group of men. As Trevor-Roper noted, 'my private life tends to be virtually restricted to...the purely homosexual world'.[62]

Disreputable practices were partly attributed to laws that produced isolation and unhappiness and prevented men from leading ordered private lives. Winter thought reform

> would make a great deal of difference to the attitude of a number of homosexuals...who are extremely embittered and rather exhibitionist...[in] protest against what they feel is an infringement against their security...the lunatic fringe of homosexuals.[63]

Yet despite this ambiguous plea for tolerance, the witnesses carefully distanced themselves from these 'absurd people', defining their own respectability by repudiating 'the pathetically flamboyant pansy', 'the corrupters of youth' and the promiscuous who dared to transgress the public domain. The 'homosexual' was both masculine and discreet. 'No one realises how many of us there are', claimed Wildeblood, because we 'behave more soberly and...more conventionally in public than the normal men I know.'[64]

By establishing the spatial and cultural boundaries of 'homosexuality' along a rigid division between public and private, Wildeblood, Trevor-Roper and Winter began to define a subject who was far from depraved, possessing what Wildeblood termed an 'austere and strict morality'.[65] Winter made this explicit when describing his own social life to Wolfenden:

> I have many [homosexual] friends...we are all completely at ease in one another's company and the world in which we live...We visit each other's houses, go abroad...[to] art exhibitions and ballet and have a satisfactory life within this sphere.[66]

Winter depicted a bourgeois lifestyle that was at once familiar to all the committee members and far removed from the West End immorality exposed by the tabloids and punished by the courts. Such conduct explicitly mirrored the wider behavioural and emotional codes of respectability, particularly the emphasis upon self-control, restraint and discretion. Asked how he found partners, Trevor-Roper explained that 'one is introduced to them by other homosexuals', thereby rejecting the implication that he cruised the public city.[67] Inhabiting the realm of domestic order and propriety meant 'there is no evidence that [the homosexual] is less prone to the emotion of love than the heterosexual'.[68]

By presenting themselves as unequivocally respectable, Wildeblood, Winter and Trevor-Roper were contriving a political fiction for a particular audience, deliberately exaggerating the fixity of the public-private boundary. Their testimony did not mention queer commercial venues, which existed on the precarious boundary between private and public, respectable and disreputable. It was also strikingly silent about their own public practices. Wildeblood argued eloquently that 'I seek only to apply to my life the rules which govern the lives of all good men; freedom to chose a partner and...to live with him discreetly and faithfully.'[69] Yet in so doing, he neatly glossed over the question of where exactly he was going to *meet* that 'partner', and failed to mention how he had met the airman McNally in Piccadilly Circus subway.[70]

The legal reforms demanded by Wildeblood, Winter and Trevor-Roper were thus limited—that the words 'in private' be removed from Section 11 of the Criminal Law Amendment Act, thereby decriminalising encounters that took place in the home. At no point did they contemplate legalising public practices or queer commercial venues, or the right to be visibly different.[71] As such, they sought to remove the stigma and danger attached to otherwise respectable lives, legitimating and protecting a private 'homosexual' realm of discretion, fidelity and intimacy. All agreed that the laws regulating *public* sexual behaviour should be retained and targeted at the disreputable queer who continued to transgress the public-private boundary. As Wildeblood noted, 'if far-reaching changes in the law were to be recommended they would...be principally concerned with...[those who] tend to live their lives with discretion and decency, neither corrupting others nor publicly flaunting their condition'.[72] Regulation of the public-private boundary was displaced onto the respectable subject. A situation where 'there is no particular advantage in obeying the universal moral rule and ordering one's private life with discretion and fidelity' was to be replaced with a model of citizenship that carefully balanced rights and responsibilities.[73]

In its own terms this intervention was unequivocally successful. Moved by their encounter with respectable 'homosexuals' and the testimony of medical and legal 'experts', the Wolfenden Report of 1957 endorsed the three witnesses' claims. The law's purpose was in its view 'to preserve public order and decency, to protect the citizens from what is offensive and injurious and to provide sufficient safeguards against the exploitation and corruption of others'. Having accepted an innate 'homosexual propensity', the report recommended that private relationships between consenting adults should no longer be criminal: 'we are charged not to enter into matters of private moral conduct except insofar as they directly affect the public good'. In emphasising the importance of 'personal and private responsibility', however, reform was made conditional on individual self-control. Quite deliberately, the report stressed how 'this limited modification of the law should not be interpreted as indicating that the law can be indifferent to other forms of homosexual behaviour, or as a general license to homosexuals to behave as they please'.[74] Creating a space outside the law, yet refusing to accept a public queer realm, the report granted the respectable 'homosexual' legitimacy, endorsing his demand for social acceptance, just as it contributed to the growing stigmatisation of the disreputable queer.

Conclusion

In publicly representing the middle-class 'homosexual', Wildeblood, Winter and Trevor-Roper were certainly not unique in post-war Britain. Rather, their testimony was one aspect of a wider challenge to dominant narratives of depravity that aimed to establish an image of the respectable 'homosexual' for whom tolerance and legal recognition should be granted. Such arguments permeated the public domain in ways that they never had between the wars. They were developed in a series of published works including Michael Schofield's pioneering sociological investigations, Wildeblood's moving autobiographical writings and popular novels like Rodney Garland's *The Heart in Exile* (1953). And in 1961 they framed Basil Dearden's seminal film *Victim*.[75] With Wolfenden, these indirect pressures for reform gained further impetus. The Report did not change the law, but it provided an authoritative focus for queer politics—an officially endorsed blueprint for reform. In 1958, a group of middle-class men thus formed the HLRS to campaign towards that end.[76] With the public support of medical and legal experts and politicians like Roy Jenkins, the pressure for reform became direct and insistent. In 1967, after a series of abortive bills, the Sexual Offences Act was passed through parliament.[77]

Like the Wolfenden Report, the Sexual Offences Act embodied a respectable, yet highly exclusive, 'homosexual' subject. For if law reform created a legitimate private space for the 'homosexual' citizen, it offered no comfort to those who could or would not conform to such rigid models of desire.[78] It was what David Bell and Jon Binnie term a 'compromise'—'*we will grant you certain rights if (and only if) you match these by taking on certain responsibilities.*' The Act thus demanded 'a modality of sexual citizenship that is privatised, deradicalised, de-erotised and *confined*'.[79] Men who frequented queer commercial venues, who cruised the public city or who were excluded from private space continued to risk arrest and imprisonment. The recorded incidence of indecency between men doubled between 1967 and 1977.[80] Though private practices had been decriminalised, the boundaries between public and private were regulated with increasing vigour. Just in case the respectable 'homosexual' did not willingly assume the responsibilities of citizenship by remaining discreet and invisible, the law would punish him.

The narrowness of this legislation represented more than simply the limitations of post-war liberal tolerance, but was embedded in the limitations of the respectable 'homosexual' imagination and in the harsh realities of power and social exclusion in post-war Britain. The claims of the 'homosexual' subject depended upon his rejection of public sexual difference—upon accepting, even accentuating, a radical distinction between the respectable 'homosexual' and the repugnant queer. At once discreet and discrete, the 'homosexual' acquiesced in the silencing and marginalisation of those placed beyond the boundaries of social acceptability and formal citizenship. Respectability—the key to law reform—crystallised the antagonisms and contradictions characteristic of modes of early twentieth-century queerness.

Both Patrick Higgins and Jeffrey Weeks discern a radical qualitative difference between interwar Britain and the 'permissive society', a seismic cultural shift that enabled the forward march of 'homosexual emancipation'. For Higgins, 'no one, in public at least, called for a reform of the laws in Britain until the autumn of 1953'.[81] Weeks similarly notes the 'self-contained nature' of the debates surrounding Wolfenden and the Sexual Offences Act, arguing that reform occurred in isolation from earlier 'homosexual' political interventions and was the result of the laws' 'inherent instability' in the 'more relaxed social climate of post-war affluent Britain'.[82] As I have demonstrated, however, the mobilisation of an effective politics of identity in the 1950s and 1960s was shaped profoundly by the discursive terrain mapped between the wars. Men regularly and repeatedly called for reform of the sexual offences laws before 1953—both implicitly and explicitly—and the reform associated with 'permissiveness' cannot be understood without reference to the increasing influence of respectable 'homosexuality' upon medical experts and progressive authority figures in that period.

Yet this article has done more than simply trace the pre-history of 'homosexual' political interventions. Rather than a linear narrative of the 'road to reform', it suggests that the history of queer politics is marked by bitter contention, fracture, exclusion and denial. The successful claims of certain men rested upon the deliberate marginalisation of others. The reforms envisaged by Anomaly or Wildeblood were passed into law; those demanded by Lady Austin's Camp Boys were not. If there are continuities within queer culture, they lie in its very diversity. The marginalisation of the disreputable queer in the 'permissive' society was—and could only be—temporary, since legal reform failed to meet the needs of so many men. In part this explains why the Act of 1967 was so soon followed by the resurgence of a public culture it had tried to render invisible and the massive fragmentation of queer culture signalled by the advent of the Gay Liberation Front.

3. *Little By Little? Arena Three and Lesbian Politics in the 1960s*

Alison Oram

> We were sick and tired of being told what we were from psychiatrists and others outside. We thought *no*, *we* know what we're about, we are the experts. And so we became rather political in *Arena Three* (Jackie Forster, 1992).[1]

This chapter reassesses the aims and strategies of the British lesbian organisation the Minorities Research Group (MRG) and its paper *Arena Three* from their launch in the mid-1960s to their demise in 1971.[2] I have borrowed my title 'Little By Little' from the 1966 hit single by the great British soul singer—and lesbian—Dusty Springfield, to indicate and challenge the reformist image of earlier 'homophile' organisations created by the Gay Liberation Front (GLF) and the Women's Liberation Movement (WLM).[3] Elizabeth Wilson, who was involved with both these groups, has described how they 'despised absolutely the polite methods of their predecessors'[4]—and historians, themselves often veterans of Gay Liberation, followed their lead in emphasising the conservatism of homophile organisations in the 1960s. According to these accounts, the members and leaders of these organisations had internalised the contemporary pathologising stereotypes of homosexuals and aimed at best for the gradual social acceptance of homosexuality.[5] During the 1970s they were represented as less authentic as well as less courageous than the confrontational GLF. The MRG is accordingly portrayed as a cautious self-help group that provided succour to otherwise isolated lesbians. In Jeffrey Weeks's view, this was a necessary first step. 'The existence of support groups, however conservative and tiny...had an important impact…[on lesbians'] sense of identity and self-esteem', he writes, but it took the women's and gay liberation movements to transform gay organising into serious sexual politics.[6]

The role of the 1960s homophile organisations has recently been reassessed much more positively in American historiography. Historians have argued that the respectable public face of the Daughters of Bilitis and the Mattachine Society belied their far-reaching demands for homosexual rights and respect.[7] This process of recuperation has been slower in Britain, though a number of oral history accounts have been published and recent scholarship has emphasised the MRG's significance as the first explicitly lesbian social and political organisation in Britain.[8]

By examining the public face of the MRG through its monthly magazine *Arena Three*, its challenge to psychiatry and its relationship with the gay and women's liberation movements, this organisation created an innovative lesbian politics well before the appearance of Gay Liberation. Indeed it should be seen as one of the 'new social movements' (or NSMs) of the 1960s. By building a lesbian network, by contesting social attitudes towards lesbians and by critiquing existing scientific stereotypes, it was the first British NSM to concern itself with sexual politics and exemplified many features of the new political style.

A New Lesbian Politics

Legally tolerated but socially stigmatised, lesbians experienced little permissiveness in early 1960s Britain. 'Even the word "lesbianism" was publicly tabu', recalled *Arena Three*'s editors in 1969: 'If Lesbians were mentioned at all, it was only by way of the smoking-room snigger or the psychiatric "case history".'[9] Journalists and writers in earlier decades had portrayed the lesbian as a social danger—a potential marriage wrecker and seducer of young women. By the 1960s, although the Radclyffe Hall-inspired stereotype of the mannish woman remained in place, the growing influence of psychiatry and psychoanalysis had transformed the lesbian from a figure of horror to one of pity.[10] She was increasingly seen as a social misfit, her sexuality being at once a product of arrested sexual development and a personal failing.[11] One supposedly liberal treatment of the subject reported that female homosexuality was 'often associated with deep unhappiness' and asserted that lesbian partnerships 'produce the twisted embittered woman, only too familiar to psychiatrists.'[12] Popular and psychiatric valorisation of a 'true femininity' centred on marriage and motherhood meant that the lesbian was marginalised as 'a sad, mad or sick girl, a girl without pleasures'.[13]

Despite the force of these social prejudices, lesbian subcultures developing since the 1930s had created the opportunities for organising around a shared sexual identity. Post-war affluence and the expansion of professional and office work for women increased the possibilities for lifestyles independent of the family and participation in lesbian networks, especially in the anonymous city. The evolution of lesbian political awareness was also aided by a change in political culture from the late 1950s as a new politics of liberal reform took shape alongside the radical critique of the Campaign for Nuclear Disarmament (CND) and the New Left. In the years following the Wolfenden Report of 1957, sexual and moral issues including capital punishment, abortion and divorce as well as homosexuality were widely debated, allowing progressive as well as traditional views to be aired. While media coverage of the lobbying for homosexual law reform was often hostile and seldom addressed female homosexuality, it did create greater public acknowledgement of lesbians and gay men than had previously been the case.[14]

Lesbianism was also increasingly visible in other post-war cultural forms, making it easier for women to define their sexual subjectivity. *The Well of Loneliness* was reissued in 1949, while the camp banter and butch style of popular radio and television personality Nancy Spain made her a lesbian icon. In the 1960s, feature films such as *Victim* (1961) and *The Loudest Whisper* (1962) dealt more explicitly with lesbian and gay themes. Both literary novels and pulp fiction circulated images of the growing number of lesbian pubs, clubs and coffee bars.[15] This nascent commercial scene, combined with increasing cultural visibility and a changing political context, provided the necessary confidence, sense of sexual identity, and networking opportunities for a political and social identity to emerge.

Some lesbians, including those who were to become involved in *Arena Three*, were aware of homophile organisations in The Netherlands and the USA and attempted to use the male-orientated groups such as the

Homosexual Law Reform Society and the Albany Trust to construct similar networks for British lesbians in the early 1960s.[16] Another catalyst was a derogatory article about lesbianism published in *Twentieth Century* magazine in 1962. It described lesbians as self-hating, eccentric and cynical, living in a Home Counties world of dog-breeding and tea-shops.[17] Diana Chapman wrote a sharp response to the article and was contacted by Esme Langley. They joined forces with three other women in 1963 and together founded the Minorities Research Group (MRG) to create wider social opportunities for lesbians and counteract cultural hostility.

The MRG and its monthly newsletter *Arena Three*, published from January 1964 to the summer of 1971, pursued two aims. The first was to foster a sense of community. *Arena Three*, edited by the energetic Esme Langley, the *de facto* leader of MRG, adopted a jolly, upbeat, and often defiant tone.[18] It invented a tradition of lesbian culture for its readers by reviewing contemporary novels and films with lesbian content and promoting the seahorse as a shared symbol of sexual identity. Readers were invited to attend MRG meetings and branches were formed across the country.[19] The MRG also linked British lesbians to others worldwide through liaising with the Dutch homophile organisation COC and reporting on the activities of the Daughters of Bilitis in the USA.

More controversial was the MRG's second aim of educating public opinion and countering detrimental attitudes. Some lesbians wished for nothing more than a meeting place, leading them to split off into a purely social organisation called Kenric in 1965.[20] But some of the original founders believed that lesbians suffered from loneliness because of social ignorance, prejudice and discrimination and so were determined to address the causes as well as the symptoms of their marginalisation. In addition to monitoring the reporting of lesbianism in the media, the MRG sought to 'promote and collaborate in unprejudiced research in this field' that would demonstrate the lesbian to be a 'normal person'.[21]

Both these aims—creating a lesbian community and changing social perceptions of lesbianism—point to affinities between the MRG and other 'new social movements' of the 1960s and reveal its distinctiveness in instigating a new type of lesbian and gay politics. There is continuing debate about the distinguishing features of NSMs, but they are generally characterised as loosely organised networks concerned with the construction and assertion of personal identity, and engaged in cultural transformation rather than traditional political activity.[22] The MRG displayed all these characteristics.

Unlike previous homosexual reform groups, which took care to shield the sexual orientation of their members,[23] the MRG was explicit about its status as a self-help group for lesbians. Defying the invisibility of lesbianism in culture, *Arena Three*'s editors often wrote under their own names and made media appearances as early as 1964.[24] In this, they were bolder than some of their contributors (lesbian psychiatrists, for example, continued to use pseudonyms), while many among their hundreds of readers led private lives of secrecy and guilt.[25] Mainly middle class—teachers, nurses, office workers and suchlike—they did not wish to jeopardise their status, respectability and employment by revealing their sexuality, yet supported an organisation arguing that lesbians were just like other 'normal' women.[26] For these members, as well as for the purposes of public education, the name of the organisation was usefully anodyne.

Arena Three emphasised its own respectability and that of its readership, partly to avoid possible legal sanctions and partly to counteract the contemporary image of lesbianism as something 'nasty and peculiar'.[27] Stressing the normality of their members was nevertheless a challenging position to take in a period when lesbianism was automatically seen as pathological.[28] The MRG acted as a resource for support and sympathetic counselling, aiming to raise members' self-esteem and fortify them against social disapproval. By suggesting alternative ways of thinking about sexuality and by asserting the position of lesbians as a distinct sexual minority, it was also building a positive collective identity.[29] Like the women's and green movements which followed it, the MRG understood the wider political significance of individual consciousness and championed the politics of everyday life.

As well as developing a lesbian community and strengthening its members' identity, the MRG sought to transform how lesbians were viewed by the rest of society. The MRG paralleled other NSMs in spurning the established political mechanisms of parties or trade unions, nor did it make specific demands of the state. Instead, it worked for cultural change 'outside and underneath' these dominant institutions.[30] The MRG and *Arena Three* engaged directly with the discourses and symbolic systems—the media and medicine—which regulated the social meanings attached to lesbianism and caused discrimination. Like other contemporary struggles (for example the anti-psychiatry movement), the MRG challenged the key discursive space which structured power relations in contemporary society—science—aiming to reshape medical views of lesbianism by producing its own forms of counter-expertise.[31]

The radical ambition of the Minorities Research Group distinguishes it from those reformist single-issue organisations of the 1960s that attempted to nudge liberal opinion, solicit tolerance or change the law. It was part of a new kind of politics, the struggle to establish identity and change frameworks of meaning. Not all readers and members agreed with this position, and some were content with the social aspects of the MRG, but the organisation remained committed to a wider political agenda. In building community, asserting unashamed sexual identities and extending the definition of the 'political' by linking it to personal feeling and experience, the MRG and *Arena Three* anticipated the women's liberation and gay liberation movements which began in 1969 and 1970.

The Challenge to Psychiatry

The MRG's attitude to psychiatry powerfully illustrates its commonalities with other 'new social movements' in that it challenged medical orthodoxies and insisted that its members were the only true experts on lesbianism. Chris Waters has argued that there were two main approaches within British medicine in the 1940s and 1950s informing explanations and treatment of male homosexuality. The first, that homosexuality was innate or constitutional, derived from the work of Havelock Ellis. The second, and increasingly influential, Freudian approach held that homosexual behaviour was caused by environmental factors (for example, family relationships) and was therefore amenable to treatment.[32] While these approaches are also evident in the much more limited medical literature on lesbians in this period, a plurality of medical frameworks for understanding and 'treating' lesbianism existed in the post-war years.[33] There was no single coherent psychological model of lesbianism and very little new research was published until the mid 1960s.[34]

Doctors generally regarded lesbianism as less anti-social than male homosexuality (only a minority of lesbians being deemed promiscuous or corrupters of younger women), while some commented on the asexual nature of many lesbian relationships.[35] In its evidence to the Wolfenden Committee in 1955, the Medical Women's Federation presented the common medical model of a mixed aetiology for homosexuality (as innate and/or environmental), but also suggested that lesbians had no 'greater predisposition to neurotic or psychotic tendencies than the average heterosexual.'[36] These sentiments were not typical. The supposedly liberal doctor Eustace Chesser used lurid case histories to portray the lesbian temperament as jealous and sado-masochistic and Freudians equated female homosexuality with 'arrested development': a refusal or inability to reach adult femininity through heterosexuality and motherhood.[37] While lesbians in the 1960s might still be subject to aversion therapy or even be threatened with lobotomies,[38] other methods were more benign. Some sympathetic psychiatrists counselled self-acceptance, while others arranged introductions for their patients to lesbian networks and clubs.[39]

Lesbians could not avoid being influenced by psychiatry when attempting to understand their own sexuality and devoted much space to it in *Arena Three*. Though concerned about the internalisation of the more negative psychiatric models, they often assumed their lesbianism was a consequence of poor parenting or broken homes, especially in the early years of the publication.[40] One of the founders of MRG later described her youthful self image in the following terms:

> I thought I was a lesbian but then I thought that it was ridiculous and awful and every book on psychology I ever read (and I had a stack of those blue Pelicans) told me that it was immature and that I should really get my act together and reconcile myself to my femininity and find myself a good man and have children. And so I thought, I must simply get on with being a normal woman. Which I tried to do without very much success.[41]

Medical discourses therefore worked through self-regulation. Individual lesbians policed themselves against a social norm of feminine heterosexuality and judged themselves to be maladjusted and in need of help. Many MRG members wrote graphically of the increased despair (and, more productively, anger) brought about by their psychiatric treatment.

Arena Three offered plenty of evidence of readers' interest in explanatory paradigms derived from psychology, even among those who believed their choice of sexual partner was basically normal. Members were enticed into research projects by the promise of individual feedback and self-knowledge, whether through Rorschach ink blot tests or the analysis of handwriting.[42] The magazine advocated the provision of sympathetic counselling services for lesbians[43] and published non-pathologising articles by psychotherapists, including an occasional series entitled 'Healthy Homosexuality' by Hippocamp.[44] Later issues always carried Freud's statement that 'Homosexuality is assuredly no advantage, but it is nothing to be ashamed of, no vice, no degradation; it cannot be classified as an illness.' And, above all, it promoted the notion that lesbians were 'normal' women, as the novelist (and sometime bisexual) Iris Murdoch argued in the very first issue:

> Anything to do with…'treating these people kindly as persons in need of treatment', must be got away from. What needs to be recognised is that homosexuals are perfectly ordinary people, and vary as much as heterosexuals.[45]

MRG leaders sought to bring psychiatry into line with their own analysis, rather than remaining subject to its interpretations. Like Radclyffe Hall some decades earlier, the editors of *Arena Three* argued that it was not homosexuality but the stigma surrounding it which caused problems for lesbians. They also used humour and sarcasm to defuse the sting of negative social images. Esme Langley wrote in the debut issue of 'the airy realm of the headshrinkers, who hear all, tell all, know all, and contradict one another like polecats in a basket.'[46] Some readers, too, saw themselves as 'non-neurotics' and were critical of psychiatrists: 'The way they define maturity makes it impossible for them to admit that homosexuals can have a proper adult relationship.'[47] In a similar vein, one medically trained contributor denounced Anthony Storr's influential portrait of lesbianism in his 1964 book *Sexual Deviation* as 'disappointingly stereotyped and facile', while an article four years later expressed exasperation with the entire research enterprise:

> After digesting the miscellany of 'expert' bewilderment...the homosexual cannot fail to survey with dismay the 'great quantity of scientific and medical material available', and become even more firmly entrenched in the belief which most of us have (despite the blinding-with-science to which we are ruthlessly subjected), that homosexuals on the inside looking out know a darned sight more about homosexuality than pontifical pundits on the outside peering in![48]

At the same time, the magazine hoped that science had the potential to challenge negative stereotypes. It drew attention to sympathetic medical research published in US homophile magazines and praised Bernard F. Riess and Ralph H. Gundlach, two American psychologists who discovered that the family backgrounds of lesbians were no more likely to be pathological than those of other women:

> The findings...confirm our own experience, that the lesbian differs in no way (other than her love-life) from the 'normal' woman. Love, after all, is love, and never a 'sexual deviation'. All the more reason, then, in this day and age, for the supposedly 'authoritative' writers on human psychology to get with it, and straighten out the kinks in their own thinking.[49]

Presenting themselves as the experts on lesbianism, the MRG sought to change the basic premises of psychiatric medicine by offering their members as 'normal' research subjects in contrast to the psychiatric patients or case studies on which the current literature was based.[50] This coincided with the move towards large-scale statistical studies of sexuality initiated by the Kinsey Reports. In 1964, *Arena Three* encouraged readers to volunteer as a 'public-spirited action' to assist Dr Eva Bene, a psychologist researching the childhood relationships of homosexuals with their families.[51] However, the editors found it necessary to allay some members' suspicions of medical research:

> While most of those we approached offered their services willingly, many others expressed uneasiness, and some, outright horror, at the

> idea of being involved in psychological research...The objections raised fell into two groups...The first showed itself as a fear of attempted curative measures. The second as a feeling of indignation aroused by the supposed implications of mental illness.

They countered these fears by stressing the scientific credentials of modern psychology and reassuring readers that the MRG would act as an effective gate-keeper by assessing the 'sincerity, qualifications, method, and respect of confidence' of all prospective researchers.[52]

Bene's study, like those conducted by Frank Kenyon and June Hopkins, compared a group of lesbians recruited from the MRG with a control group of heterosexual women across a range of psychological or physical measures. It is clear that the MRG expected 'unbiased' research to reflect their own views. They believed that the 'truth' of their own minds and bodies could reshape the scientific agenda, away from pathologising lesbianism and towards their concept of lesbian normality. Its largely middle-class and educated readers were possibly more inclined to believe in the ultimate neutrality of science, whose authority could be used to make their case to the general public.[53] If so, their hopes were disappointed, since the results of these studies were decidedly mixed.

Bene's research, published in *The British Journal of Psychiatry*, did not overturn stereotypical depictions of lesbians. Instead, she argued that there was a relationship between parents' wish for a son and the homosexuality of their daughter and suggested that lesbians were much more likely to be 'hostile towards and afraid of their fathers'.[54] *Arena Three* at first simply reported Bene's conclusions, but an article six months later contrasted her findings with those of the more positive American study by Riess and Gundlach, implying that the latter was more reliable due to its larger sample size.[55]

Frank Kenyon's study of physical and attitudinal differences between lesbians and heterosexual women was similarly unhelpful to the cause. *Arena Three* initially described him in glowing terms: 'he has himself helped a number of our members already, and they speak very warmly of his fair-mindedness, integrity and genuine desire to collaborate in our aims of improving the "public image".'[56] But his findings tended towards psychological orthodoxy. Only 29 per cent of the lesbian group felt 'fully feminine', while less than half considered that their parents had been happily married. Fewer lesbians experienced pre-menstrual tension than married women, but more resented menstruation. The lesbians studied by Kenyon were also inclined to be heavier and shorter than the control group, having bigger busts, waists and hips.[57] Though such claims drew no immediate editorial discussion, the magazine published a letter that exposed his survey to ridicule:

> Dear Miss Langley—Research is very shattering to the illusions! No doubt we are mostly stocky, "hippy" and well endowed bosom-wise—but I did hope there were a few long-legged, lissom ladies in our ranks! (*à la* Emma Peel?) Ah well, love is blind, fortunately, and physical perfection is rare.[58]

Arena Three remarked that Kenyon's findings in a later paper were 'a little naïve'.[59]

There was a more encouraging outcome from research conducted by June Hopkins and published in *The British Journal of Psychiatry* in 1969. Hopkins's hypothesis was that there were no significant differences of personality between lesbian and heterosexual groups of women. In fact she discovered that her lesbian sample (once again recruited from the MRG membership) were more likely to be independent, resilient and self-sufficient: 'In brief, not more but notably LESS "neurotic" than the heterosexual study group', as *Arena Three* gleefully reported.[60] Within a year, Hopkins's findings were quoted in an article in *The Times* on 'one of society's loneliest minorities'. This was quite an informative and factual piece, which also discussed lesbian clubs and social groups, much of its content having probably been supplied by the MRG.[61] From a recognised medical journal to an authoritative newspaper, it appeared that positive research outcomes could begin to create alternative representations of lesbianism in the media.

US historians differ about the efficacy of homosexuals trying to yoke psychiatrists to their cause. Jennifer Terry argues that they entered into an unequal and potentially damaging relationship, while Martin Meeker emphasises that the collaboration of the Mattachine Society aided radical sexologists whose work led to the liberalising of attitudes.[62] The British evidence likewise points both ways. *Arena Three* had considerable confidence that lesbians' expertise on their own sexual identities could counter psychiatric discourses. Yet, however sympathetic the MRG believed psychiatrists to be, it could not control the conclusions they might draw from their research. Even so, *Arena Three* prided itself on having created a public dialogue on lesbianism by the close of the 1960s. One 1969 article claimed that, whereas the most scurrilous myths about lesbianism had been allowed to flourish unchecked before the foundation of the MRG, *Arena Three* had allowed 'women who really knew what they were talking about' to speak not only to each other but to the public at large. 'Before very long', it stated, 'the hitherto tabu topic was being widely discussed by every other channel of communication with the general public.'[63]

Liberation Movements and the MRG

Arena Three's interest in psychiatry waned and its tone became less defensive by the end of the 1960s, in part because alternative images of lesbianism were beginning to appear in debates on 'permissiveness'. Some relatively unpathologised interviews concerning lesbian sexual experience were published as part of a 1970 survey sponsored by *Forum*, the magazine of the straight sexual revolution. Cultural representations of lesbianism featured more prominently, most notably in the film *The Killing of Sister George* (1968) with its scenes set in London's Gateways club.[64] Positive new images of homosexuality also emerged from the women's and gay liberation movements.

The internationalist perspective of *Arena Three* made it aware of the American gay power movement from the 1969 Stonewall riots onwards.[65] Yet, just as the MRG is not generally viewed as a new social movement, nor is it considered part of Gay Liberation, being at most a precursor. Some of the older members of MRG certainly kept their distance from these new movements. One of the original founders, Diana Chapman, described how she welcomed women's liberation as 'absolutely marvellous' but did not like the 'brashness and anger' of Gay Liberation. Another member joked that she identified less with the Gay Liberation Front than the Townswomen's Guild.[66] But *Arena Three*'s response to Gay Liberation was diverse and to some extent reflected a generational divide, with a new group of younger editors expressing more interest in the GLF.

When we consider what Jeffrey Weeks identifies to be three novel principles of the Gay Liberation Front—the importance of collective action and self-help, asserting the validity of homosexuality ('Gay is Good') and openness about one's sexuality ('Coming Out')—it can be seen that the MRG and *Arena Three* played a pioneering role in every respect.[67] In terms of collective action, it was the first organisation in Britain to be led by self-declared lesbians representing their own interests. Its leaders were neither ashamed of nor covert about their sexuality in the hostile environment of the mid-1960s. And, as its readership grew over the remainder of the decade, *Arena Three* came to see itself as the main voice of British lesbians, with a key position in the spectrum of gay groups and organisations and in public debates. Gay Liberation brought a new vision of utopian change and inspired the MRG to become more forthright and confrontational. But it had already helped to forge a lesbian community and its emphasis on the rights and citizenship of lesbians link it to later political activism for local authority services, partnership rights and unprejudiced cultural representation.

Arena Three's attempt to correct psychiatric stereotypes of lesbianism demonstrated its belief in the validity of homosexuality. This assertion of lesbian authenticity, and MRG's encouragement to its members throughout the 1960s to understand their sexuality as a positive attribute, parallels that of Gay Liberation. It is striking that *Arena Three* could express such a degree of confidence in its anti-psychiatry position well before the Gay Liberation movement took up the cause.[68]

As for 'coming out', whereas Gay Liberation saw it as a political action to confront straight society, *Arena Three* treated the public declaration of sexuality in a different way, by both seeking publicity in the mainstream press and by suggesting the benefits of openness to its individual members. The 1970 'campaign for press freedom' represented a new phase of coming out, one that drew upon *Arena Three*'s longstanding efforts to recuperate the image of lesbianism. The magazine protested against the censorship of the mainstream press, which refused to carry their classified advertisement announcing that 'Homosexual women read *Arena Three*' lest it offend their readers.[69] *Arena Three* pointed out that the editorial pages of these newspapers made continual references to homosexuality and complained that

> The weird and wildly distorted 'views of homosexuality' presented by so many writers, film makers, playwrights and others must on no account (say the Fleet Street bosses) be challenged by a publication such as *Arena Three* which sets out simply to present the TRUTH to the general public...WHY should we, as women, as voters, as citizens, be discriminated against in this manner?

The editors drew strength from the example of gay power in the US: 'The GAY LIBERATION movement is going great guns in the States. It is high time we had a little more positive action over here.'[70]

The campaign convinced some advertising managers to change their policy and, despite the Press Council's rejection of *Arena Three*'s formal complaint in 1971, the magazine felt it had exposed the hypocrisy of the newspapers. *The Times*, for example, had solicited *Arena Three*'s help when preparing an article about the magazine, yet refused it a classified advertisement the following month.[71] During 1971 activists directly approached newsagents to sell *Arena Three*. This attempt to circumvent press censorship was another form of coming out, requiring the self-exposure both of the women who persuaded their newsagents to stock the magazine and of those who bought copies publicly rather than through the mail.

Although *Arena Three* refrained from using Gay Liberation's language of being 'out and proud', it increasingly recommended this strategy to its readers. A 1970 article in the 'Healthy Homosexuality' series examined 'the lesbian's most common bogey..."social disapproval" and the haunting fear of being "found out"'. The author debunked the assumption that disasters such as job loss and family rows would inevitably follow coming out. She suggested that many closeted lesbians wrongly dismissed the heterosexual world and ended up in little prisons of their own making. They should find gentle ways to 'tell' people and take part in office or family discussions of lesbianism rather than feigning lack of interest, ignorance or—worse still—disapproval. 'In the year 1970 that kind of protective colouring is old hat, completely unnecessary, and extremely destructive', she wrote.[72] The article sparked a discussion in the letters pages on the pros and cons of 'discretion', followed by another article arguing that heterosexual people were more tolerant of homosexuality than many lesbians assumed.[73]

Despite their commonalities, the two faces of gay collective action had very different political strategies. The GLF, with its Marxist perspective, sought revolutionary change and many of its supporters undoubtedly saw *Arena Three* as irredeemably conventional and old-fashioned. Yet, though *Arena Three* and the MRG sought to work within the system, this did not make them conservative or reformist. Published correspondence with Kenric in 1971 indicates that *Arena Three*'s editors saw their magazine as an ally of Gay Liberation, a stance reflected in the new style and tone of the magazine.[74] The previous year's open meetings of the Press Freedom group brought new women into the editorial group, and a relaunch that November aimed to achieve a higher profile and more readers.[75] The magazine sported a glossy new cover featuring a women's symbol encircling two women and printed some articles in the *bricolage* style of the Underground press. A 1971 report entitled 'A3 Grooves with GLF at LSE' described the issues discussed at a meeting of four hundred lesbians and gay men and explained the politics of the GLF magazine *Come Together.* It quoted the countercultural argot of its members—'Brothers and sisters have been busted by the fuzz and bread is needed for bail, for fines, for solicitors'—complete with a jokey glossary.[76] At the same time, the MRG continued to work with non-militant organisations such as the Campaign for Homosexual Equality and the Albany Trust for basic rights and services of particular relevance to isolated or closeted lesbians. *Arena Three* was enthusiastic about joint initiatives including the short-lived National Federation of Homophile Organisations (NFHO), established in 1970 with the goal of providing counselling services, meeting places and public education: all aims that the MRG had been pursuing since 1964.[77]

Arena Three's readers were similarly divided over political ideologies and methods in the early 1970s. While some attended GLF meetings and dances, and proposed marches declaring 'why should we have to hide?',[78] others were still keen that action should continue along moderate lines. Splits were apparent at the MRG's screening of a 1971 television documentary on lesbianism, 'The Most Important Thing is Love' which included interviews with members.[79] Among the large audience of *Arena*

Three readers and members of various other gay and lesbian groups,

> The discussion ranged from impatience with self-imposed oppression…to [advocacy of] much more cross-fertilisation between homosexual groups and organisations! This was punctuated with let straight society stay sick, while homosexuals stay an in-group, to pleas for homosexuals to speak to community groups of all ages and sexes…proposals for counter-action against social oppression by aggressive demonstrations were hotly contested by proposals of 'reasonable' approaches through responsible bodies.[80]

The 'hotly contested' reactions to this screening demonstrated that the early 1970s was an inauspicious time to form alliances.

As well as remaining ambivalent about the politics and tactics of Gay Liberation, *Arena Three* also critiqued it on gender grounds. The magazine had expressed a nascent feminism since it was first published. In the early to mid 1960s, new expressions of discontent about women's position were voiced, anticipating the renewal of feminist energies in the Women's Liberation Movement (WLM). Many readers were professional women who were well aware of sex discrimination and proud of their achievements in overcoming it. In 1971, *Arena Three* issued a forthright editorial outlining its relationship to Gay Liberation and the women's movement:

> GAY LIB–WOMEN'S LIB–YOUNG LIB–ANTI-APARTHEID…
> all the talk and most of the doing in Britain today is of liberation and freedom from age-old oppressions. And where do we stand on all this? Let's always remember that we are women first, homosexuals second. *ARENA THREE* has always stood up to be counted in the battle for equal status with men—and this whether the men are hetero, homo or bisexual.[81]

What they had in mind was the manner in which the male-dominated American gay liberation movement treated lesbians as second-class homosexuals. Their warning that Gay Lib would not necessarily work for the interests of lesbians was extremely prescient, for a year later many lesbians left the London GLF on just these grounds.[82]

Yet *Arena Three*'s relationship with the Women's Liberation Movement was less enthusiastic than that with its gay counterpart. It carried regular references to the WLM, reporting on the establishment of the Women's Liberation Workshop and its newsletter *Shrew*, and published a favourable review of Germaine Greer's *The Female Eunuch*. Members also joined the GLF on the women's liberation demonstration in London in March 1971.[83] However, the subtext of its reports indicated a slightly tense relationship between lesbians and heterosexual feminists. Women's liberation supporters were frequently derided as lesbians and, in this period, often chose to stress their heterosexuality rather than challenge the notion that 'lesbian' was an insult. Some of the main concerns of the Women's Liberation Movement—marriage, childcare, contraception and abortion—were also not day-to-day issues for lesbians.[84]

As a long-established political and cultural magazine for lesbians, *Arena Three* was engaged with and challenged by the new liberation movements. But the magazine was unable to maintain its focus and expand its readership in this turbulent period. There were significant editorial disagreements, Esme Langley announced that she was emigrating and, its relaunch having overburdened its finances, the magazine closed in the summer of 1971. A number of the other women involved in the editorial team went on to found *Sappho*, which took a similar political approach.[85]

The Minorities Research Group was more akin to Gay Liberation than the latter ever recognised. Viewing it as a new social movement allows us to recognise that it was already taking on important political battles in the hostile mid-1960s in a way that no other British homophile group was doing, thus making gay liberation possible. *Arena Three* was instrumental in creating a national community of lesbians, a network in which women could participate by reading the magazine, writing letters to the editors or attending meetings and social groups. The largely middle-class membership of the MRG included very diverse perspectives and lifestyles, but it was a constituency that was ready, in the mid 1960s, to develop self-acceptance and pride and hold society to account for their difficulties.

Above all, *Arena Three* pioneered the politicisation of sexual identity, with the crucial recognition that in modern society, power was centred around representation—especially, for lesbians, in the media and medicine. By attempting to change psychiatric discourses through asserting their subjective knowledge, they were engaging in a battle over the very meaning of lesbianism. Their engagement with the 'trick-cyclists', as some *Arena Three* readers scathingly termed prejudiced psychiatrists, was not altogether successful.[86] But the group could claim credit by the late 1960s for presenting alternative perspectives on lesbianism through sympathetic journalists and mental health professionals.

The MRG also proved able to evolve with the changing political context. Gay liberation re-energised *Arena Three* and emboldened it to engage with a younger generation of lesbians and feminists. Its existing principles were strengthened during the years 1969–71 and there was an increasing cross-over of membership and activities between the MRG, women's liberation and the GLF. *Arena Three*'s renewed emphasis on press freedom and its encouragement to readers to come out was a forceful articulation of its claim for social justice and their rights as women and as lesbians. Little by little, the MRG had achieved a great deal.

4. *Homosexuality, Permissiveness and Morality in France and Britain, 1954–1982*

Julian Jackson

> At various moments there are 'hot spots' where the future of the planet is played out; in politics it is at the moment Vietnam; on the front of sexual liberty, whether one likes it or not, the 'hot spot' of the struggle is today England.

These words were written in April 1966 by a member of the French homosexual reform movement, Arcadie.[1] A British gay activist who visited France a decade later was not impressed by what he saw: 'The French believe themselves to be free though when you argue with them, it turns out that they mean they are free to come and go as they please in the bars and the clubs…In England we take our liberation, meagre as it is, for granted, but the French are not even aware of its possibility.'[2]

This cross-Channel comparison is surprising. In Britain, with its reputation for sexual puritanism, homosexuality had been legal only since 1967; in France, with its reputation for sexual tolerance, it had been legal since 1791. The purpose of this chapter will be to explore these differences in the hope that a comparative perspective will illuminate the specificities of each country's experience. My focus will be on the more conservative homosexual reform movements in each country: Arcadie in France and the Homosexual Law Reform Society (HLRS) and the Campaign for Homosexual Equality (CHE) in Britain. This choice is dictated by three considerations: first, despite recent work on pre-gay liberationist homosexual movements like *Der Kreis* in Switzerland or the Mattachine Society in the United States,[3] little has been written on such movements in France or Britain; second, the membership of these movements was higher than that of the more radical movements which have been studied more closely; and third, it was these movements which had most difficulty in dealing with some aspects of the 'permissive society'.

France

France had no tradition of homosexual activism before 1945, the most obvious reason being the decriminalisation of homosexuality in the Revolution.[4] Of course homosexuals were persecuted in various ways, but Paris had a thriving homosexual subculture centred on Montparnasse in the interwar years and on St Germain de Prés after 1945. One guide book in 1945 described Paris 'as a world centre for homosexual activities.'[5]

In reality, the situation was less rosy. Since the late nineteenth century France had been a privileged site of what Foucault called the 'proliferation of discourse' about homosexuality.[6] One reason for this was that the precocious decline in the French birth rate encouraged strongly pro-natalist rhetoric. Pro-natalism had reached its apogee under the Vichy regime, which introduced the death penalty for abortionists. In August 1942 the government passed an ordinance punishing homosexual acts when committed by individuals under the age of twenty-one.[7] This introduced a distinction between homosexuals and heterosexuals for the first time since the Revolution, the age of consent now being six years lower for the latter.

The ordinance was retained at the Liberation as article 331.3 of the Penal Code. This was no oversight. Pro-natalist discourse was very present in 1945, prompting de Gaulle to call for 'twelve million beautiful babies in ten years'. Furthermore, the Resistance's celebration of 'virility' often verged into homophobia, as in Jean-Paul Sartre's essay associating homosexuality with collaboration.[8] The number of prosecutions of homosexuals rose between 1945 and 1954, as did the severity of the punishments.[9] A 1949 ordinance by the Prefect of Paris forbade men from dancing together in public. One reaction to these developments was the appearance in October 1952 of the newspaper *Futur*, which devoted itself primarily to denouncing anti-homosexual persecution. It particularly attacked the Catholic MRP, christening it the Mouvement des

Refoulés Pratiquants (Movement of Repressed Churchgoers). *Futur* folded after nineteen issues in April 1956 after its publishers were convicted of offending public morality.

Such was the background to the emergence of Arcadie.[10] Its founder, André Baudry, was born in 1922 and trained as a seminarian but never took holy orders. In 1952 he started writing for the Swiss homophile review *Der Kreis*, and was in touch with the Amsterdam-based International Committee for Sexual Equality (ICSE). He contributed to *Futur* but, finding it too strident, he decided to start his own review in the spirit of *Der Kreis*. The first issue of *Arcadie* appeared in January 1954. Baudry's attempts to mobilise the support of prominent figures were mostly unsuccessful. The homosexual writers Marcel Jouhandeau, Julien Green and Henri de Montherlant refused his advances, Jouhandeau denouncing this 'ridiculous' enterprise that would provoke a 'terrible persecution against non-conformists in love'.[11] The only known names to lend support were Jean Cocteau and Roger Peyrefitte. Recently feted for his 1944 novel of boy love, *Les Amitiés particulières* (*Special Friendships*), Peyrefitte contributed a story to the first issue, and retained links with *Arcadie* over the years. He also devised its name. Conjuring up, as one contributor put it, images of 'young Greek shepherds, of tender charms, playing the flute',[12] the title encapsulated the vision of the organisation. In a similar spirit, *Arcadie* preferred the word 'homophile' to 'homosexual'. Coined by the Dutchman Arendt van Sundhorst in 1949, 'homophile' was the term used by all the homosexual reform movements of this period: *Der Kreis*, America's Mattachine Society and the Dutch movement Cultuur en Ontspanningscentrum (COC).

Baudry's initial team of collaborators all used pseudonyms and included several teachers, a magistrate and an archivist at the Archives Nationales, Michel Duchein. Within six months, Baudry had amassed approximately 2,500 subscribers. His journal described itself as a 'Literary and Scientific Review' and adopted an austere tone. There were no photographs and the erotic short stories were extremely discreet. Even so, it was banned from public display in 1954 and fined the following year for offending morals through the press after the judges denounced its 'proselytism' as a 'danger for youth'.[13]

This hostile climate helps explain Arcadie's obsession with respectability, its fear of antagonising the authorities, and Baudry's desire to preserve his independence from other organisations that might compromise his reputation. This was demonstrated in November 1955 when he withdrew from the ICSE conference at the last moment because of the failure of Arcadie to become France's sole accredited representative.[14] To complement the review, Baudry created an organisation in 1957 called the Club Littéraire et Scientifique des Pays Latins (the Literary and Scientific Club of the Latin Countries, otherwise known as Clespala). Subscription to the review conferred automatic membership. Baudry leased premises in the Rue Bérenger, which offered lectures, films, poetry readings, and dancing on Sunday afternoons along very much the same lines as COC's club in Amsterdam. Baudry was also keen to establish Arcadie outside Paris. He had 'regional delegates' in Lyons, Bordeaux, Marseilles, Nice and elsewhere, but he failed to establish any club outside Paris. By the end of the decade Arcadie had about 4,000 members. Membership primarily meant receiving the review; in Paris, it might also mean frequenting the club. In addition, subscribers to the review received mimeographed circulars with information on Arcadie's cultural events, and also some personal ads.

Just when Arcadie seemed to be establishing itself, an event occurred which threatened to transform the situation of homosexuals in France. On 18 July 1960, during a parliamentary debate on the 'social scourges' of tuberculosis, alcoholism and prostitution, a Gaullist deputy named Paul Mirguet proposed an amendment adding homosexuality to the list and granting the government full powers to take all necessary measures to combat it. Baudry wrote to Mirguet repudiating the association of homosexuality with prostitution. He warned that further repression would lead to 'anguish, terror and ruin' for innumerable ordinary Frenchmen and reported that a number of them were considering whether to 'sell everything up, liquidate their affairs, prepare their cases and depart.'[15] The legislative consequences of the Mirguet amendment were limited to an ordinance in November 1960 doubling the penalties against homosexuals committing indecent acts.

The late 1950s and early 1960s were a paradoxical time for French homosexuals. Although the legal situation had worsened, there was also, as elsewhere in Europe, a burgeoning youth culture and a degree of social liberalisation. In 1959 there appeared a new homosexual publication,

Juventus: revue littéraire mensuelle (Juventus: a Monthly Literary Review). Although claiming not to be a rival of *Arcadie*, its declared preference for the term 'homosexual' over 'homophile' was a challenge to it.[16] Moreover, it boasted a glossy format, gossipy style and sexy photographs. *Juventus* may have been more in tune with the times than *Arcadie*, but it lasted only one year before it fell foul of the law.[17] Thus *Arcadie* remained on the defensive for much of the decade. Baudry discontinued the inclusion of small ads and announced that he had decided to 'accentuate the scientific nature of the review' in order to avoid the risk of seizure.[18] He confessed that he no longer dared to publish stories which could have appeared ten years earlier.[19]

Such tactical adaptations did not require any fundamental alteration of Arcadie's strategy. The fundamental objective was the integration of homosexuality into society by demonstrating its normality and respectability. The key words were 'dignity' and 'prudence'. As Baudry incessantly repeated, 'Homophiles are not prostitutes, depraved, eccentric and mannered individuals…[they are]…in society…alongside everyone else, in all professional, spiritual, political, cultural milieus…We do not ask for any special dispensation for homophiles.'[20] Baudry expended as much energy denouncing homosexuals for their frivolity as denouncing society for its persecution of them. His circular of June 1956 warned Arcadians to '*watch the way you dress*, watch how you behave' when on holiday.[21] Ten years later, he declared that 'If you are looking immediately for adventure, encounters in bed, ABSTAIN. Don't behave like a boor as people so frequently do. Oh, how vulgar, nasty, low, inhuman, bestial men can be.'[22]

Baudry's tirades were delivered in his 'personal letters', his articles in the review and his famous monthly speech at the club—the 'mot du mois' derided as a sermon by his opponents. Arcadie's emphasis on respectability was partly a question of tactics. It believed in operating behind the scenes, cultivating the authorities and opinion-formers. Homosexuals needed to be discreet: 'we are a minority and we will always be a minority. Our only possible policy is to convince intelligent people. They are in all parties, in the professions, in all the Churches…It is they who, little by little, form opinion.[23] At the Arcadie banquet a 'representative of the public authorities'—generally a high-ranking official from the prefecture de police—sat at Baudry's right-hand side. Baudry sometimes had to defend itself from rumours that he provided the police with membership lists. He was unabashed about these contacts and believed that his private interventions following the passage of the Mirguet amendment had prevented further damage.[24]

To critics who alleged that Arcadie had achieved little, Baudry replied in 1958 that 'in the present state of things, we think our energies should go towards stating the issue, educating, helping homophiles.' He accepted that more might be possible in the future, but 'for the moment history forces this tactic upon us.'[25] In fact, Arcadie never considered itself to be a primarily political movement. It was more of a 'spiritual family', Baudry explained, describing his own role as 'an apostolic mission, a priestly vocation' and urging people to visit him as one might 'the doctor, the teacher or the priest'.[26]

Yet Arcadie did want to transform social attitudes. Its review was directed to three constituencies: homosexuals themselves, opinion-formers, and the wider public. This was the reason for its seriousness: 'in the review we don't try to "please"...We prefer 66 pages of text to four photographs.'[27] The aim was 'to produce, starting from philosophy, biology, history and sociology, evidence, irrefutable conclusions which allow the homophile to live in a world when he will no longer be the man to destroy'.[28] Baudry invoked two authorities in the first issue of *Arcadie*: Alfred Kinsey and Marc Oraison, a Catholic priest who wrote in an exceptionally open-minded way about sexual matters from a Christian standpoint. The second issue had an article by the French sexologist René Guyon.[29]

Science, history and religion were three constant preoccupations of *Arcadie*. The role of science was to establish the natural roots of homosexuality: 'Everywhere men…and women…have been homophile, have remained homophile, as they were born homophile.'[30] One issue had an article on homosexual tendencies in childhood; another on homosexuality in monkeys. The past was excavated by the journal's resident historian Michel Duchein through potted biographies of such notables as Frederick the Great, Michelangelo, and Tchaikovsky, which aimed to 'demonstrate that that the sexual desire of man for man is as natural as the sexual desire of man for woman'.[31] *Arcadie* also engaged in a constant dialogue with religion.[32] Many articles denounced the obscurantist attitude of the Catholic Church, but it was necessary to tread delicately since there were many Catholics in Arcadie. In December 1971 Baudry asked the 'Arcadian' Gérald de la Mauvinière to organise a roundtable on Christianity and homosexuality, out of which emerged the organisation David et Jonathan. Although Arcadie's staunch independence precluded any formal connection, David et Jonathan initially used Arcadie's headquarters as a meeting place and mailing address.

As well as addressing non-homosexuals, Arcadie aimed to educate homosexuals themselves into a new way of living, 'spiritualising' their existence. Homosexuality was distinguished from effeminacy, prostitution and exhibitionism. The homosexual scene of St Germain des Prés represented what was to be avoided. Baudry wrote that 'Homophiles do not want to be confused with these caricatures, the merchants of love...these exhibitionists, these "boys who no longer have anything of boys about them".'[33] As he explained in 1960,

> Homosexuality is about one's nature, one's way of loving, one's way of living, a 'vocation' in the noblest meaning of the term. To be homosexual is not to prostitute oneself in the Place Pigalle nor to corrupt schoolboys. It is about love, in one's body and soul, for our fellow. It is not a choice. Socrates, Plato, Michelangelo, Shakespeare, Walt Whitman, Gabriel Lorca, who were all homosexuals (I cite six but I could cite a hundred) were in no way corrupters of youth.[34]

For Arcadie, effeminacy and promiscuity were responses to the treatment of homosexuals by society: 'the idea of adventure, soon associated with the idea of pleasure, pushes homophiles to change their partners ceaselessly and to multiply their encounters, in ever more risky conditions.'[35]

If Arcadie pointed the way to the new life, the club offered the chance to live it away from the gaze of a hostile society. Baudry, who was not ashamed of the 'glacial visage with which people reproach me', policed the morals of the club ferociously: 'as long as I am director of this club it will be thus: MORALITY ABOVE EVERYTHING, ABOVE EVERYTHING.'[36] Although his motive was partly to avoid problems with the authorities, it was also to provide a model for homosexuals to live a more responsible life. The club was to encourage friendships over the search for transient encounters:

> People think too much about the body...that is the terrible and awful drama of the homophile milieu...Arcadie is an elite in the homophile milieu...Don't just visit the club in the hope of leaving with someone...Establish a current of sympathy, of confidence and of freedom in the club. And if the 'rest' follows, so much the better...[37]

In the late 1960s the prevailing climate became less hostile to homosexuality. There was an expansion of the commercial scene in Paris which moved to the Rue St Anne on the Right Bank. In September 1969, Arcadie moved to bigger premises in the Rue du Chateau d'Eau. The prohibition against public display of the journal was lifted in 1975, and Baudry received unprecedented publicity that same year when he discussed homosexuality on the flagship television programme, 'Les Dossiers de l'Ecran'.[38] In this less repressive atmosphere some rank-and-file members of Arcadie began to find Baudry's moralising irksome. One member wrote to Baudry: 'why must we be so careful not to make any noise on the stairs? Why are we not allowed to gather outside the club to chat and laugh?'[39]

Such criticisms took on a more ideological caste with the emergence of radical gay politics in France in the early 1970s and the founding of the Homosexual Revolutionary Action Front (FHAR) in 1971. Although the FHAR rapidly succumbed to sectarian disputes, it was replaced by a series of local Homosexual Liberation Groups (GLH) that included some expelled members of Arcadie's youth wing.[40] These gay liberationists attacked Arcadie for an 'accommodationism' which tried to 'normalise' homosexuality. Duchein was shouted down as a fascist in a meeting at the University of Vincennes, while one of Arcadie's few prominent female members, Françoise d'Eaubonne, told Baudry that homosexuals should seek to disintegrate society rather than integrate into it.[41] The near impossibility of dialogue under such circumstances was discovered by the writer Jean-Louis Bory, who spoke at Arcadie's 1973 Congress and also co-authored a book with Guy Hocquenghem of FHAR. Whereas FHAR argued for the 'le droit à la différence' (the right to be different), Bory pleaded for 'le droit à l'indifférence' (the right to be treated with indifference).[42]

Gay liberationists argued that Arcadie had internalised heterosexual repression. Baudry's more extreme utterances lent credence to this view, but the reality was more complex than 1970s gay radicals allowed. While he inveighed against casual encounters in gardens or baths, *Arcadie* provided information about sexually transmitted diseases and cruising venues. It also systematically denounced negative representations of homosexuality in the media and applauded positive ones in an attempt to create a supportive homosexual culture. Despite *Arcadie*'s insistence on respectability, its objective was a society in which homosexuals could live openly and without shame:

> homosexuality is not a crime. It must cease to be a stigma or an object of derision. How many terrible dramas would be avoided the day when, in the metro, one could hear a woman say quite naturally to her friend: 'my second son is not marrying because he is a homosexual.' So we say to homosexuals: assume your condition courageously.[43]

Furthermore, although Arcadie theoretically rejected FHAR's ideology of difference, it remained open-minded as to whether all the values of heterosexual society were appropriate for homosexuals. André Lafond, one of Baudry's closest collaborators, refused to condemn homosexual promiscuity unconditionally on the grounds that 'the matrimonial and familial norms of our society' were meaningless for homosexuals whose only 'norm' should be the realisation of 'happiness and equilibrium'. Rather than falling into the trap of subscribing to the 'fallacious mirror offered to them by heterosexuals', homosexual couples had the 'delicate but exalting task of inventing…the life in common of two men.'[44] Arcadie's championing of 'authenticity' in homosexual relationships may have been vague, but its distaste for the commodification of the 1970s gay 'scene' mirrored that of gay activists.

Gay politics became more reformist towards the end of the 1970s. The

GLH collapsed and was replaced in 1979 by the Emergency Action Committee against Anti-Homosexual Repression (CUARH), an umbrella movement of gay organisations working to repeal article 331.3 of the Penal Code.[45] Arcadie shared CUARH's objectives, but kept aloof in order to preserve its autonomy. Nonetheless Arcadie did regain some credibility in this period for featuring Michel Foucault at its 1979 congress and Robert Badinter, a close aide of soon-to-be President François Mitterrand, at its banquet the following year.

At last Arcadie seemed to have acquired recognition and Mitterrand duly repealed Article 331.3 in July 1982. But Arcadie was no longer there to witness the event. The lease on the Club's premises had expired and mounting costs made its renewal problematic. Baudry, increasingly out of sympathy with gay activism, had had enough. In May 1982 he announced the end of Arcadie, proclaiming with customary melodrama that 'far from the tumult of these people all of whom I have loved, I will await my death.' Interviewed a month later by the gay magazine *Gai pied*, he was asked for his views of contemporary homosexuals in America. 'They make me vomit', he replied.[46]

Britain

British homosexual politics displayed many parallels with those in France, the big difference being all male homosexual acts had been illegal in Britain since 1885. This meant that homosexual activism concentrated initially on legal reform. Opening a club in the style of Arcadie would at this stage have been against the law. On 7 March 1958, six months after the Wolfenden Report recommended that private homosexual acts between consenting adults be decriminalised, thirty-three liberal worthies called for its implementation in a letter to *The Times*. Out of this initiative emerged two organisations: the Homosexual Law Reform Society, to campaign for the legalisation of homosexuality, and the Albany Trust, a complementary body to enlighten public opinion through its journal, *Man and Society*, and its newsletter, *Spectrum*. The two organisations were inextricably linked, and shared a secretary in Antony Grey (the pseudonym of Edgar Wright).[47]

The HLRS was a middle-class pressure group much like those

concerning abortion and capital punishment. Besides lobbying opinion-makers, Grey spent much of his time addressing rotary clubs, mothers' unions and university debating societies. In this sense the HLRS was not really a 'homophile' movement at all. It required no endorsement of homosexuality from its members, only the conviction that the law was wrong. Its first secretary, the Anglican clergyman Andrew Hallidie Smith, was married with two children, and the committee of the HLRS prevaricated over appointing Grey on account of his homosexuality. Grey later reflected that the organisation had to remain low key in order not to stir up opposition.[48]

The HLRS's low profile meant that it lacked the muscle to impose its views once the issue was taken up in parliament. The parliamentary sponsors of reform—Lord Arran in the Lords and Leo Abse in the Commons—were both mavericks far from favourable towards homosexuality. Lord Arran, having been informed by Grey that he was secretary of the HLRS 'because I am a homosexual', replied: 'I wish you hadn't told me that.'[49] Abse, meanwhile, urged Grey to distinguish the HLRS from the 'ham-fisted' Abortion Law Reform Association by taking 'no action which could be regarded as a public campaign'.[50] For all its behind-the-scenes lobbying, the HLRS was not directly consulted on the wording of the bill and proved unable to prevent parliament from imposing several restrictions: the age of consent for homosexual relations was fixed at twenty-one (as opposed to sixteen for heterosexual relations), homosexuality remained illegal in the armed forces, and the law did not apply to Scotland or Northern Ireland. The spirit in which the bill was passed found expression in Arran's comment that 'no amount of legislation will prevent homosexuals from being the subject of dislike, derision or at best pity.' Grey 'almost puked' on hearing these words.[51]

The question was where to go next. However restrictive, the new law had opened up a legal space for homosexual activity. But Grey was pessimistic about the immediate outlook:

> In spite of all the progress in informing the public about these things, and despite law reform, there is still far too little real understanding of the true nature of homosexuality. Very many people, even today, still do not understand that in essence it is about love,

> and not simply some behaviour which immoral people indulge in for 'kicks'. While unreserved social acceptance of the homosexual may seem a legitimate and urgent goal for 'homophile' organisations to campaign for, it is surely unrealistic to expect most people who are not themselves homosexual to regard homosexuality as being other than a personal misfortune.[52]

Grey believed that establishing a club for homosexuals might be a means of dispelling such attitudes. It would aim to 'integrate' rather than 'separate off homosexuals from society' and to help them build 'permanent relationships based on affection in place of casual promiscuous ones'.[53] Although Grey's direct inspiration was the Dutch COC, his vision was entirely in line with that of Baudry.[54] In May 1968 he proposed a meeting with Home Office officials, senior policemen, representatives from the Dutch and Danish clubs, and possibly Arcadie.[55]

But Grey was hamstrung by the caution of the HLRS and Albany Trust. Arran deplored the prospect of homosexuals 'flaunting themselves in public places' and wished them to bear the 'distaste and ridicule' of society 'modestly and in quietness'.[56] Grey conceded that some London clubs were 'jam-packed nightly with teenagers (not to mention dope pushers and other vicious types)', but considered this all the more reason to establish 'a well-run social centre where the timid, shy and maladjusted can safely and beneficially go'.[57] Arran was not persuaded. He anticipated demands for 'similar clubs for lesbians and sadists' and declared that 'what is good enough for the Dutch is not good enough for us.'[58]

While Grey shelved his plans until the Albany Trust chose to pursue a 'more satisfactorily "radical" line', action was being taken by an affiliated organisation, the North Western Homosexual Law Reform Society (NWHLRS).[59] Founded in 1964 by a Labour councillor named Allan Horsfall, it proposed to take advantage of the 1967 reforms by launching a chain of 'Esquire' Clubs on the COC model.[60] After it was clear that no such initiative would be undertaken by the Albany Trust, the NWHLRS decided to go it alone. Rechristened the Committee (and later Campaign) for Homosexual Equality (CHE) in April 1969, it was the first homophile organisation to be founded in Britain.

Plans to open the first Esquire Club in Burnley were blocked by the local council in 1971, but the issue remained on the agenda and the CHE executive dispatched a fact-finding mission to Holland in 1972.[61] The objective was to create a homosexual community distinct from cruising and the emerging commercial 'scene'. CHE generally avoided the explicit moralising of Arcadie but there was an implicit assumption that promiscuity was an undesirable by-product of ostracism and persecution. Though no club was ever founded, local CHE groups did provide discreet and decorous social activities for their members.

Almost immediately after the emergence of CHE, however, the whole matter of establishing a club was somewhat eclipsed by the emergence of the Gay Liberation Front (GLF) in 1970. The GLF was founded by two LSE students, Bob Mellors and Aubrey Walter, who had both been exposed to the new wave of gay activism in the United States. Like the French FHAR, GLF rejected integration and linked the oppression of homosexuals to capitalist society. Most revolutionary was its openness: 'gays' were exhorted to 'come out' and assert their identity with 'pride'. It repudiated any formal organisational structures and its meetings were cacophonous. By the summer of 1972 the energy of GLF was consumed by acrimonious divisions between men and women, libertarians and socialists, radical queens and Marxist feminists. But nothing would ever be quite the same again.[62]

The GLF challenged the assumptions and strategy of existing British homophile organisations in much the same manner as the FHAR in France. One of those who attended the first meetings of GLF was Antony Grey, and his initial verdict was more open-minded than Baudry's. He applauded 'the real sense of brotherhood' and accepted that this 'new spirit' might do more to 'help the timid and isolated "closet queens" towards greater self-acceptance...than all the do-goodery in the world'.[63] But Grey personified the do-goodery so despised by GLF activists. They suspected him of trying to take control of the movement, even of being a CIA agent.[64] He later wrote that 'GLF people looked on the past period of gentle law reform as Uncle-Tomism. I feel that I was Stalinised, treated like Trotsky because the past history wasn't popular.'[65]

During the 1970s the Albany Trust confined itself to a largely counselling role. The challenge of GLF-style activism was irrelevant to it, since the two organisations operated in different universes. The same was not true of CHE which, having been founded out of frustration with the HLRS, now found itself outflanked on the left. CHE was unsure how to respond. In January 1971, a CHE member wrote to Horsfall that, although gay liberationists managed to 'alienate more people than they encourage', their activism made CHE seem moribund.[66] But its Secretary General, Paul Temperton, felt that any superficial similarities between the aims of CHE and GLF were outweighed by the fact that 'We are non political and don't believe that prejudice against homosexuals has anything to do with capitalism.'[67]

Relations were not always as bad as such polemics might suggest. After a conference in Leeds in June 1971 attended by representatives from the two organisations, Temperton noted that 'the most hostile people on both sides cooled down a bit and some of the rest of us managed to put more emphasis on the common ground between CHE and GLF.'[68] An attempt to forge formal links between the two organisations came to nothing,[69] but cooperation occurred over specific issues. The GLF supported CHE's attempt to establish its Burnley club and they both campaigned against the anti-homosexual bias of David Reuben's book *Everything You Wanted to Know about Sex, But Were Afraid to Ask* (1969).[70] CHE risked 'getting our message swallowed up in a GLF demonstration' when it attended the first Gay Pride event in July 1972, while members of both organisations helped to found *Gay News* that same year.

The arrival of *Gay News* coincided with the end of GLF. Nonetheless its new style of activism continued to pose problems for CHE, with one executive member resigning in 1972 on account of its conservatism and integrationism.[71] There were related and justifiable complaints that much of its membership was 'quiet and discreet...middle-aged, middle-class and middle-sexed'.[72] Moreover, CHE was chronically exercised by the problem of combining and prioritising its social and campaigning activities. The London groups were criticised by Temperton for their '100 per cent concentration on social events'—possibly because the GLF had siphoned off the political activists there—and one of their members wrote to complain that they 'seem to be little better than micro-gay bars for inadequates'. The National Council decided in 1971 that CHE should not have groups which were purely social, but that purely social groups could serve a purpose for their members.[73] What this meant was anybody's guess.

CHE became notoriously obsessed with its own structures, as if these offered some magic organisational cure for its members' lack of militancy. To this end, its 1974 national conference committed itself to campaign vigorously to reduce the age of consent to sixteen years and to repeal discrimination against homosexuals in the armed forces. *Gay News* applauded its newfound 'self-confidence'[74] and it subsequently acquired something of the spirit of the GLF, gaining membership and participating actively in Gay Pride marches. But its efforts came to nothing, as the House of Lords refused to lower the age of consent in 1977 and Margaret Thatcher's 1979 victory scotched any immediate chance of further reform. CHE lost its impetus and its membership started to fall. In 1982 yet another restructuring plan was introduced, allowing members to be either in the campaigning groups or in social organisations (GCOs), in effect dividing the organisation into two. But the rise of commercial gay venues reduced the demand for CHE's social activities and it played little part in the revival of gay activism in response to the notorious Clause 28 in 1988.

Comparisons

Arcadie ceased to exist in 1982, the same year that CHE effectively abandoned its role as a campaigning organisation. In both countries, gay politics were to be transformed from the mid 1980s by the arrival of HIV/AIDS. This seems, therefore, an appropriate date to end these two parallel histories. What conclusions can we draw from the comparison between them?

In many respects there was a broadly similar pattern in both France and Britain even if the chronologies were not synchronised. In both countries, 'reformist' movements emerged from the 1950s onwards (Arcadie in 1954; HLRS and the Albany Trust in 1958, CHE in 1969). Radical gay politics, inspired by America, arrived at the end of the 1960s (FHAR in 1971–3, GLF in 1970–2). These radical movements quickly burnt themselves out, although their influence endured in the form of gay newspapers (*Gay News* in 1972, *Gai pied* in 1980) and gay bookshops (Gay's the Word in London in 1979, Mots à la bouche in Paris in 1983). Finally, from the middle of the 1970s there was a return to the theme of law reform and civil rights (the establishment of CUARH in 1978, CHE's national conference in 1974).

These parallel histories were also intersecting ones. FHAR activists attended Britain's first Gay Pride week in 1972. Michel Duchein wrote about Britain in *Arcadie*, enjoyed good relations with Antony Grey, addressed the Albany Trust in 1966 and attended CHE's 1974 conference,[75] while Grey in turn spoke at one of Arcadie's colloquia. Both Arcadie and the HLRS preferred lobbying to mass campaigns and, together in large part with CHE, they subscribed to an 'integrationist', anti-materialist and moral vision of homosexuality. In that sense they were both unhappy with aspects of the 'permissive society'.

In the end, however, the differences are more striking than the similarities. Arcadie was undoubtedly more conservative than any of its British equivalents. In 1959 Duchein argued that the HLRS had polarised opinion before the British elections and pushed the government into taking a more hostile stand than it might otherwise have done. 'Minorities should not adopt aggressive attitudes', he commented.[76] But it was in the 1970s that the British and French experiences diverged fundamentally. While CHE was able to engage in some sort of dialogue with GLF, and indeed absorbed quite a bit of its activism, Arcadie evolved little, and consistently refused to cooperate with any other organisations. One British visitor observed in 1974 that 'Arcadie is far more discreet and respectable than CHE has ever been.'[77] To some extent this was simply a reflection of the powerful personality of Baudry, whose Jansenist morality imprinted itself indelibly on the organisation. But the historical context also played an important role. Arcadie was born at a moment when the cultural climate was particularly unfavourable to homosexuality and becoming more so, as the Mirguet amendment demonstrated. France in the 1960s, at least as far as homosexuals were concerned, was not a period of liberalisation. The HLRS was founded when the mood seemed, however gradually, to be moving in its favour. Arcadie, then, became frozen in a prudential strategy which might initially have been appropriate to ensure survival—after all *Arcadie* was the only homosexual newspaper to survive more than a few issues before the 1970s—but became less so once the context had changed. *Arcadie* also suffered from the fact that it represented the homosexual establishment in France in the eyes of the FHAR . It was the 'homosexualité de papa' which had to be combated. In Britain, the HLRS rather faded from the scene once law reform arrived, while CHE was a product of the same cultural moment as GLF and able to absorb some of the same influences.

There is ultimately a more profound reason for the divergence between the experiences of France and Britain that is visible still in the respective position of homosexuality in each country today. Thanks to the introduction of 'PACs' in 1999, homosexual couples in France are entitled to set up legally recognised civil unions. Although analogous legislation has been recently introduced in Britain, the legal position of homosexuals in Britain still remains inferior to that in France. On the other hand, the visibility of homosexuality in public life is much greater in Britain than in France and there is possibly a greater degree of public tolerance (the act of 'coming out' is much less prevalent in France than in Britain).

The origins of this difference lie in French resistance, both on the right and the left, to the idea of 'identity politics'. This resistance derives perhaps partly from traditional Catholic morality—the whole language of 'coming out' is suffused with Protestant notions of the primacy of the individual conscience—but more importantly it derives from the Republican notion, stemming from the French Revolution, of a necessary distinction between the public and the private, between the 'citizen' and the 'individual'. Any breach in this tradition of Republican 'universalism' is seen as a slippery slope towards 'communitarianism' and multiculturalism.[78] This difference between the French and 'Anglo-Saxon' models became evident as early as 1964 in an article in *Arcadie* by Duchein entitled 'le plus grand danger', denouncing the American 'ghetto' culture of homosexual bars, restaurants and shops.[79] Thus even its detractors on the left could share at least that part of Arcadie's vision of the world. Perhaps, too, that is why Michel Foucault—the inspiration of many queer activists, though never himself one and never favourable to 'coming out'—was able to write a surprisingly nostalgic and favourable 'obituary' of Arcadie in the left-wing newspaper *Libération*.[80] In the end, the strange history of Arcadie is a very French story.[81]

5. *Beatniks, Moral Crusaders, Delinquent Teenagers and Hippies: Accounting for the Counterculture*

Colin Campbell

This chapter puts forward an account of the 'cultural revolution' of the 1960s that highlights the interaction between three socio-cultural movements and subcultures differentiated along lines of class, cultural response and age. Two of these—the contrasting political and cultural wings of middle-class youth radicalism that originated in the nineteenth-century—appeared in post-war Western Europe and North America in the form of the moral crusades of the civil rights and anti-nuclear movements on the one hand, and the Beat and café-existentialist subculture on the other. The third factor which, when added to these two, gave rise to the 1960s cultural revolution, was the adolescent or 'teenage revolution' of the middle to late 1950s. A combination of demographic, economic, technological and social factors combined in the 1950s to enable male, working-class teenagers to develop their own subculture, one centred on music, dress and personal transport.

Until the early 1960s, these three youthful socio-cultural movements existed in a state of mutual suspicion if not antagonism. This changed in the mid-1960s when the teenage subculture spread up the social scale to embrace the middle-class young. Its main expressive forms, especially its music, consequently became a catalyst, or unifying factor, that enabled a rapprochement between the two middle-class forms of radicalism. The result was a temporary alliance between all three youthful subcultures that transcended the traditional boundaries of class and age and resulted in the emergence of the counterculture.[1]

As a sociologist whose principal interests lie in understanding and explaining cultural change, I can hardly conceive of a more daunting challenge than trying to explain the 'cultural revolution' of the 1960s, which is arguably the most important cultural event of modern times. What follows is therefore only the outline of an argument, one that is necessarily panoramic as well as non-place specific, for the phenomenon I am interested in explaining was not confined within national boundaries and cannot be understood in purely national terms.[2] I shall begin by introducing the Beat-bohemians, moral crusaders and teenage delinquents together with their associated subcultures. Then I shall proceed to describe how their relationship changed over the period from roughly 1958–59 to 1967 from one of separation and suspicion to that of cooperation and collaboration, thereby creating a fourth type—the hippie—and hence the counterculture.[3] For the sake of brevity and simplicity, I shall use musical genres to 'represent' each subculture, using what happened to the different styles of music as a way of illustrating what actually happened to the subcultures themselves.

Beat-Bohemians

Bohemianism can be described as an unconventional and irregular way of life, voluntarily chosen by, and frequently involving the artistic pursuits of, Romantics who are self-consciously in revolt against what they see as a utilitarian and philistine society, and who find mutual support against its 'corrupting' influence in coterie behaviour.[4] It is a modern phenomenon, making its first appearance in Paris in the 1840s and thereafter spreading to all the major cities in Europe and North America. Its most recent manifestation, prior to the counterculture of the 1960s, was the Beat movement of the 1950s. This was a largely American social and literary movement, whose members—true to the bohemian tradition—rejected what they saw as the prevailing materialistic, philistinic and sterile anti-life culture of the modern United States. Beats wished to 'drop out' of a society dominated by such values, and to carve out lives that, if not redeemed, were at least made worth living through a concentration on direct experience and artistic endeavour. They tried to live communal or semi-communal lives with like-minded friends, occupying their time with drug-taking, sex and listening to (or creating) music and poetry, together with a certain dabbling in Zen Buddhism and Existentialism. According to *Life* magazine's Paul

O'Neil, the typical Beat 'live[d] with such basic furnishings as a mattress, a few cans of tinned food and a record player, recorder, or set of bongo drums'.[5] Part-time jobs, borrowing from family and friends or occasional drug dealing generally provided the meagre funds necessary for this lifestyle, allowing Beats to congregate in low-rent city districts such as North Beach in San Francisco, Venice West in Los Angeles, and Greenwich Village in New York.[6] However the Beats' influence was certainly not confined to the United States, for British students in the late 1950s were likewise busily reading Jack Kerouac's *On the Road* (1957), as Paul McCartney recalled.[7] Also to be found on both sides of the Atlantic were 'beatniks', the term coined by San Francisco columnist Herb Caen for that wider segment of the young with little or no literary ability or pretension who nonetheless aped the lifestyle of the Beat literary elite.[8]

Moral Crusaders

Bohemianism is a cultural and essentially non-political form of radicalism. Allen Ginsberg described himself as a rebel but not a revolutionary, while William Burroughs observed that 'the Beat movement had few if any political overtones'.[9] Yet the 1950s also spawned a second, more politically oriented form of youthful radicalism best articulated by the 'Angry Young Men' group of British writers. Though the Angry Young Men's revolt against established society bore some resemblance to that of the Beats, they were closer to the tradition of political than cultural radicalism. Gene Feldman and Max Gartenberg, the American editors of a 1958 anthology of Angry and Beat writings, shrewdly noted that while the Beat generation was 'beyond caring', the Angry Young Men still cared.[10] Or, as Paul O'Neil put it, 'Unlike England's Angry Young Men, who know what they want of society and bay for it with vehemence, the Beat finds society too hideous to contemplate and so withdraws from it.'[11] In fact, the Angry Young Men were not so much angry as bitter and disappointed. They were idealists who did not want to drop out of society as the Beats had done, but rather work to improve it: 'social reformers not world-rejecters', in the words of sociologist John Barron Mays.[12]

However, the Angry Young Men could not find any viable social reform ideology or programme to embrace. Indeed, their lack of an outlet for idealism contributed at least as much to their outrage as what they judged to be the 'immoral' society they saw around them. This position was clearly articulated by Jimmy Porter, the anti-hero of John Osborne's 1956 play *Look Back In Anger*. Jimmy envies those who 'seem to have a cause' and have 'a revolutionary fire about them'.[13] At the same time, he declares that 'there aren't any good, brave causes left.'[14]

Angry Young Men shared the frustration of much of their generation with having inherited inadequate ideologies or worldviews. They flatly refused to commit themselves to an 'Old Left' discredited by its authoritarianism and the failure of the 'Russian experiment', leading Feldman and Gartenberg to describe them as 'resembl[ing] the militant socialists of the thirties except that they didn't believe in socialism'.[15] Moreover, as the American anarchist Paul Goodman argued in his influential *Growing Up Absurd* (1960), many of the most sensitive, intelligent and idealistic of the young realised that what he termed 'the radical-liberal program' had effectively been curtailed, compromised, or even abandoned and betrayed.[16] Goodman claimed that they saw political leaders as dishonest and the churches as hypocritical: 'the flag and the cross have become objects of contempt in their eyes.'[17] Bereft of any clear, defined 'lofty purpose' to which they could commit themselves, the young were prone to scepticism and disillusionment.[18]

Since they had eschewed ideology, young middle-class idealists had little choice but to settle for simple moral outrage as the manner of expressing their reformist zeal: the dominant form of non-cultural radicalism in the post-war period. Whereas such systems of ideas might once have provided an intellectual framework for the expression of idealistic hopes and dreams, moral and humanitarian postures now had to suffice. Hence the popularity of specific moral crusades launched against singular transparent evils, the principal ones being the civil rights movement in the USA and the Campaign for Nuclear Disarmament (CND) in the UK.[19]

These moral crusades were not political in any conventional sense. Indeed, they had more in common with such earlier causes as suffragism, the anti-slavery movement or even the temperance movement than with political movements such as communism, fascism, trade unionism or social democracy, for they were independent of traditional class-based politics and focused on moral rather than socio-economic reform. The sociologist Frank Parkin discovered that support for CND arose from a 'deeply felt ethical commitment' that embodied moral judgement rather than political calculation.[20] Unilateralists were therefore just as likely to come from a religious as a political background, so that Quakers and Canons of the Church of England marched alongside Trotskyists and communists in protest against nuclear weapons. Likewise, Southern US black church figures such as Martin Luther King were joined in the American civil rights struggle by Northern white divinity students, ex-communists and left-leaning political activists.[21] The choice of tactics such as civil disobedience and direct action also revealed that these were moral rather than political campaigns in that they were not guided primarily by any instrumental calculation of their effectiveness but were rather expressive of a deep moral commitment.

So far I have identified two important, but different, cultural responses by the new generation to their disillusionment with Western civilisation as they experienced it in the 1950s. The one, principally manifested in the Beat movement, was a cultural radicalism expressive of alienation and despair. The other, manifested in the moral crusades of civil rights and CND, was closer to the tradition of political radicalism insofar as it was an expression of a Utopian idealism. However, since this response was also anti-ideological, these movements were essentially humanitarian in character and best described as moral crusades.[22] There was, however, a third player on the scene, one that initially seemed to have little connection with the other two, and yet was destined to play a vital role in effecting their eventual union and thereby bringing the 1960s' counter-culture into being. This was the subculture of the teenage delinquents.

Teenage Delinquents

Post-war prosperity brought a new affluence to the urban working classes in the USA and Western Europe. Among the first to benefit from this were young, single males who held semi-skilled or unskilled manual jobs. In receipt of a good wage and yet with few commitments, this group had significant disposable income. Later, teenagers without full-time jobs began to share in this prosperity, either because of part-time employment or more generous allowances from their parents. In addition, the baby boom meant that there were now enough teenagers for their combined spending power to create a sizeable yet distinctive market too important to be ignored. As Mays remarked, 'for the first time [in British history] the adolescent age group has enough purchasing power to make it a worthwhile target age group for commercial exploitation.'[23] Understandably, teenagers used their newly acquired wealth to satisfy their own distinctive needs and tastes, ones that were not only very different from those of their parents but which were currently not being catered for. The need that was most prominent among teenage males at this time was the need for excitement. Bored yet full of the impulsive energy of young manhood, they craved stimulation in all its forms. Sexual stimulation certainly, but also the thrill that could be gained from the speed and power of cars or motor bikes, or indeed that which accompanied danger, violence, or the direct challenging of adult authority. It was the search for stimulation of this kind, or 'kicks', that led to the much-discussed link with delinquency.[24]

Delinquency mainly took the form of status offences such as truancy, sexual activity and under-age drinking, or violence associated either with gangs or direct challenges to authority. The 'Teddy Boy' was for a time the stereotypical teenage delinquent in Britain, before being superseded by the rocker or biker-hipster, as immortalised by Marlon Brando in *The Wild One* (1953). However, what best defined this subculture was their music: rock 'n' roll. Rock 'n' roll first hit Britain in September 1955 with the premiere of *Blackboard Jungle* at the Trocadero cinema in the Elephant and Castle, featuring the single 'Rock Around the Clock'. Soon, however, Bill Haley and the Comets were eclipsed by performers like Elvis Presley, who combined a rock beat with both a rebel image and sex appeal.

The result, as Kenneth Hudson notes, was that teenagers in the 1950s became what they had never been before, a subculture. What he calls the 'Teenage Movement' had at its centre 'an insistence that adolescents should be regarded as a force in their own right, entitled to make their own rules and observe their own standards, without interference from the adult world'.[25] This is not to say that teenagers were an 'invention' of the 1950s.[26] However, whereas the teenagers who had previously come to public attention because of their dress or taste in music—such as the 'bobby-soxers' of the 1940s—had been drawn largely from the middle classes, the most visible teenagers in the 1950s were first and foremost working class, a far more frightening prospect for those in authority. In addition, earlier teenage generations had not possessed their own subcultural style and music, but rather tended to share one with adults, as had been the case with bobby-soxers and the 'jitter-bug'. Now, for the first time, there was a teenage subculture that was not merely distinctive of this age group but exclusive to them. Indeed, it served as a barrier, a boundary, something that marked them off from the adult world. Distinctive music, clothing and slang became the hallmarks of this new teenage-delinquent subculture.

The Three Youth Subcultures

It is important to stress that these three subcultures were separate and sharply divided in the late 1950s and early 1960s. They subscribed to very different values and beliefs and often existed in a state of mutual hostility and suspicion. Drawing upon a long-established history of animosity between the cultural and political wings of middle-class youth radicalism, Beats tended to characterise moral crusaders as self-righteous moralisers. Moral crusaders accused them in turn of being self-indulgent hedonists. Their desire to distance themselves from the 'immorality' of the Beat-bohemians manifested itself in the Berkeley student protests of 1964 and 1965, when the moral crusaders involved in the Free Speech Movement flatly refused to lend their support to the Filthy Speech Movement, a Beat-bohemian offshoot that demanded the right to shout obscenities in the name of freedom of expression.[27] Conversely, the bohemians, first as Beats and later as Haight-Ashbury hippies, tended to regard politics as 'a bad trip'.[28] British commune-dwellers in the early 1970s similarly considered 'politicos' to be 'up-tight' and 'very uncomfortable and uncool to be with.'[29]

The differences between teenagers and the two middle-class youth groups were even more pronounced, because both age and class tended to separate its members from those of the other two. Beat-bohemians and moral crusaders customarily dismissed teenage delinquent subculture as vulgar, mindless and infantile, thereby echoing a traditional middle-class critique of the lower classes.[30] Rock 'n' roll was not only despised by the mainly middle-class student idealists who formed the bulk of the audience for folk singers like Bob Dylan.[31] The Beats also 'rather looked down on rock 'n' roll music' and its teenage fans, according to Tuli Kupferberg, the onetime Beat poet and founder member of The Fugs.[32] The nature of the critique nonetheless differed somewhat between the cultural and the moral rebels. It was the intimate association with delinquency that tended to outrage the moral crusaders. Like most adults, they were appalled at the drug taking, sexual licence and apparently mindless violence. Such issues did not overly concern the Beat-bohemians, who were more likely to criticise the subculture of teenage delinquents for its lack of aesthetic sophistication and intellectual significance.

In order to understand how the counterculture came into existence, it is vital to grasp how these differences were eventually overcome or, at least, how they were set aside sufficiently for a widespread sense of common purpose to emerge. In essence, my thesis is that the teenage delinquent subculture acted as the critical catalyst, enabling a 'merger' of the Beat-bohemians and moral crusaders to occur, and therefore the counterculture itself to emerge. This happened because the two middle-class groups appropriated or 'adopted' the subculture of the teenage delinquents for their own ends. Both groups grew to regard teenage rebelliousness—and hence the subculture itself—as an expression of their own beliefs and values. The Beat-bohemians began to see the teenage delinquent as someone akin to the 'noble savage', a vital, uninhibited, authentic and 'natural' human being, untainted by an effete and soul-destroying suburban Puritanism. The moral crusaders on the other hand came to perceive the teenage delinquent as a heroic yet unconscious revolutionary, an individual whose defiant stance against authority revealed him (the juvenile delinquent at this period was an unambiguously male figure) to be actively resisting the unjust and oppressive bourgeois adult world. In that sense each group succeeded in 'reading into' the essentially inarticulate teenage delinquent response precisely the message they wished to find. However, because this enabled both groups to 'adopt' the teenage delinquents in this way, a rapprochement of sorts became effected between them.[33]

This still leaves the question of how the acrimony that originally characterised the relationships between these three groups was overcome and replaced by sufficient fellow feeling for them to become allied if not entirely fused. I think that the best way I can answer this crucial question is by describing the role that music played for each group, and how the development of different musical styles is indicative of how the subcultures converged.

The Music

Each group had its own music—the protest song (and folk music more generally) for the moral crusaders, modern jazz for the Beat-bohemians and rock 'n' roll for the teenage delinquents—which formed a major component of its subcultural identity. In the late 1950s and early 1960s, enthusiasts for each of these genres typically hated the other two musical forms and their associated subcultures, an understandable attitude given the different values they embodied and functions they fulfilled. The protest song (or topical song, as it was often known at the time) was a simple and tuneful variety of folk song in which the lyrics mattered most, as they aimed to bind a moral community to its chosen cause. Such songs had long been part of folk singers' repertoires prior to the 1960s, but the causes to which they referred were generally those of times past and few had any contemporary relevance.[34] This changed with the civil rights movement, which served not only to revive old songs such as 'We Shall Overcome' (a Negro spiritual that had been used in the labour movement of the 1930s), but also to inspire performers to write new ones.

In sharp contrast, rock 'n' roll was music in which the lyrics hardly mattered at all—indeed they were often virtually meaningless—but in which the beat, loud and insistent, was overwhelmingly important. Indeed, what was revolutionary about rock 'n' roll as a musical form was that melody was of secondary importance to the underlying beat. The beat had to be regular, insistent and loud so that, as Kenneth Hudson put it, 'Rock was not so much to be listened to as felt.'[35] It was music to move to, whether that meant dancing or something stronger—the cultural commentator George Melly wrote of rock 'n' roll as an 'incitement to mindless fucking and arbitrary vandalism: screw and smash music'.[36] Modern jazz was for its part a musical genre in which lyrics did not feature at all, but in which subtle and complex harmony and improvised elaboration mattered most. This was music to 'dig', which not merely meant that one liked it, but that also one appreciated it intellectually.

Each of these musical forms was characterised by its own distinctive musical instrument or combination of instruments. For protest songs, this was the unaccompanied acoustic guitar (its portability making it ideal for marches and demonstrations). For rock 'n' roll, it was the electric guitar, usually backed by at least one other guitar and drums. For modern jazz, it was a combination of instruments, or 'combo', in which drums and double bass typically accompanied two or more brass or wind instruments.

None of these genres could adequately fulfil the function of either of the other two. One could not protest to the sound of Dizzy Gillespie, for example, or find moral inspiration in 'Rock Around The Clock'. There was little possibility of appreciating the subtle musical complexity or skilful improvisation displayed by Bill Haley and The Comets, or indeed Dylan's singing of 'Blowin' in the Wind'. And one could hardly dance vigorously or fight either to 'We Shall Overcome' or the music of Charlie Parker. However, these sharp distinctions in form and function were beginning to collapse by the mid 1960s, as the three musical genres, along with their respective subcultures, started to overlap, intersect, and finally blend into one. The result was not merely the emergence of a new musical form but also a new youth subculture—the counterculture—of which it was the principal expression. This new music, rock, was clearly an amalgam of features from the three contributing genres.[37] Rock 'n' roll contributed the basic rhythmic structure as well as the standard line-up of electric guitars with drum backing. It also contributed some of the basic material that featured in rock songs, such as the specific concerns of teenagers and the focus on romantic love. The folk protest tradition contributed not just the idea that lyrics were important but more specifically that they should carry a message that aroused people to change the world for the better. The Beat tradition contributed the notion that the rock musician was not simply a performer but an artist, someone who should ideally write his or her own material and take charge of the whole creative process. The assumption that rock musicians should have the opportunity to demonstrate their skill and virtuosity in solo improvisations also came from the modern jazz tradition favoured by the Beats.

To say that this new form comprised a mixture of ingredients from the previous three is not to deny that something new was added. For there clearly was. Other instruments, such as electronic synthesisers, often supplemented the basic group line-up of drums, bass and lead guitar (especially in the recording studio). Technological developments led to the introduction of the fuzz-box and wah-wah pedal together with techniques such as feedback and multiple tracking.[38] The music itself also changed, being required to carry richer and more diverse meanings, ones in which variations in tone, colour, texture, density and volume were all explored. At the same time, established song forms gave way to new, more experimental ones involving 'shifting meters, radical stanza patterns and changing time signatures', as one contemporary critic noted.[39] The lyrics were expected to carry more profound and variable messages, while the song increasingly became seen as only one part of a total artistic package that included the album sleeve, the musicians' appearance and the stage 'set' accompanying the performance. All these changes contributed to the notion that rock music was an art form and that the rock composer-performer was an artist. The traditional division between elite and popular musical forms appeared to be breaking down at this time, symbolically mirroring the similar erosion of the traditional division between working-class and middle-class forms of youthful rebellion. The manner in which material from three very different musical forms was used to create an entirely new one was largely achieved by the two most outstanding influences on the development of the counterculture, Bob Dylan and the Beatles. If we look briefly at their careers, we can see how and when this process occurred.

Bob Dylan's 'conversion' or 'apostasy' (depending on one's point of view) is one of the most dramatic and for some, inexplicable, events in the history of popular music.[40] Protest songs such as 'The Ballad of Emmett Till', 'Masters of War' and especially 'Blowin' in the Wind' had made him almost a saint—'a sort of reincarnation of Woody Guthrie', to quote music critic R. Serge Denisoff—in the eyes of the moral crusaders who were his most devoted fans.[41] They were duly shocked and appalled when he apparently turned his back not simply on protest songs, but on the folk music tradition more generally. This happened at the 1965 Newport Folk

Festival where, instead of wearing his usual folk-singer uniform of boots, jeans and work shirt, Dylan came on stage in a black leather jacket, black trousers, a dress shirt and pointed, high-heeled boots, toting a solid-body Fender guitar.[42] There could be no clearer statement of his identification with rock 'n' roll than this, one that was comprehensible even to those fans who had conveniently overlooked the style of his latest record, 'Like A Rolling Stone'. He was duly booed and heckled and though he later exchanged his electric guitar for an acoustic one and played songs that were more in the style of the 'old' Dylan, this did not disguise his change of musical direction.[43]

At almost precisely the same time as Dylan appeared to be abandoning folk protest music for rock 'n' roll, the Beatles appeared to be abandoning rock 'n' roll for something else. Yet while Dylan jeopardised his old fanbase of moral crusaders while gaining new teenage fans in the process, the Beatles did exactly the opposite. The Beatles had started out as an unambiguous rock 'n' roll group and clearly identified in their Hamburg days with the associated teenage-delinquent subculture. The toning down of their image at the hands of Brian Epstein did not really eliminate this basic identification during their early years of fame. However, they subsequently underwent a transformation which, though less sudden and dramatic than Dylan's, was if anything more far reaching. Between 1965 and 1967, they gave up touring, spent more time in the recording studio, made films, and, after the death of Brian Epstein, formed their own recording company. At the same time, their lyrics began to deal with topics other than romantic love and their music became far more experimental, a process that culminated in 1967 in the path-breaking 'Sgt. Pepper' album. Most intriguingly, in view of Dylan's conversion, they began to include, if not protest songs, then at least songs with a message such as 'The Word', 'Within You Without You', and 'All You Need Is Love'.

These 'conversions' are instructive. In the first place, they involved the creation of an entirely new musical genre. This upset many long-time fans, who considered that, by abandoning their former musical style, the performers were rejecting the corresponding subculture and its values. At the same time, both conversions also involved a process in which new fans were acquired from another subculture. They therefore constituted precisely those 'cross-overs' between the three subcultures that were necessary for the counterculture to emerge.

There remains the question of how this process was possible. In fact more than one process is involved but I shall explore just one—one in keeping with my emphasis upon music—the 'taming' and consequent 'intellectualisation' of rock 'n' roll. Arguably, middle-class bands turned rock 'n' roll into rock music somewhat accidentally, largely as a consequence of efforts to appropriate and moderate this seemingly threatening genre of music.

It is important to remember that there was enormous hostility towards rock 'n' roll on the grounds that it was 'Negro music' that incited violence and lewdness. Yet countervailing pressure against censorship came from entrepreneurs in the music business eager to exploit its money-making potential. The result was effectively an understanding that rock 'n' roll would be exempt from a total ban just so long as it was tamed. Considerable effort went into knocking the rough edges off the music. In addition to promoting more 'wholesome' rock performers such as Pat Boone and Cliff Richard, a key tactic was to shift the emphasis away from raw power and energy toward romance. This strategy largely worked in the sense that rock 'n' roll became acceptable, a process in which the Beatles played a crucial role. As music critic Arnold Shaw observed, 'what disarmed the older generation' was that the Beatles 'were *for* adolescents without being *against* adults'.[44]

The immediate consequence of this 'taming' of rock 'n' roll was that it spread up the social scale. Middle-class teenagers venturing into the lower-class world of rock 'n' roll would have been deemed rebellious in the mid 1950s, but by the early 1960s this was no longer true.[45] However, the taming of rock 'n' roll was to prove to be more apparent than real. Indeed, the stage was set for a far more widespread and fundamental assault on the *status quo*. This was because, having crossed first the race barrier from blacks to whites and then the class barrier from working-class to middle-class teenagers, rock 'n' roll now threatened to cross the age barrier between teenagers and young adults and become what has been described as 'the central communication system of youth'.[46] Since rock 'n' roll's basically rebellious, anti-adult ethic core was still intact (albeit somewhat muted at the beginning of the 1960s), there now existed the potential for a truly widespread revolt of the young. 'Protesting' and 'alienated' middle-class youth subcultures already existed in the form of the moral crusaders and the Beat-bohemians. Were they to decide to join forces with the teenage-delinquents, a unique and powerful alliance of anti-adult and anti-establishment forces would have been created. However, for this to happen, protest music and jazz would have to be replaced as the essential 'signature tunes' of these two middle-class forms of youthful revolt by rock 'n' roll, or something closely resembling it. This is precisely what Dylan and the Beatles accomplished.

Conclusion

This necessarily condensed analysis suggests that the counterculture came into being as the result of a largely accidental and serendipitous conjunction of different strands of youthful rebelliousness. Quite simply, the power and suddenness with which the counterculture burst on to the scene in the second half of the 1960s is to be understood as the outcome of the successful harnessing together of three distinct forces. These were, first, Beat-bohemian disgust with a society and culture dominated by a shallow, bourgeois 'moneytheism'. Second, moral revulsion at a complacent, unjust and hypocritical establishment and social order coupled with idealistic expectations of a coming Utopia. And third, adolescent resentment and frustration against behavioural restrictions and controls imposed by adults. It was largely because these very different modes of cultural resistance and rebellion came to overlap and coincide—or at least to be represented as coinciding—that a large-scale movement was born that appeared to be 'counter' to the established order.

At the heart of this movement was a unique alliance of generational and life-cycle conflict, one in which two separate critiques appeared to overlap—that of teenager against adult and that of generation against generation (the babyboomers versus their predecessors). No wonder then that, for a time at least, it seemed as if society was divided between young and old. Although generational conflict was nothing new, what made the crucial difference was the emergence of a distinct and distinctly rebellious teenage subculture, open to all those who could afford to buy into its music and fashions. Once this teenage-delinquent subculture spread up the social scale from the working class to the middle class—in the process effecting a mediation between the moral and the cultural radicals—the way was open for age and generation to take precedence over class in determining the allegiance of the young. The outcome was a fully romantic movement, comparable in nature and extent to the first Romantic Movement, and destined, like its predecessor, to bring dramatic changes to the civilisation of the West.

6. *Down the Rabbit Hole: Permissiveness and Paedophilia in the 1960s*

Mark Jones

Though debates on permissiveness in 1960s Britain encompassed everything from drug use to abortion, perhaps nothing attracted as much attention as sex and the young. In the early 1960s, anxiety focused on the guidance being offered to children by fairly traditional sources of authority, including the clergy, teachers and academics. In 1960, Eustace Chesser asked *Is Chastity Outmoded?*,[1] and was soon answered in the affirmative by fellow psychologist G.M. Carstairs in the 1962 Reith Lectures ('Charity is more important than chastity')[2] and by theologian John Robinson in 1963's *Honest to God* ('Nothing prescribed—except love').[3] Concern soon transferred to the actual behaviour of young people, with the phenomenon of Beatlemania providing an early battleground for moral commentators. The journalist Paul Johnson pitied the 'pathetic and listless' fans at a Beatles concert: 'young girls, hardly any more than sixteen, dressed as adults and already lined up as fodder for exploitation.'[4] A few years later, the prosecution of 'School Kids' *Oz* on the charge of corrupting 'the morals of children and young people within the realm' marked the climax of both the political threat of the counterculture and the debate over the sexual morality of the young.

Both the opponents and proponents of permissiveness recognised the revolutionary potential of youthful sexual agency. In Mary Whitehouse's view, the defence of traditional moral standards at the *Oz* trial represented resistance to social revolution. 'Are we not justified in our fears for what may be the long-term effect of this new kind of adolescent licence, not least upon the young themselves?' she asked: 'How can democracy defend itself from what an increasing number of people recognise as a new technique in ideological warfare?'[5] Enthusiasts for the 'youthquake' conversely regarded adolescent sex as an index of emancipation. In his celebratory *The Teenage Revolution* (1965), Peter Laurie asserted that 'The real dynamo behind the teenage revolution is the anonymous adolescent girl from twelve to sixteen, nameless but irresistible'. He cited the nine-fold increase since 1939 in prosecutions for illegal intercourse between adult men and thirteen- to sixteen-year-olds as evidence that 'girls are now celebrating a sensational breakdown in adult oppression.'[6]

However, the intergenerational nature of much teenage sexual activity ultimately questioned the equation of permissiveness with liberation. In the *Oz* trial, counsel for the prosecution Brian Leary identified sex between adults and underage youths as anarchism of the most licentious kind: 'The alternative society puts forward as a way of life, sex as being something to be worshipped for itself, until you reach the ultimate state, which has been called fucking in the streets. Kicks, promiscuity, sex with minors.'[7] Increasingly, though, sex between adults and adolescents would be characterised not simply as symptomatic of political revolution or juvenile delinquency, but as involving the abuse and exploitation of children. In 1979, the Paedophile Information Exchange's (PIE) contact magazine was charged with the same offence of 'conspiracy to corrupt public morals' that had faced *Oz* eight years before. Yet it was being put on trial not for political subversion, but because paedophilia and child pornography had come to be viewed over the course of the 1970s as the logical and extreme outcome of the removal of sexual restraint.

Paedophilia would ultimately prove to be the most effective bogeyman marking the dangers of sexual liberation, but it was not until the mid-1970s that it began to be used explicitly in the campaign against permissiveness. Although most of the major prosecutions for obscenity in the late 1960s and early 1970s ostensibly involved issues of child protection,[8] 1960s' permissiveness has seldom been examined in relation to the sexual exploitation of children. In part, this is because an organised paedophile movement only began in earnest in the 1970s, leading to a paucity of evidence concerning the practice of—and public attitudes towards—intergenerational sex. In this chapter, though, I will show that there are markers in cultural production, and in some aspects of counter-cultural politics that offer insight into the relationship between paedophilia and the permissive society. Fiction, music and films from 1960 onwards show how an unmentionable subject gradually became represented and debated, at least as far as heterosexual experience was concerned. (Homosexual paedophilia—even as sex crime—almost never featured in the legally available texts of the period, and as such is not dealt with in this chapter). In the late 1960s and early 1970s, an increasing number of texts tended to defend, and even celebrate, childhood sexual experience on libertarian grounds. Traces of paedophiliac politics began to surface in the counterculture at the same time as child pornography became more available. This generated an effective reaction from conservative moralists, who were aided by a broadly similar response from otherwise permissive thinkers who believed that intergenerational sex might be one liberatory move too far. In effect, the unacknowledged coalition of traditional moralists and political radicals has silenced the debate on the extension of sexual liberation to children, and heterosexual intergenerational sex survives in contemporary culture largely as the repressed dark side of permissiveness.

Criminal Sex

Despite the controversial appearance of *Lolita* in Britain in 1959,[9] the paedophile had a very low cultural profile at the beginning of the 1960s. Recent histories of the subject have shown that systematic (and often incestuous) domestic abuse was effectively invisible, with child sexual abuse associated with the stereotypical 'dirty old man'.[10] It is therefore unsurprising that fictional representations of paedophilia prior to the late 1960s are rare, reticent about describing sexual acts and largely dependent on the generic apparatus of the 'deviant psychology' crime novel.

Dianne Doubtfire's *Lust for Innocence* (1960) typifies the early 1960s' fictional attitude to the topic by being structured around an anticipated but ultimately avoided act of abuse.[11] Eight-year-old Angela inadvertently causes the death of her cruel mother beneath the wheels of a tube train. The deed is witnessed by Leonard Otter, who assures the police that he knows Angela and offers to take her home. He promises to buy her a new dress, gives her sweets, claims magical powers and, when all else fails, threatens to reveal her culpability in her mother's death. In this way, he arranges for Angela to visit him regularly without her father's knowledge. Otter's alternately charming and menacing behaviour seems a textbook example of the paedophile's technique. Similarly, his appearance—'the bland pink face, the smile, friendly and yet in some way sinister, and, most of all, the…queer eyes'[12]—conjures up the archetypal child molester.

Angela occupies the centre of the narrative throughout most of the novel. Otter's mindset remains resolutely closed to the reader, with the only clues to his psychology coming in a brief exchange with the child:

> 'Why don't you have a wife?' she asked, suddenly seeing a solution to his loneliness.
>
> Otter stiffened and winced. 'Oh no—no—I don't want that…' His eyes swerved away from her, and he pointed to a photograph on a bureau near the window. 'There—that's my mother,' he said…He picked it up and planted a kiss on the glass, leaving it steamy and moist...
>
> 'We were always together. My father left us, went away, when I was about your age. But my mother was never lonely—she always told me—because I was with her. And neither was I—until she died.'[13]

Significantly, the text makes no attempt to explore this area in any detail. It is simply used as an indicator of potential deviance, and no further explanation for Otter's behaviour is required. The externalisation of the character is such that we are even left uninformed as to whether Otter is responsible for a child abduction and subsequent murder, news of which is casually sprinkled through the latter part of the novel as a warning about 'bad men about who do awful things to little girls'.[14] Owing to the lucky accident that Otter is run over by a bus, Angela is spared anything worse than a short struggle. Molestation, abuse, or any other kind of sexualised physical contact between an adult and a child seems to be unspeakable. As an early permissive text, *Lust for Innocence* can only allude to its ostensible subject matter, and Angela remains as pure as her name would indicate.

Despite the tabooed nature of child molestation, childhood sexuality appears in *Lust for Innocence* in the form of Janet, the daughter of Angela's father's girlfriend. She is a heavily pregnant seventeen-year-old, who started wearing lipstick, going to dances, and passing as sixteen when she was twelve. While Otter remains a mysterious and external—albeit potentially fatal—threat, Janet also signals the dangers to childhood innocence. Already indolent and sexually blasé, and metonymically represented by her long blonde hair and a glowing cigarette, Janet functions as a warning against youthful sexual experimentation and, by extension, the dawning permissive society. While Angela is clearly identified with 'innocence' and Otter with a 'lust' at odds with 'normal' sexual desire, Janet serves as a reminder that all unregulated sexual activity is potentially a social danger. Her provisional re-admittance to the familial structure towards the end of the novel, as she attempts to warn Angela away from Otter and communicates civilly with Angela's father for the first time, indicates that a sexually wayward generation might still be retrieved. For Otter, though, no reinsertion into the social order is possible. 'Lust' marks its bearer as ambiguously gendered and sexualised: antipathetic to, rather than a product of, the social system.

The crude portrayal of the child molester as self-evidently deviant to all except the most naïve—and thus easily subject to social control—would be exposed as fatally simplistic by the Moors murders trial of 1966. Although the press has retrospectively portrayed Ian Brady and Myra Hindley as icons of evil, contemporary commentary wrestled with the apparent normality of the perpetrators. Faced with child murderers who had passed as socially ordinary, writers sought to identify the social determinants which created their deviancy. Pamela Hansford Johnson's *On Iniquity* (1967) virtually ignores the specificity of the killers in its indictment of permissiveness in general,[15] while Emlyn Williams' *Beyond Belief* (1967) intermingles detailed biographies of the killers with numerous, if somewhat inchoate, references to the social and cultural context.[16]

A similar concern to place a child killer's psychology within a wider societal perspective is seen in Peter Loughran's *The Train Ride* (1966), in which a young man rapes and (accidentally) kills a seven-year-old girl whilst on a long train journey to London.[17] Narrated by the unnamed killer, the novel shifts attention from the child victim to the adult perpetrator, and is a clear attempt to replace the symbolic protection of 'innocence' with a forensic exploration of 'lust'. On the whole, though, the text is at pains to emphasise the relative normality of the killer. The first-person account—replete with mild expletives, recollections of previous sexual encounters, complaints about the state of the world, and self-indulgent moralising—reads like a cross between *Catcher in the Rye* and *Saturday Night and Sunday Morning*. The narrator's activities, which include frequent brawling, patronising prostitutes and reading pornography, do not make him socially isolated like Leonard Otter. Although anti-social, he has clearly undergone a fairly normal masculine socialisation.

Despite the plethora of detail given about the narrator's criminal and immoral practices, the rape and killing take place in a textual lacunae. Although this lack of information may be partly due to the literal unspeakableness of the crime, as in *Lust for Innocence*, there are indications that the killing is a result of a momentary lack of control or a temporary madness. This period of apparent insanity is brief and, rather than serving as a rationalisation for the assault, it is related to 'years of dirty talk, dirty books, dirty thinking, dirty women'.[18] Afterwards comes self disgust, fear, and then mitigation as the narrator conducts an imaginary conversation with a court:

> 'You think I'm all wrong, don't you—think I've gone in the head?' They all start looking relieved, yeah, that's it, he's gone in the head, there's nothing really the matter with *us*.
>
> 'But just let me ask you something. You there, the women—how many of you would trust me with your kids?' They all look horrified. 'None of you…because you reckon I'm filthy and not normal?' Yes, yes, they all nod, he's abnormal.
>
> 'Well then, I'm an outcast, so leave me out of it—but ask yourselves this…How many of you would trust your girls—girls any age at all—would trust them with any man in this court…? [H]ands up all those who would…' There's not a move from no one.
>
> 'I knew it, I *knew* it—not one of you. Not one of you would trust your girls alone with any man alive, some of you not even with the father…because *all* men are the same, posh or scruffy, rich or poor, high class or low class, every man that walks this earth is after the same thing, and he'll take it off anything female between the age of six and sixty.'[19]

Rather than functioning to expel the perpetrator from a normative social system, the text continually reinstates him within a violent, exploitative and largely masculinist society. Yet sexual abuse and intercourse with children remain proscribed, for even the narrator recognises that his actions are not just illegal but unacceptable. In his exploration of the apparent consequences of the permissive society, Loughran's novel recognises that a child killer can be both the product of, and antithetical to, wider society. Not wholly or solely paedophiliac, Loughran's protagonist is placed at one extreme of a continuum of male behaviour. To portray him as being normally socialised and his act of abuse as occurring within a recognisable framework of male exploitation of women does not lessen the unacceptability of paedophiliac practice, but it does bring it within the discourses on sexuality and gender being challenged by permissiveness. In depicting a sexual assault on a child as existing on a continuum with other sexual behaviour, it marks the entry of the child molester into permissible speech, and prepares us for the possibility of representing a paedophile as non-abusive.

By 1966, it was therefore possible for a British novelist to depict a paedophile as a motivationally complex figure. Two years later, Marianne Sinclair's *Watcher in the Park* (1968) pushed the boundaries of permissiveness still further by portraying paedophilia as the basis for a fictional intergenerational relationship, rather than a violent crime.[20] Sinclair's protagonist initially appears to be a stereotypical dirty old man akin to Otter in *Lust for Innocence*. Fritz is middle-aged, single, perhaps 'mentally retarded', with 'brown eyes [which] bulged and were not quite even in size'.[21] His brutal father died during his childhood and his cold, domineering mother followed suit when he was twenty-one. The narrative relates a slowly developing relationship between Fritz and ten-year-old Pamela, beginning with sweets and chats on a park bench, progressing through tea and cakes in a café, and culminating in regular visits to Fritz's flat during which the two play increasingly physical games. The novel ends with discovery by Pamela's parents, a police investigation, and Fritz on his way to prison.

However, the text maintains a more complex view of the events than that imposed by the judiciary. The relationship between Fritz and Pamela is explored and considered *as* a relationship, with 'ups and downs',[22] disagreements, conflicts, tenderness and oscillations in dominance and subservience: 'It amused her to turn their association into a cat-and-mouse game, which in fact it was. But contrary to what she believed, Pamela was not the cat.'[23] Pamela is nonetheless an independent agent, albeit only partially aware of the exact nature of the situation, and it is she who initiates a degree of physical contact by suggesting that they pretend to be dogs: 'The little girl's genius had truly manifested itself at last. They had found the one element in which their association could evolve without becoming criminal...Not that it could be called good clean fun...[b]ut they now had a medium for physical communication which could satisfy Fritz without outraging Pamela.'[24] This sub-sexual relationship is maintained until Pamela selfishly and unthinkingly betrays Fritz. Only when he is in custody does Pamela comprehend his paedophilia:

> [S]he looked at Fritz for the first and last time with understanding and said, 'Poor man.'...
>
> 'Fuck off,' he said. It was the first time in his life that he had ever used bad language.
>
> Everyone gasped audibly...But Fritz's face relaxed, became almost tranquil, as though he knew in that moment that he had finally become an outlaw.[25]

The novel recognises that the paedophile remains a social outcast. Opprobrium is no less forthcoming than before, and there is no suggestion that intergenerational intercourse is legitimised either in the text or in the society of the late 1960s that it represents. As in the other texts examined here, the permissive society *per se* is noticeable by its absence, and the possibility of paedophilia becoming a generally acceptable practice is never even a subtextual suggestion. However, although it remains outside of the social order, paedophilia is no longer unspeakable. None of the novels examined here is pornographic or clearly countercultural. Indeed, it is their relative respectability that most convincingly signals a shift in the discourse on intergenerational intercourse towards recognising that paedophilia is part of a sexual continuum shared with other inclinations or preferences, and is socially constructed rather than an unnatural deviation.

Sexual Agency

British fiction featuring intergenerational sex became more liberal in three significant respects during the late 1960s and early 1970s. First, whereas *Lust for Innocence* and *The Train Ride* portrayed permissiveness as a debasement of moral standards, and perhaps conducive to sex crime, a more liberatory view is apparent in such novels as Leslie Thomas's *His Lordship* (1970). In it, an older character looks on enviously as two schoolchildren—a fourteen-year-old girl and a slightly older boy—have sex: 'I couldn't help thinking to myself that I didn't enjoy it my first time nearly as much as that. I was nineteen and I was in the Army at the time, and I'd paid for it…It's different now, ain't it. Looking at them made me think I'd started much too late.'[26]

The second change is that, in contrast to the care with which earlier novelists approach the theme of the molestation of pre-pubescent children, popular fiction of the late 1960s and early 1970s typically depicts post-pubescent girls enjoying sex with older men. Whereas sexual contact involving eleven-year-olds or younger is clearly identified as criminal behaviour, the law is seen as an arbitrary inconvenience rather than an expression of natural justice as the child nears the age of consent. Indeed, the criminal justice system is frequently stymied in these post-*Lolita* narratives by an implicit agreement that, although nominally illegal, such sexual activity is understandable and justifiable. In Leslie Thomas's *His Lordship*—a comic novel influenced at least as much by St Trinian's as *Lolita*—thirty-five-year-old tennis coach William Herbert has sexual relationships with six schoolgirls before making a full confession to the police.[27] He goes free, however, when every girl refuses to testify against him. A narrative tension in the novel is maintained between the manner in which Herbert is seduced by the girls and the attribution to him of clear paedophiliac characteristics, notably voyeurism. The novel's narrative ambiguities and the arbitrariness of its legal outcome, which could go either way until the very end, are an acknowledgement that the legal, moral and psychological status of sexual contact between adult men and post-pubescent girls has become subject to negotiation, rather than outright denunciation.

What makes intergenerational sex seem justifiable is the third key change effected by these novels: the ascription of sexual agency to the teenage girl. The pro-active nymphet is a common trope in these fictions, and virtually replaces the initially reluctant, deflowered young girl prevalent since Victorian pornography. Her first experience of intercourse is generally between the ages of twelve to fourteen, though she can start as early as eleven. Even with the youngest girls, the sexual contact is frequently conceived as initiated by the child. In this, the novels seem to reflect a more general shift in sexual mores. The received wisdom concerning adolescent female sexual expression before the 1960s was that it was either 'accidental' or a symptom of delinquency. A standard sex manual of the late 1950s, Kenneth Barnes's *He and She* (1958), asserted that girls often 'have no idea of what they are doing to men and boys...[because] no one has told them how easily a boy is sexually aroused.'[28] A decade later, however, John James's *The Facts of Sex* (1969) claims that

> these days it is as often as not the girl who makes the advances; and this is quite a new thing...One great difficulty has only lately been admitted: there has always been great natural indignation when adult or elderly men have been found to have interfered sexually with young girls. Unfortunately, as has been shown, the 'seducer' is quite often the young girl, who, in all innocence perhaps, has introduced the sexual element.[29]

One trans-Atlantic example of this new treatment of intergenerational sex can be found in John London's *Seductions* (1969). Its wealthy American female narrator is followed from childhood into an adulthood in which, recognising England's internationally swinging status, she embarks on a *ménage à trois* in Hampstead. Her first experience of intercourse occurs at the age of eleven with her private tutor. 'You might say that it was Nino's business as an adult to extricate himself...And I say to you that the woman in me was not to be denied.'[30] Six years later, the narrator appears to be unaffected by her earlier experiences—'for all intents and purposes...the perfect virgin'—though is nonetheless 'primed' for sexual advances.[31]

In a *Bildungsroman* such as *Seductions*, youthful sexual activity is generally portrayed as a relatively insignificant though titillating stage in the development of a healthy adult sexuality. However, it is more often problematised in texts that concentrate on childhood sexuality, as in Tina Chad Christian's *Baby Love* (1968). 'To the family that gave her a home, fourteen-year-old Luci is a fragile, pretty, orphan in need of protection', states its blurb: 'But her frail appearance conceals a demon which drives her to destroy the lives of those around her. Luci's chosen weapon is her own precocious sexual talent.'[32] Luci narrates her own story and, though emotionally disturbed as a result of having discovered the corpse of her unloving, prostitute mother, she is also portrayed as being 'typical of [her] generation'.[33] She is newly aware of her sexual attractiveness, and experiments with its effects with both a friend of her foster-father, and a group of mods in a racially mixed nightclub. The prime object of her desire is Robert, her foster father, although she first seduces his wife and thirteen-year-old son. 'She throws herself at me—in her nudity', Robert tells his wife: 'They're bloody appealing at that age! If you knew what control I've had to exercise…'[34] Robert resists Luci's attempts at seduction, and she is ejected from the family.

Luci's attempt to kill her stepbrother, together with repeated suggestions that Robert may be her biological father (although the ostensible timescale within the novel makes that impossible), makes *Baby Love* a psychodrama rather than a strictly realistic text, but Luci's vacillation between childish and adult behaviour is depicted as explicable within its social, psychological and familial context. Given the relatively plausible characterisation of the young narrator, *Baby Love* suggests that a polymorphously perverse adolescent female sexuality is within the bounds of normality. And whereas it is frequently inchoate, its natural object is the adult male. 'I prefer older men',[35] says Luci, as did the nymphets in *Seductions* and *His Lordship*.

Paedophilia and Popular Culture

In its earnest exploration of sexual psychology, *Baby Love* has something in common with *The Train Ride* or *Watcher in the Park*. The same could not be said of the many late 1960s works concerning schoolgirls. A favourite marketing strategy in pulp novels is to refer vaguely to schoolgirls without specifying their age. This is especially common in reprinted American titles, where high school students could be as old as eighteen, whereas secondary schooling in Britain tended to end at fifteen or sixteen. This difference is seldom pointed out, so that the British edition of John Farris's *Harrison High* carries a comment from the *Daily Mirror*: 'Can we risk these sex-mad schools?'[36] Girls' schools in particular are portrayed as being productive of a self-consciously perverse eroticism which is simultaneously castigated and exploited by adult interlopers. Female teenage sexuality in these texts is polymorphously perverse, usually bisexual and often ritualised. In another example of the convergence of interest between the paedophile and the sexually active adolescent, it requires a responsible male adult to direct it towards its appropriate outlet.

Depictions of schoolgirls as sexual agents also featured prominently in soft-core pornography of the period.[37] *Schoolgirl Sex*, a photographic collection from 1971 containing fatuous notes on such things as 'Innocence' and 'The Awakening of the Senses', carefully intermingles partially clothed, apparently underage girls with nude seventeen-year-olds. While the publisher's prefatory note maintains that a commercially exploitable interest in schoolgirl images is a new phenomenon,[38] the introduction claims that

> the innocence of the schoolgirl has always exerted a most powerful and potent effect on the male sex. But it has also been a taboo subject since it conjures up in most minds a picture of corruption, with the innocent child translated into the victim of mature male lust. The attraction of the schoolgirl has, in short, long been regarded as a perversion…[But] men are not attracted to schoolgirls at all, but fascinated by the image of youth…In a society which is in the throes of change and modification, concerned to question freedom and responsibility, it seems not impossible that innocence has a genuine attraction which must surely be a source of optimism in a pessimistic age.[39]

Although not invariably paedophiliac—in fact, the sexualised schoolgirl is usually above the age of consent—such pornography functions as a titillating indication of sexual activity marked as perhaps only temporarily illegal. Coinciding with the near-invisible beginnings of the commercial child pornography industry in Denmark,[40] this more public soft-core pornography is similarly a marker of the exploitative elements of permissiveness, contrary to its emancipatory rhetoric.

Significantly more politically and culturally important than soft-core pornography was rock music, which in the late 1960s and early 1970s similarly showed an interest in the depiction of sexual encounters between adults and children. Recent high-profile investigations have revealed hitherto unknown paedophiliac behaviour of prominent individuals in the rock industry of the late 1960s and early 1970s. But much popular music of the period made no secret of its fascination with intergenerational sex. Even ignoring the numerous songs about 'little girls', 'school girls' and 'teens', a collection of tracks of the time about intergenerational sex would fill an album or two. The Who's 'Fiddle About' relates an experience of domestic abuse of a boy by an adult male; Jethro Tull's 'Aqualung' portrays the stereotypical child-molester; 'Sarah Crazy Child' by John's Children features a seductive thirteen-year-old girl; sexual encounters with fourteen-year-old girls are described in Donovan's 'Mellow Yellow' and 'Superlungs My Supergirl', as well as Van Morrison's 'Cyprus Avenue'; and the cover of Blind Faith's sole album depicts a naked eleven-year-old girl.[41] The Rolling Stones were perhaps the artists most devoted to the theme of intergenerational sex. Their recorded (though not always released) output includes 'Family' (which refers to father-daughter incest), 'Cocksucker Blues' (concerning a schoolboy prostitute) and 'Stray Cat Blues' (which features sex between an adult male and a girl aged either fifteen or thirteen).[42] A painting of the Stones in Nazi uniforms with a group of naked pubescent girls by Guy Peellaert may have met with their approval as he was commissioned to provide the cover art for *It's Only Rock 'n' Roll*, which also features a group of young girls (clothed this time).[43]

Paedophilia and the Counterculture

By the end of the 1960s, countercultural figures were routinely citing children's sexual autonomy, experimentation and even participation in intergenerational sex as evidence for the extensive percolation of permissive ideology into youth culture. Sometime editor of *International Times*, William Bloom, wrote a novel entitled *A Canterbury Tale: A Game for Children* (1971) that was advertised thus: 'Eighteen-year-old Kelvin, fat, frustrated, and bitterly humorous, badly needs love...His sexual fantasies are fulfilled by the aid of a telescope and the erotic experiments made by sweet guileless Jenny, and fourteen-year-old virgin Tristram'.[44] The children are viewed as occupying a self-sufficient, erotic Utopia from which all grown-ups are excluded, even teenage Kelvin, allowing the novel to promote children's independence and sexual autonomy. 'Providing both people are nice, [sex] can't be anything but nice as well, can it?', Kelvin asks Jenny: '[I]t's the most normal thing in the world to do, no matter how old you are.' Jenny questions this—'Do you really think it doesn't matter how old you are?'—but Kelvin reiterates that 'Providing no one gets hurt or anything. Thirteen or eighty, there's nothing stopping anyone.'[45] *A Canterbury Tale* is careful to extend sexual rights only to the post-pubescent. This suits Kelvin, who is a paedophiliac bisexual voyeur. His voyeurism means that, although the novel exclusively depicts children having sex with each other, their sexual activity is continually filtered through his masturbatory fantasies. Childhood sexuality presented in such a manner, however ostensibly liberatory and idealistic, is demonstrably of paedophiliac interest.

Associating sexual activity with adolescent agency allowed some counterculturalists to incorporate intergenerational sex within their wider liberatory agenda. *Oz* editor Richard Neville breaks off from his descriptions of countercultural revolutionary activity in his best-selling manifesto, *Play Power* (1970), to relate an encounter with a schoolgirl:

> I meet a moderately attractive, intelligent, cherubic fourteen-year-old girl from a nearby London comprehensive school. I ask her home, she rolls a joint and we begin to watch the mid-week TV movie...Comes the Heinz Souperday commercial, a hurricane fuck, another joint. No feigned love or hollow promises...A farewell kiss, and the girl rushes off to finish her homework.[46]

This apparently extraneous passage actually serves manifold revolutionary purposes. The elder participant is transgressing the social norm by participating in an illegal act, while the child is being initiated into the counterculture as well as expressing her inalienable sexual rights. As Neville argued elsewhere, 'the post-pubertal child should regard any voluntary sexual relationship as freedom, and therapeutic.'[47]

Several other significant figures in the counterculture argued for the permissibility of consensual sexual contact between adults and children. For example, Germaine Greer observed that 'From the child's point of view and from the common sense point of view, there is an enormous difference between intercourse with a willing little girl and the forcible penetration of the small vagina of a terrified child.'[48] Fellow co-editor of *Suck* and founder of the Arts Lab, Jim Haynes, co-edited *Hello I Love You!* in 1974, a belated attempt to reinvigorate the sexual revolution. The volume contained 'A Child's Sexual Bill of Rights', issued by the Childhood Sexuality (or Sensuality) Circle (CSC). Number seven is '*Choice of a sex partner.* Every child has the right to loving relationships, including sexual, with a parent, sibling, other responsible adult or child, and shall be protected and aided in doing so by being provided with contraceptives and aids to prevent venereal disease.'[49] CSC was actually a paedophile rights campaigning group formed in California in 1971, and its advocacy of children's (sexual) rights was also a feature of other paedophile organisations. The use of this strategy was learnt directly from their parent liberation movements. CSC was associated with the San Francisco Sexual Freedom League, which campaigned for hetero-, homo- and bi-sexual rights.

In Britain, paedophile organisations formed on the fringes of the gay liberation movement, with Paedophile Action for Liberation beginning within South London Gay Liberation Front and PIE, originally part of the Scottish Minorities Group.[50] In their attempts to manage the public discourse on sexual contact between adults and children, these groups adopted the strategies of other civil rights campaigns. The early activities of CSC and PIE coincided with the counterculture's extension of liberation campaigns beyond race and gender, to include the issues of rights for 'sexual minorities' and children. Attempts by paedophile groups to enlist the support of other politically and sexually radical activists were not wholly unsuccessful and—to a limited degree and for a short period—the twinned issues of paedophilia and children's sexual rights were two of the touchstone arguments for sexual liberation.

Culture Wars

The increasingly open representation of adolescent sexuality and the activism of paedophile groups might have been expected to reduce the taboos against intergenerational sex in the 1970s. However, this was not to be, as an unannounced coalition of forces gradually gathered to expel permissiveness's unacceptable stowaway. In retrospect, it is remarkable that the forces of Moral Rearmament and their associates did not earlier identify occurrences of paedophiliac or abusive sex as symptomatic of moral decline. The absence of this strategy during the 1960s and early 1970s might signal that there was no significant perceived connection between permissiveness and paedophilia.[51] However, it might otherwise indicate that adult/child sexual contact was generally accepted, or tacitly ignored. The evidence I have presented above might indicate that certain kinds of intergenerational sexual contact was tolerated, and the practice and representation of it was becoming increasingly legitimised. However, the coincidence of interests among various groups of liberals, libertarians, paedophiles, and pornographers was met by a similarly diverse anti-permissive lobby which seized on child sexual abuse as the most outrageous outcome of the 'new morality'. Although attacks on permissiveness had dealt with the moral effects on children before, it was only in the 1970s that this moral rhetoric hardened into a 'real' bogeyman, identifying a physical danger to young people.

The early legislative successes of the campaigns against child pornography and the sexual exploitation of children were the responsibility of moral conservatives, with Mary Whitehouse leading the campaign for the Protection of Children Act in 1978. Whitehouse had previously exhibited concerns about the sexual abuse of children, but in an evasive manner that itself reinscribed its unspeakableness.[52] However, she had dealt at some length with paedophilia and incest as 'abnormalit[ies] on the list for "normalisation"' just prior to the debate over the Protection of Children Act.[53] She concentrated her ire on PIE's attempts to lower the age of consent and sought to implicate key players in the permissive revolution including the National Council for Civil Liberties, the British Humanist Association, the Abortion Law Reform Association, and the Campaign for Homosexual Equality. Coming immediately prior to the election of the morally conservative Thatcher government, Whitehouse's campaigning helped to secure the passage of the Indecent Displays Act of 1981 and Video Recordings Act of 1984. The latter was particularly significant, marking the first instance of state censorship in Britain since the repeal of the Lord Chamberlain's power to preview plays in 1968. It was a highly symbolic marker that the permissive society was over. Also pressing for anti-pornography and child protection legislation were many feminist groups, whose disengagement from their fellow inheritors of the liberation agenda was a similarly stark indication of the end of permissiveness.

As paedophilia came under sustained attack from both moral conservatives and radical feminists, the 1960s vogue for blurring the boundaries between child pornography and legitimate cultural production began to be challenged. In popular fiction of the 1970s, child abuse became confined to horror novels, often represented symbolically as its unspeakability became reinscribed. More serious representations, as in several short stories by Ian McEwan, generally focused on the nature of the paedophile and avoided the eroticisation of children prevalent in both the popular and literary fiction of the previous decade.[54]

However, some ambiguity over the cultural representation of paedophilia remained in the early 1970s. The stereotypical child molester in *Straw Dogs* (1971)[55]—Henry Niles (David Warner)—is largely tolerated by the local community until he accidentally kills a girl, and is then protected from the vengeful drunken villagers by an American interloper, David Sumner (Dustin Hoffman). The film does not actively engender sympathy for paedophilia, yet renders it less uniquely horrifying by locating it in a network of sexually exploitative behaviour including rape, voyeurism and exhibitionism.[56] The child sexual abuse exhibited in *Get Carter* (1971)[57] is similarly only partially condemned, being introduced as titillating and amusing, and becoming offensive only when Jack Carter (Michael Caine) realises that the young girl in a pornographic film is the daughter of his murdered brother. However, the film also allows for a reading in which Carter comes to a realisation of the individual and domestic implications of socially permitted licence, and thus it can be seen as an ambiguous meditation on permissiveness and its discontents.

The Offence (1973) contained a clearer denunciation of paedophilia.[58]

Detective Sergeant Johnson (Sean Connery) beats to death a suspected child molester (Ian Bannen) during interrogation. While Bannen's character hovers around some of the stereotypical features of the paedophile, the focus is on Johnson and his degradation after years of investigating violent crimes. The film suggests that Johnson also has paedophiliac inclinations, and his murder of the suspect becomes a symbolic expulsion of his own abusive fantasies. In portraying paedophilia as a product of both moral decay and masculine excess, *The Offence* anticipates the critiques of moral conservatives and radical feminists and the use of the issue as a marker for the limits of permissible behaviour.

Falsified Memories

The 1960s retain their fascination for contemporary culture as a symbol of the transcendence of potential over achievement. Its image of anarchic affluence, in which the breaking of societal restrictions was a revolutionary act, has resulted in its becoming a fantasy referent, a textual locale into which can be inserted material which might otherwise be unacceptable. A recent example of this occurred with 'lad culture', which bypassed the politics of anti-feminism through a knowing use of 1960s' icons and attitudes. The retrospective legitimacy of otherwise prohibited expression extends to other aspects of permissiveness, including the eroticisation of children. A certain amount of 1960s' and early 1970s' artwork featuring these themes is still readily available, including works by photographer David Hamilton, fantasy artist Patrick Woodroffe and Underground comix artist Robert Crumb. And the somewhat disingenuous excuse of historicity extends to reprinting vintage titillating material as a form of sexological archaeology.

A notable example of such quasi-pornographic nostalgia is *Baby Doll*, a collection of photographs by Peter Whitehead recording 'a month staying in a château with Mia [Martin]—an heiress cum teenage model'.[59] The images, which were photographed in 1972 but not published until 1996, fully exploit the 'age reduction' techniques favoured in early 1970s 'schoolgirl' pornography, while the text by Jack Sargeant and Iain Sinclair is similarly evasive about the nature of the photographs.[60] It is not paedophilia itself that has now become eroticised, but permissive culture's ability to allude to it. Whitehead himself functions iconographically to allow this allusion, as he was a significant figure in the 1960s counterculture, making films about psychedelia and the Rolling Stones. Although his 1960s output shows little interest in teen sexuality,[61] his subsequent work exhibits a continuing fascination with the subject. Mia Martin appears in Whitehead's *Daddy* (1973),[62] an ambiguous sexual psychodrama between the young girl and her father. In *Nora and*…(1990),[63] a novel illustrated with photographs from *Baby Doll*, Whitehead sets an apparent incest narrative against the background of Paris in 1968. The novel seems to claim the late 1960s as a unique era in which 'the various levels of public fantasy…cross the level of our own private fantasies and the third level of our private lives':[64] a sort of psychosexual year zero that allowed the reinvention of sexual, familial and political relationships. A further intervention by Whitehead into 1960s history occurs in *Tonite Let's All Make Love in London* (1999), based around the International Poetry Incarnation at the Royal Albert Hall in June 1965, and intertwining a CIA plot to destabilise the counterculture with sexually precocious fifteen-year-old Swedish nymphets.[65] What might be considered child sexual abuse in other situations is tolerated or even celebrated in the prehistory that permissiveness has come to signify.

Many recently published novels associate the permissive era with deviant intergenerational sex. Gordon Burns's *Alma Cogan* (1991) ends its investigation of early celebrity culture with the inescapable events of the Moors murders. Simon Mawer's *The Fall* (2003) involves two generations of sexual promiscuity and abuse. David Peace's *Nineteen Seventy-Four* (1999) features the journalistic and criminological investigation of a multiple child murderer active from 1969.[66] Nicci French's *The Memory Game* (1997) begins with the discovery of the body of Natalie, a sixteen-year-old who went missing in 1969. When her body is discovered, Jane, her best friend, enters therapy and 'remembers' seeing Natalie being raped and murdered by her father. This incestuous murder comes as no surprise—it was the 1960s, after all. Jane's memory is incorrect, however. The actual murderer was her husband and Natalie's older brother (and lover), Claud. In a move which mirrors the cultural confusion over the pornographic exploitation of adolescent sexuality since the 1960s, the novel retreats from the paedophiliac scenario and replaces it with one which implicates the schoolgirl protagonist in sibling incest. As before, female teenage sexuality is bound up with both criminality and desire.[67]

The exploitative ambiguity around the nature of intergenerational and incestuous sex during the permissive era allows it to be maintained as an erotically charged fantasy in post-permissive popular fiction. The use of similar themes in more clearly serious fictional narratives is less obviously exploitative, but they are similarly referencing a permissive space in which the unspeakable can be not just spoken but performed. This varied but recurrent eroticisation of paedophilia through allusion rather than direct reference has led to permissiveness and the 1960s becoming figured as essentially, if largely symbolically, paedophiliac. The permissive society has, in fact, become the fictional space within which contemporary culture can safely insert its own abusive fantasies.

7. *Rupert Bare: Art, Obscenity and the Oz Trial*

Gerry Carlin

Many of the key debates concerning the permissive society reached their climax at the 1971 conspiracy trial of the editors of *Oz* magazine, Jim Anderson, Felix Dennis and Richard Neville, for publishing and distributing

> a magazine containing divers obscene lewd indecent and sexually perverted articles cartoons drawings and illustrations with intent thereby to debauch and corrupt the morals of children and young persons within the realm and to arouse and implant in their minds lustful and perverted desires.[1]

But, though the trial encapsulated a number of political, moral and legal debates, it hardly resolved them. Conservative moralists failed to realise that obscenity trials publicised the material that they sought to suppress and unrealistically represented teenagers as being corrupted by counter-culturalists little older than themselves. For their part, the defendants implausibly argued that the case had 'nothing to do with obscenity' and found it easier to defend their magazine against political censorship than to justify its contents.[2] The Underground knew what it was against more clearly than what it was for. The harsh custodial sentences imposed by the original trial judge were suspended and reduced on appeal due to his 'serious misdirection of the jury', and the legal aftermath was equally ambiguous. The trial at once helped to secure freedom of political expression and consolidated the trend towards obscenity prosecutions being justified on the grounds of protecting children.

The reason for this focus on childhood was that the cartoon at the centre of the *Oz* trial was not only created by a child, but also featured one: a young, anthropomorphic bear called Rupert whose representation in an erotic montage provoked a wide-ranging discussion of youth, aesthetics and sexuality in the permissive society. It is my intention here to contextualise this cartoon in order to draw out the issues in this late and inconclusive confrontation between the Underground and the Establishment. Furthermore, I would like to suggest that the *Oz* trial simultaneously marked the heyday and the death-knell of the counterculture: a point after which its coherence and influence waned due to ideological contradictions as much as to any legal persecution. As such, it offers a case study of the complex fate of the Underground.

Oz magazine served as the irreverent 'colour supplement' of the London counterculture from January 1967 until November 1973. *International Times* (*IT*) had preceded it by a few months and both magazines began fairly conventionally before finding a different audience. '*Oz* took off in the way *IT* did: there was a community responding to it', recalled *IT*'s founding editor, Barry Miles: 'The first edition was a cynical pale attempt at *Private Eye* but that was only on the stands for a few issues before it completely changed its direction and from being deeply cynical of hippies, the next issue was super-hippie.'[3] The 'hippie' or countercultural community that was reflected (and in many ways constructed) by the Underground press loosely cohered around confrontational, libertarian and permissive principles.[4] 'The statement of our values is "dope, rock-'n'roll and fucking in the streets"', declared one *Oz* contributor: 'We know what we mean by this even if straights don't.'[5] The history of the Underground press was accordingly punctuated by a series of skirmishes with the authorities, from the 1967 police raid on *IT* to the *Oz* trial four years later. The conspiracy charge brought against *Oz* rather transparently revealed that it was on trial for its politics and its championing of alternative lifestyles as much as for its obscenity. As a 'Friends of *Oz*' poster put it,

> While it is *Oz* that is on trial at the Old Bailey, it is in fact an entire community which is being prosecuted. If you care about your freedom to think, communicate and experiment, if you care about

> freedom of the press, freedom to live the life you wish, then you also are in the dock.[6]

The offending issue was *Oz* 28, which appeared in May 1970. This 'School Kids' edition was primarily the work of a group of fourteen- to eighteen-year-olds invited to guest-edit the magazine.[7] The issue contained *Oz*'s customarily provocative mix of 'alternative' graphics, cartoons, articles, reviews and advertisements, but additionally included teenagers' thoughts on sex, drugs, rock 'n' roll, corporal punishment and institutionalised abuse. It was anti-authoritarian in tone and presented itself, as Richard Neville argued at the trial, as a radical experiment in adolescent autonomy. However, Neville would find himself forced, rather disingenuously, to stress the fact that *Oz* 28 was put together *by* school kids, and targeted at the usual *Oz* readership, rather than being specifically marketed *at* school kids, as the prosecution constantly implied.[8]

The prosecution especially targeted one item within the issue: a montage created by fifteen-year-old Vivian Berger that fused a Rupert Bear cartoon with one by the American cartoonist Robert Crumb. Rupert Bear had first appeared in the *Daily Express* in 1920 and had long offered an innocent, nostalgic and quintessentially 'middle-English' version of childhood. By contrast, Crumb was one of the most prolific and explicit of the American Underground cartoonists: a bizarre and somewhat tragic figure who put his sexual hang-ups and sado-masochistic obsessions directly onto the page.[9] The Crumb strip used by Berger was part of a long cartoon called 'Eggs Ackley Among the Vulture Demonesses', published in the first issue of *Big Ass Comics* in 1969.[10] What appeared in the *Oz* montage was a sexually excited Rupert Bear apparently violating the virginity of a prone female. Although the basic drawings and speech-bubbles were Crumb's, Rupert's head and scarf had been carefully superimposed on the male character, and the frame titles and narrative in rhyming couplets had been retained from the Rupert strip.[11]

Some aspects of this cartoon could not be said to shock or startle. Reproductions of American Underground comics were a common enough sight in British countercultural magazines of this period. What's more, such comics regularly featured mainstream cartoon characters.

'Characters like Batman and Superman, with impeccable overground credentials, are usually parodied or placed in embarrassing sexual situations', noted Roger Lewis in 1972: 'Mickey Mouse is shown shooting up heroin, Olive Oyle lays into Popeye on the subject of Women's Liberation, and Clark Kent desperately tries to don his Superman outfit in a public lavatory.'[12] But the Rupert montage *did* startle, not least because it satirised the middle-Englishness of the *Daily Express* and, more specifically, seemed to distort and pervert a version of English childhood.

The prosecution of literature and art for corrupting the young had been a common feature of British legal history since 1895, when Oscar Wilde had unwisely rhapsodised about the love 'of an elder for a younger man as there was between David and Jonathan' when asked in court to explain the meaning of his poem, 'Two Loves' (1894).[13] Wilde's trial initiated a curious legal fusion of textual practices and lifestyles that stressed the protection of childhood innocence. Cartoons first became a major concern in the 1950s, when the Communist Party orchestrated a campaign against the base morals and baser aesthetics of American pulp comics that resulted in their censorship under the terms of the 1955 Children and Young Persons Harmful Publications Act.[14] And, in 1969, there was a Wildean touch to the 1969 prosecution of *IT* for publishing gay contact ads placed by men below the age of consent.[15]

By this point, the Underground was considered by conservative moralists to be the greatest threat to the nation's youth. The prosecution of *Oz* overlapped with that, on identical charges, of *The Little Red Schoolbook*, the British edition of a radical Danish text that provided schoolchildren with advice on civil rights, education, drugs and sex. Though many of its demands were subsequently implemented, Mary Whitehouse considered the book to be a 'revolutionary primer' that advocated a 'value-free society' for the younger generation, while fellow reactionary Ross McWhirter declared it to be 'not only obscene but also seditious'.[16] Two years later, the British 'Adult Comix' *Nasty Tales* would face obscenity charges, with a Robert Crumb cartoon once again forming the centrepiece of the prosecution's case. The prosecution of these publications introduced a new and explicitly generational element into the assault upon the counterculture. Inspector Frederick Luff, the Obscene Publications squad officer responsible for the *Oz* bust, acknowledged such a motivation to editor

Jim Anderson when he stated 'I think *Oz* should be closed down. I'm doing this for the sake of my children.'[17]

The prosecution charged that *Oz* exploited children. They even portrayed Rupert Bear as a child, and posed pointed questions about what constituted appropriate behaviour for a bear cub, the size of his sexual organs and Rupert's age ('He's a young bear isn't he?', 'He goes to school doesn't he?' asked prosecutor Brian Leary).[18] Yet the *Oz* camp turned the tables on their accusers by presenting themselves as children's true champions. *Oz* issued a 'Draft Charter' of children's rights in 1971 and Richard Neville argued in *Play Power* (1970) that workaday adult lives needed to be infused with a childish sense of fun:

> There is one quality which enlivens both the political and cultural dimensions of Youth protest; which provides its most important innovation; which has the greatest relevance for the future; which is the funniest, freakiest and the most effective. This is the element of play...[19]

Neville's views reflected the counterculture's glorification of youth, and this proved a ready target for conservative moralists. 'Let's all be kids together' was how Mary Whitehouse characterised the creed of the 'New Libertarians', as if 'only the fantasies of child's play help them to come to terms with what they have made of the world.'[20] It also distinguished the counterculture from liberal progressives, who were prepared to concede the case for protecting children. Whereas he wished to treat adults as adults, Sir John Trevelyan defended his role as film censor when it came to sheltering young minds.[21] Liberal progressives likened permissiveness to a maturing process that allowed adults to accept responsibility for their own actions in a suitably sober manner. Sir John Wolfenden wrote in 1973 that individual freedoms had increased at the expense of restrictive legislation while, paradoxically, it was 'only *within* the law that people can *have* freedom'. He acknowledged that minorities often drive social change (for better and for worse) and suggested that the young seem biologically determined to rebel. He viewed humanity as undergoing its own 'turbulent, tiresome, troubled, worried' adolescence and closed his essay with the thought that 'the writer trusts his children and their children to do, far better, what he himself has failed to do.'[22]

If childhood was one central issue in the *Oz* trial, then art was another, not least because the 1959 Obscene Publications Act exempted works of literary or artistic merit from censorship. The prosecution followed the logic of the earlier censorship of American comics in assuming cartoons to be inherently worthless. From their perspective, the Rupert montage represented the sexualisation and contamination of a British icon by an alien and degenerate culture. The defence nonetheless sought to mount an artistic defence in emulation of the landmark *Lady Chatterley's Lover* trial of 1960 and recruited a similarly illustrious body of defence witnesses. However, their case proved difficult to argue. One problem was that there had been an acceleration in media technologies and diversification of audiences and markets in the intervening decade. *Oz* was one of what Pierre Bourdieu has termed 'new cultural intermediaries', engaged in challenging traditional hierarchies by embracing hitherto marginalised aspects of culture.[23] Its treatment of rock music, popular art, alternative lifestyles and experimentation with drugs was notable for its seriousness but, from a legal point of view, tarnished its cultural credentials.

Another difficulty was that *Oz*'s anarchic editorial policy raised awkward questions about the clause in the 1959 Act requiring that the work be 'taken as a whole'. Each issue included graphics, articles, current and alternative news, reviews, polemic, comment, gossip, poetry, nonsense, 'lively and original propaganda as well as garbled and sub-literate war cries' and an increasing amount of advertising.[24] The prosecution, however, tended to overlook the written content of *Oz* 28 (which included much perceptive social commentary and no fewer than three pages of letters criticising either the magazine or the Underground) and focused on the cover, cartoons, graphics and small ads.[25] Richard Neville was himself most worried when questioned about the detailed descriptions of fellatio that featured in an advertisement for *Suck* magazine:

> 'Why was that put in the magazine?'
> 'It's a miniscule advertisement for a European sex paper.'
> 'But it has nothing to do with the children who produced this magazine?'
> 'No.'[26]

The *Oz* team hedged its bets about the literary merit of issue 28, at once portraying it as a valid expression of a customarily voiceless minority and commenting that 'the authorities in this country take our publishing venture more seriously than we do'. However, there was less hedging when it came to the Rupert montage. This was *art*. Editor Jim Anderson had described it as 'youthful genius' in the issue itself and, at the trial, almost all of the defence witnesses characterised it as a valid statement with some artistic merit. The artist Feliks Topolski made the strongest case for its specifically aesthetic value. While admitting under cross-examination that the Crumb and Rupert elements were 'not art' when considered in isolation, he maintained that Berger's montage became 'satirical art' through its 'juxtaposition of hitherto unrelated elements'. By refusing to accede to the prosecution's attempts to 'separate' the elements of the montage, Topolski was insisting that the work be considered 'as a whole' in accordance with the new obscenity law.[27]

Montage has been an important aesthetic technique at least since the invention of photography. It became a staple element of Dada, Surrealism and political satire and propaganda in the first half of the twentieth century, and also featured prominently in post-war Pop Art, in which it was often used to express the breakdown of cultural boundaries or the commodification of culture.[28] *Oz* had used montage extensively before the 'School Kids' edition, most notably in issue 16 (November 1968), described by art critic Robert Hughes as 'one of the richest banks of images that has ever appeared in a magazine'.[29] That issue had been designed by the magazine's in-house artist, Martin Sharp, and had virtually no copy in the accepted sense. Instead, it consisted of 24 pages of montaged images and scraps of text drawn from a wide range of printed sources, featuring headlines, adverts, scientific images and photographs, nudes, cartoons (including Crumb's), images from pop culture, art books, fragments of John Heartfield's photomontages and a lot of René Magritte and Vincent van Gogh.

The way in which montage functions in the field of semiotics and interpretation is that it drains, diverts or hijacks an image or object's original meaning. For example, a photomontage breaks apart the 'truth' of the photographic image. If we can take the original image as a statement of 'what is'—a visual representation of 'nature'—then montage might be considered as 'nature' (visuality) forced into a kind of writing, producing invisible comments and captions.[30] More mundanely, montage takes 'found' objects (images) and modifies them or imports them into new contexts, and *anyone* can do it. Montage democratises art in interesting ways, and plugs directly into what the art critic Norbert Lynton labelled the 'artist-jester' impulse in a 1969 *Guardian* collection concerning the permissive society. Lynton claimed that art in its most significant modern traditions had no obligation to depict 'beauty' (in fact it often produces disturbance and discord); that it proceeded through a dialectic between the sublime vision of Vincent van Gogh and Marcel Duchamp's shocking 'art-as-gesture'; and that its contemporary democratic proliferation should be celebrated.[31]

Such arguments might support the contention that the Rupert cartoon was a work of art when taken 'as a whole' and when related both to twentieth-century modernism and to the magazine's previous aesthetic experimentalism. Moreover, affinities with earlier avant-garde traditions had been claimed by Jeff Nuttall's *Bomb Culture* (1968), which traced the roots of the Underground back to jazz, Dada and the Marquis de Sade.[32] What this chain of succession glossed over, however, was the breakdown of distinctions between high art and popular forms in the multimedia 1960s. Implicit throughout *Oz*, but certainly not fully expressed at the trial, was the levelling postmodern aesthetic expressed by Duchamp in 1957 in his comment that 'bad art is still art in the same way that a bad emotion is still an emotion'.[33] While the counterculture and culture at large were being redefined by breakdowns, levellings and expansions of cultural categories, it seemed rather anachronistic to redraw the aesthetic boundaries in one's own favour, such as when Topolski insisted that Berger's cartoon was art in a manner that the Rupert and Crumb cartoons were not. Claims for the cartoon's worth signalled out its humour, honesty and use of montage, yet none of these things differentiated it from other examples of permissive culture with no artistic pretensions. Vivian Berger admitted that the Rupert montage was 'the kind of drawing that goes around every classroom, every day, in every school' and, when placed alongside the ribald artefacts examined in Leon Hunt's *British Low Culture* (1998), it appears to be just a product of a pre-PC age.[34]

The Rupert montage seems in hindsight to be more indebted to a form of montage specific to the 1960s. British fashion of the decade often consisted of items of historical costume—recycled Victoriana and imperial finery—*bricolaged* in ways that parodied, refashioned and relativised them as 'styles'.[35] Peter Blake's cover for the Beatles' *Sgt. Pepper* album (1967) is a classic example of this. The ultra-hip Beatles stand in pastiched military uniforms before a montage of assorted celebrities whose juxtaposition questions the traditional hierarchies of cultural value.[36] Psychedelic montage and its parallels in other fields of expression both decodes and recodes the past, draining it of its power and emphasising the provisionality of its values by forcing it, usually irreverently, into the present.

George Melly characterised this tendency to treat history as 'a vast boutique' as a means of rendering the past harmless by 'wrenching these objects out of their historical context'.[37] But British psychedelia of the late 1960s also re-examined the past *critically*, particularly when dealing with the early twentieth-century childhood experienced by the parents of babyboomers (and signified by Rupert Bear). Though British psychedelia is often seen as glorifying childish innocence,[38] its portrayal of childhood was often uncanny, grotesque and ironic. Take the canonical psychedelic record, the Beatles' 'Strawberry Fields Forever'. In it, the musical complexity and verbal archness pull against any sense of a pastoral or 'innocent' childish vision. Rather, 'Strawberry Fields' attempts to replicate altered states, uncertain memories, and psychological discontinuities. Here as elsewhere, the psychedelic return to childhood has overtones of the gothic and psychotic. It is often refracted through drug experiences that promote critical scepticism as much as hedonistic indulgence and as music critic Jon Savage noted, 'LSD was not an escape but a reckoning'.[39] In a real sense, psychedelia's concern with childhood might be considered as a concern with childhood *betrayed*. Conventional versions of childhood become myths of magic and innocence which the adult world uses to mesmerise and infantilise children. Seen in this light, *Oz*'s Rupert montage represents a late example of psychedelic historical interrogation and its demythologisation of childhood.

However, the sexual elements of the montage nudged it out of the realms of art and into much more contentious areas. In line with their somewhat elitist defence of the Rupert cartoon's artistic worth, supporters of *Oz* similarly contrasted the magazine's treatment of sexual matters with their exploitation by the popular media. Feliks Topolski defended *Oz* as 'a satirical send-up of erotic, pornographic, commercial publications', John Lennon suggested that the police should 'arrest Soho' rather than magazine editors and Vivian Berger's mother, who chaired the National Council for Civil Liberties, maintained that her son's artwork represented a healthy expression of sexual curiosity when compared with Fleet Street's 'innuendo'.[40] Richard Neville pointed out that more graphic material was available in soft-core publications 'on sale at W. H. Smith's, and much more likely to catch the eye of young people primarily interested in sex', and went so far as to claim that the magazine was 'trying to redefine love':

> It is true that contained within this re-interpretation of the concept of love, is a more candid sexuality. But I think this is indicative of a healthier and more honest relationship between men and women.[41]

It was a hard sell. Brian Leary, counsel for the prosecution, refused to see any treatment of 'love' in the magazine at all, citing representations of underage sex, necrophilia, homosexuality and flagellation to claim that 'this magazine does not deal with love. It deals with sex with a capital S.' His accusation was echoed in sections of the popular press, which claimed that the magazine and its ethos promoted 'sex without tenderness; lust without love'.[42] Moreover, whereas the defence emphasised the differences between *Oz* and 'street' pornography, prosecutors stressed the similarities. They had a point, since the issue immediately preceding 'School Kids' *Oz* had featured a centrefold of three barely pubescent naked girls.[43] The distinction between subversive or satirical sexual explicitness and mainstream exploitation was becoming difficult to maintain and, as will be shortly seen, it was a distinction increasingly contested within the Underground itself. However, an unspoken countercultural rationale for such explicitness was intimated by one of the adolescent contributors to *Oz* 28, who stated that society's attitude towards an 'alternative' activity was always to 'Take it over, package it, sell it back to itself.'[44] Perhaps the only way to interrupt such cycles of appropriation, in countercultural terms, was to make the representation of sexuality so *excessive* that it became literally unmarketable. Such a strategy derived intellectual justification from the writings of Herbert Marcuse, whose notion of 'repressive desublimation' highlighted the coercive nature of liberal regimes that permitted 'the systematic inclusion of libidinal components into the realm of commodity production and exchange' in order to limit and control potentially subversive instinctive energies.[45]

The complex ways in which *Oz* simultaneously satirised, critiqued *and* exploited the commodification of sex is well illustrated by a poster insert in *Oz* 24 that reproduced a page of *The People* headlined 'Can YOUR Kids Buy This?' Alongside pictures of a bare-breasted woman from an advertisement in *Oz*, a similarly unattired woman hanging onto a Hell's Angel featured on the cover of *Oz* 20 and a photograph of a bearded and dreadlocked editor, was *The People*'s indictment of the magazine's alleged promotion of drug use and underage sex. However, the poster also included a counterblast from the *Guardian* that critiqued *The People*'s hypocritically titillating moral crusade and revealed that their interview with *Oz*'s editor (an impostor) was actually a set-up by the magazine itself. Here, while collaborating with the permissive society's circulation of sexually explicit images, *Oz* satirises the tabloids' craving for moral panics. However, the reverse side of the poster features a Robert Crumb cartoon of a bare-breasted girl entitled 'Jail Bait of the Month: "Honey Bunch" Kaminski, 13, of L.A.'[46] The Underground's peculiar mix of radical thinking and sexual exploitation is readily apparent in *Oz*'s decision to publish an image suggestive of sex with a minor. In order to reveal the control that the supposedly permissive society actually practises, *Oz had* to be excessive and thereby encourage its own prosecution. The obscenity of the Rupert montage was an index of the magazine's Underground resistance to mainstream appropriation and, if it set out to interrogate the limits of society's apparatus of 'repressive desublimation', then the initial guilty verdict should be seen as a success for defence and prosecution alike.

Yet the road of excess led to an own goal. The Rupert montage intended by Vivian Berger to 'shock your generation' of elders also shocked many young activists due to its brutal *machismo*. Sexually explicit images that had served as a generalised symbol of countercultural liberation in the 1960s had come to be seen as a display of heterosexual male power by those involved in the 1970s' gay and women's liberation movements. As David Widgery commented in the final issue of *Oz*,

> What finally knackered the Underground was its complete inability to deal with women's liberation…Because the Underground remained so utterly dominated by men, sexual liberation was framed in terms saturated with male assumptions, right down to the rape fantasy of 'Dope, rock 'n' roll and fucking in the streets'.[47]

One unnamed woman accordingly refused to be a defence witness at the trial on the grounds that the Rupert cartoon 'violated' her childhood memories. Its callous treatment of sex heightened her consciousness of 'male antagonism to women' and the manner in which 'men had the arrogance to portray sexuality in *their* terms.' Another, Martha Rowe, dismissed the cartoon as 'puerile' rather than pornographic, but was appalled by the subsequent 'commercial' direction of *Oz* and its uncomplicatedly 'pornographic' images devoid of any 'redeeming aesthetic nor any political allegorical point'.[48] She would quit her job as secretary of *Oz* to become founding editor of the feminist periodical *Spare Rib*. The magazine *Come Together* also recorded deep splits within the Gay Liberation Front over whether or not to support the *Oz* defendants in 1971:

> The objections (which were many and strongly held) sprang from what many of us thought was the blatant sexism in *Oz* magazine's treatment of women (and also gay people) as sex objects, subject to male superiority, inferior tools of male pleasure, objects of ridicule. Others in GLF either could not see the sexism in *Oz*, or felt that if it was sexism, it was something that GLF should deal with at a later date.[49]

Perhaps the *Oz* trial should therefore be as famous for widening schisms within a fragmenting—or, more accurately, an expanding and diversifying—Underground as for rallying it against the Establishment in an epic showdown. The magazine's doctrine of permissive liberation and anarchic opposition had run its course. Obscenity and outrage had become blunt instruments, while what cultural critics Simon Frith and Howard Horne describe as 'the pressing need to stay one cultural jump ahead' was less keenly felt.[50] For Martha Rowe to characterise the Rupert cartoon as 'puerile' suggested that the counterculture had to mature before its rebelliousness could be turned into either a constructive critique or an effective alternative politics. She was one of many who joined New Social Movements that were, as she put it, both 'a product of the counterculture and a reaction against it'.[51]

The use of sexuality as a symbol of permissive freedom, liberation and transgression has faded from our cultural landscape. Sexual images are omnipresent, and to a great extent 'naturalised', but they now signify something other than a generalised freedom even though, as the internet has shown, most things sexual are permitted. The idea of school children as a potent force in some anarchic process of social change has also vanished. But, in an uncanny return of the issues at the centre of the *Oz* trial, children are now used to define the limits of sexuality and permissiveness. It could be that the trial helped to increase the accountability of parents (or, for that matter, editors) for the actions as well as the treatment of children.

In the end, *Oz* 28 and the Rupert montage became and remain emblematic not only of the rebellious energies, but also of the limitations and eventual exhaustion of countercultural 'desublimations'. The Underground had grown up by 1971 and, like a disassembling montage, was separating out into varied and new groupings, new spaces, and new publications. One of the most important effects of the Rupert montage was to demonstrate that moments of rebellion rapidly become outmoded in a period of accelerating change and remain bound up with, and prey to, recuperation by the system that they oppose. What better lesson could we learn from the Underground in the afterglow of the radical 1960s?

8. 'Questioning and Dancing on the Table': The Ludic Liberalism of Richard Neville

Rychard Carrington

In the late 1960s and early 1970s, Richard Neville was arguably the most prominent spokesperson for the London branch of the international youth movement known as 'the counterculture', 'the Underground' or 'the Movement'. Born in Australia in 1941, Neville possessed an articulacy uncommon in this milieu and, as editor of *Oz*, possessed an ideal medium for his ideas. The publication of his manifesto *Play Power* in 1970 and his starring role in the *Oz* obscenity trial the following year raised his profile still higher, before he abruptly returned to Australia in 1972.[1]

Richard Neville has generally not received a good press. He tends to be regarded either as a fatuous proselytiser akin to Timothy Leary, or as a media-courting, middle-class quasi-hippie. His writings have likewise been criticised as exemplifying the counterculture's frivolity, sexism and crude contempt for 'straight' society. From the left, *New Statesman* critic Mervyn Jones described *Play Power* as 'coarse, shallow and nasty', and from the right Commander Rees Millington dubbed it 'the *Mein Kampf* of an international conspiracy to overthrow the Anglo-Saxon way of life.'[2] Fellow counterculturalists also subsequently distanced themselves from *Play Power*. The novelist Angela Carter characterised it as 'tacky, tacky, tacky' in 1988, while a decade later Neville's one-time colleague at *Oz* Jonathon Green denounced it as a 'massively-flawed…combination of the hip, the hysterical, the downright embarrassing and the occasional razor-edged *aperçu*.'[3] Even the cultural critic Julie Stephens, for all her insistence that we should take Yippie politics seriously, declines to defend Neville's 'scatter-brained and dated' ideas. Though accepting that *Play*

Power is 'replete with self-conscious parody', she concludes that 'it seems at times to be just plain foolish.'[4]

Yet Neville's advocacy of the Underground manifested more integrity and discernment than he is usually given credit for. What has been interpreted as flippancy and inconsistency can be viewed as an interest in dialogue and openness of mind that contrasts favourably with the zealotry of some of his contemporaries. Indeed, contrary to the fears of Commander Millington and the hopes of more militant counterculturalists, Neville's fashionably incendiary catchphrases belied his larger goal of reconciling classical liberalism to countercultural experientialism. This, after all, was a man who listed John Stuart Mill, William Wilberforce and Bertrand Russell among his influences as well as Jack Kerouac, Lenny Bruce, Abbie Hoffman and Jerry Rubin—and who once stated that 'I never used the word "hippy" about myself except in a jocular way. I was and still am a liberal.'[5] This chapter explores these affinities between social liberalism and Neville's political philosophy; how the ensuing tensions between his liberalism and the trajectory of the counterculture made his position as its mouthpiece increasingly untenable; and, most speculatively, how the liberal aspects of the Underground were its most permanent legacy inasmuch as they helped cause a cultural, but not a political, revolution.

Liberalism and the Counterculture

Political radicals in 1960s' America coalesced around the idea that their government and society had failed to live up to the nation's professedly liberal ideals. With McCarthy's purges still a recent memory, the Civil Rights, anti-Vietnam and student movements identified and exposed the thoroughly illiberal nature of much contemporary political authority, including the nominally liberal Johnson administration. This led to an explicit rejection of liberalism by the American New Left that drew sustenance from Herbert Marcuse's critique of 'repressive tolerance'.[6] Its increasing antipathy to liberal values evolved from the temperate critique of the SDS's founding Port Huron Statement through SDS leader Carl Oglesby's denunciation of the Vietnam War as 'fundamentally liberal' to the Leninism or Maoism of such late 1960s' organisations as Progressive

Labor and the Weathermen.[7] The Yippies accepted the New Left's association of liberalism with capitalism, but developed a more defiantly anti-rationalist stance. Yippie leader Abbie Hoffman made 'corporate liberalism' (a term coined by Oglesby) a particular target of abuse in his memoir-cum-manifesto *Revolution for the Hell of It* (1968). Rather than take issue with corporate liberalism on its own terms, Hoffman disdained the rationality and sheer earnestness of its discourse—a tactic he also deployed against the 'straight' left.[8]

While explicit identification with liberalism became increasingly rare in a movement rife with inflated revolutionary rhetoric, much countercultural ideology was nonetheless a revitalised version of the liberalism classically expounded by John Stuart Mill. However *passé* this might have seemed to political philosophers, it posed a radical challenge to the laws and values of societies that were still far from liberal. Richard Neville was a key countercultural exponent of the tradition sometimes referred to as 'social liberalism' or 'left-liberalism'. Liberalism upholds the paramount freedom of the individual. The Underground articulated this in terms of 'permissiveness', defined by Neville as the doctrine that 'each individual should be freed from the hindrance of external law and internal guilt in the pursuit of pleasure, so long as it does not impinge on others.'[9] He also embraced the cardinal liberal principles of diversity and tolerance, as he explained to me in an e-mail interview conducted in 2001. In answer to my request that he elucidate his concept of a liberal, he replied: 'a free-speech nutter, upholding democracy and the rights of others, especially those you don't agree with, a philosophy in decline. Total tolerance is my credo.'[10]

Neville recognised the potential for conflict between 'the right to pleasure…and social responsibility', yet argued that liberty need not degenerate into licence.[11] In contrast to libertarian anarchists, social liberals such as himself are prepared to accept that certain governmental restrictions on individual freedom can be justified in the name of preventing harm to other individuals or of establishing 'positive' freedoms that advance the goals of equality and community. The Underground was sympathetic to struggles for social and economic justice by minorities and developing countries: hence *Oz*'s sponsorship of the rights of women, children and homosexuals. It was also keen to perceive itself as an 'alternative' community, counteracting the alienation it saw as being endemic in society at large. Neville was attracted to such a 'feeling of belonging—to what, exactly, no one knew.'[12] Communitarian sentiments of this kind distinguish social liberalism from a neo-liberalism that is sometimes mistakenly regarded as an extension of Underground philosophy.

The social liberal shares the empiricist's suspicion of dogma and the doctrinaire. Thus a liberal manifesto is inclined to be provisional, contingent and tentative in its arguments, in contrast to the deductive rationalism of much Marxist thought. Antipathy towards Marxism is not so much on account of its egalitarianism as its totalising and scientific pretensions. Neville particularly identified with this aspect of the liberal creed:

> Sometimes...I thought I ought to be a little more revolutionary, but I've always loathed violence and bloodshed and every time I dived into Marxism all I could think of was Lenin shooting the anarchists. I could never come to terms with the Big Idea.[13]

Many Underground thinkers accordingly believed that subjective sensibility should develop through experience, rather than 'alienated' rational thought and knowledge. 'We do not need theories,' stated R.D. Laing, 'so much as the experience that is the source of the theory.'[14]

The respect paid by social liberals to individual autonomy is not merely a negative matter of allowing individuals to 'do their own thing'. It also involves exposing people to a lively, plural culture that offers a wide spectrum of experientially fulfilling activities. The greater variety of 'own things' there are legitimately available, the greater are the opportunities for each individual, and the richer society becomes as a whole. This argument was frequently employed at the *Oz* trial by Neville, his lawyer John Mortimer and the expert witnesses called in his defence.[15] Yet, while society plays a crucial role in providing or denying opportunities, social liberalism holds that ultimately a person's subjective perspective should determine his or her own choices instead of an authority claiming to know what is best for that individual.

Mention has to be made of social liberalism's relation to capitalism. The social liberal upholds the virtue of liberal principles *per se*, rejecting the automatic equation of liberalism and capitalism made by both Marxists and neo-liberals. Whereas Marxists condemn liberalism for this association, neo-liberals invoke liberal values in order to extol capitalism's virtues. The social liberal, on the other hand, is likely to be critical of capitalism's inegalitarian and competitive aspects, but neither regards capitalism as the root of all evil nor considers its downfall to be the prerequisite to a truly free society. Though social liberalism may wish to direct and limit the free market, it does not offer a thorough alternative to it (*Play Power* being a case in point). It might be described as being capitalist by default, rather than by proud identification. From such a perspective, the relationship between counterculture and capitalist enterprise is more ambivalent than a grim Situationist narrative of recuperation by hegemonic forces.[16]

A Liberal's Dilemma

Neville's liberalism, which became increasingly explicit during the 1970s, enabled him to trumpet what was genuinely progressive in the Underground, but at the same time made him uneasy about both its hardening militancy and its exuberant anti-rationalism. When he commented that at *Oz* 'we are still old-fashioned enough to try to evaluate', he was really describing his opposition to tendencies he observed elsewhere in the counterculture.[17] His qualms were exacerbated by the manner in which his enthusiasm, articulacy and charisma propelled him into becoming the principal mouthpiece for the Underground. As his girlfriend Louise Ferrier remarked to him in 1970, 'I knew the [straight] media would eat you up. They need you. Everyone else in the Underground is too stoned to finish a sentence.'[18] His editorship of *Oz*, the commission to write *Play Power*, and finally the *Oz* trial obliged Neville to remain, in his own words, 'a megaphone for the counterculture'. Yet privately he always had 'a weakness for seeing the other person's point of view'.[19]

One reason much of *Play Power* now seems quite intellectually weak is that, in absolute contradiction of a key countercultural injunction, its author was not following his instincts or doing his own thing, which was to thrive on the independence of the unallied liberal. Neville has stated that 'I felt marginally useful in propagandising the Movement and denigrating the values of straight society, from which I always felt alienated.'[20] Yet by nature he was never a propagandist and his dislike of theory and doctrine are evident throughout *Play Power*. He dismisses ideologues of the 'sober, violent, puritan' left, belittles such intellectual heroes of the counterculture as Marcuse and Reich, and pointedly ignores oriental gurus. 'I was suspicious of all religions', he later acknowledged, 'including imports from the East'.[21]

The liberal politics of *Play Power* also fit awkwardly alongside its ludism. For instance, the sober documentation of police brutality in Appendix One loses much of its impact by appearing immediately after a peroration that proclaims that 'In the land where the court jester is King, there is only one question—is he funny enough?'[22] The pleasure Neville derived from playing at revolution and generational warfare disguised his lack of interest in revolution and detracted from his promotion of radical new lifestyles capable of being incorporated within a pluralist capitalist society. Kenneth Tynan shrewdly observed that the countercultural types described in *Play Power* 'exist within the status quo, to which they offer no political threat...Neville is right about play, but terribly wrong about power.'[23] Fellow reviewer and occasional *Oz* contributor Clive James recognised that the revolution was a less pressing concern in Britain than the United States:

> The lesson in the United States is that capitalism can give ground to the new life-style but that the state can't...In Britain the straight/freak confrontation is softened to the point of workability by the presence in government and the media of the meritocratic elite—the older alternative society which identified absorptive flexibility as the essential characteristic of British politics and furthered the work of institutionalising it.[24]

In retrospect, *Play Power* displays how his role of proselytiser for an amorphous and fissiparous 'Movement' was becoming a strain for Neville, whose honest, if rather slapdash, liberal empiricism did not allow him to shelter behind the audacious irrationality of Hoffman's *Revolution for the Hell of It* or Rubin's *Do It!* (1970). At the end of 1970, some months after the publication of *Play Power*, Neville allowed himself to express his reservations more assertively in an *Oz* editorial in which he lambasted the Underground for its violence, elitism, dishonesty, hypocrisy, crude 'freaks versus straights' rhetoric and lack of genuine fellow-feeling: 'We...blithely declare World War Three on our parents and yet have already forgotten how to smile at our friends.'[25] One senses that he was, with considerable relief, finally exorcising some of the baser extravagances of the Yippie, Provo and Situationist philosophies which he had been officially endorsing for too long, against the judgement of his now not-so-latent liberal conscience and down-to-earth good sense.

The paperback edition of *Play Power* published in January 1971 contained a new paragraph summarising many of the same misgivings. He notes sourly that 'Movement people steal from each other more than from Harrods. Arts Laboratories can be stoned, unproductive vegetable patches, and manifestos in Underground newspapers can make Goebbels seem like E.M. Forster.' And he suggests a test: 'Cut your hair. The resultant hippie ostracism is a flashback to the days when it was the other way round.'[26] That summer's *Oz* trial required him to revert to the role of countercultural spokesperson, but his defence progressed from an initially ludic posture to a plea for tolerance that rested upon familiar liberal arguments: 'There is greater freedom now than ever before in entertainment and the arts, but none of it is compulsory. If you don't want to see *Oh! Calcutta!*, there is a Noel Coward revival just around the corner.'[27]

By this point, it was clear that radical politics had strayed far from Neville's liberal ideals. Tolerance was a rare commodity in the climate of violence and polarisation engendered by sectarianism in Northern Ireland and the 'urban guerrilla' bombings of the Angry Brigade.[28] Trade union militancy directed against the Heath government reoriented the Left towards a dreary materialism at odds with Neville's ludic agenda. The increasingly autonomous stance taken by the Women's Liberation Movement was in Neville's view instrumental in the 'general fragmentation' of the counterculture, so shattering the 'tremendous feeling of solidarity and harmony' he had earlier experienced.[29] And, as its original advocacy of social liberal values became increasingly obscured by militant posturing and rigid and divisive revolutionary doctrine, the Underground was becoming less and less credible as a coherent alternative community.

Neville's clarification of his philosophy consequently led him to break from the counterculture, a break which was itself an affirmation of the autonomy and empiricism that represented the guiding values of Neville's subsequent career. He publicly cut all ties in the valedictory editorial of *Oz* in January 1973, declaring that 'To be explicit, consistent and truthful has rendered it impossible for me to sign on the dotted line of any particular brand of *ism*.'[30] He did not wish to disown the Underground so much as to free his assessment of its pros and cons from the constraints imposed by any public allegiance. As revealed by his two 1990s publications, *Hippie Hippie Shake* (1995) and *Out of My Mind* (1996), Neville has continued to indulge in this internal debate ever since.

Conclusion

Richard Neville played a valuable role as a sceptical enthusiast for Underground culture, being justified in both his enthusiasm and his scepticism. His unique position as both Underground spokesperson and 'Overground' commentator upon the Underground enabled him to experience the counterculture's virtues while retaining sufficient detachment to recognise its follies. From 1970, as Neville's scepticism about the Underground increased, his honest questioning helped to expose the limits of the counterculture's social liberalism. Yet his later reflections recognise the worth of an important social movement, one that is still dismissed far too casually by both right and left.

Neville admitted in 1988 that 'time has overtaken some of the *Play Power* ideas', and so it had.[31] It conspicuously ignored some fundamental facts of life when it presented the Underground as a blueprint for a future society. Society as a whole needs to work in order to survive. Basic material needs cannot be obviated by LSD, by anything narrowly cultural, by any mass change of attitude. Neville's conflation of the work ethic with the need for work is a classic instance of the Underground's philosophical idealism and its focus on culture to the exclusion of the underlying economic system. This exclusion, socialists commonly argue, is also an essential weakness of social liberalism.

Yet his ethos of 'questioning and dancing on the table' did not actually necessitate revolution.[32] The ludic, hedonistic experientialism of the

Underground translated as easily into liberalism as into insurrectionism. Western capitalist society underwent the liberalising process of incorporating many of *Play Power*'s areas of concern within its cultural pluralism. 'Behavioural options have multiplied', Neville commented in 1976: 'The sixties let us take risks: to start a paper, to hit the road, to fight for a cause, to pick up a guitar, to play at politics, to go communal or merely to enjoy an extended vacation.'[33]

As such, the Underground is best justified from the perspective of a liberal pluralism rather than a revolutionary one. It reinvigorated liberalism as a progressive influence by confronting a society that was much more censorious than it liked to believe. The debate at the *Oz* trial was not between straight and freak sensibilities, but between conservatives who sought to restrict social and cultural pluralism and liberals in favour of extending it. Neville's defence counsel John Mortimer eloquently advanced the liberal position:

> We have heard a lot during this case about an alternative society. The truth of the matter is, however, that our society, our country, contains many alternative societies. All of them may have different ideas about bringing up their children; all of them may have different ideas about sexual morality. But the important thing is that we should live with each other and that we should be tolerant of the alternative ideas which we debate. We should be free, and one sort of person should not seek to stifle another. 'Doing your own thing' is a phrase that [prosecuting counsel] Mr Leary criticised and used as if it were something that only applied to the Underground. But all of us, Members of the Jury, in one way or another, do our own thing.[34]

The successful appeal of the *Oz* defendants played its part in broadening the limits of tolerance in the 1970s. The balance eventually swung decisively in the liberal direction and the affair became the subject of nostalgia rather than controversy. There was no protest when the BBC dramatised the trial in 1991, thereby exposing the original 'obscenities' to a nationwide television audience. The trial still made good theatre, but it had lost its revolutionary potential and was far from the cutting edge of outrage.

Arthur Marwick has rightly asserted that 'the various countercultural movements and subcultures, being ineluctably implicated in and interrelated with mainstream society while all the time expanding and interacting with each other, did not confront that society but *permeated* and *transformed* it.'[35] While Marwick suggests that credit for 1960s liberalisation should go to 'the existence in authority of men and women of traditional enlightened and rational outlook who responded flexibly and tolerantly to countercultural demands', it is also due to the Underground for forcing such demands onto their agenda and for repainting liberalism in bold new colours.[36] In 1959, the greatest parliamentary champion of permissiveness, Roy Jenkins, had called for an end to 'puritanical restriction, to petty-minded disapproval, to hypocrisy and to a dreary, ugly pattern of life.' The following decade, his vision of 'gaiety, tolerance, and beauty' formed the *raison d'être* of the Underground.[37] 'I just thought that people on the whole looked unhappy', Neville recalled: 'they seemed to be pinched and grey and silly and caught up with trivia and I felt that what was going on in London in the 60s would bring colour into those cheeks and those grey bedrooms. With a bit of sexuality and exciting music and flowers, if not in their hair at least in their living-rooms, somehow the direction of society could be altered.'[38]

By the end of the 1970s British society had become less formal, less inhibited and less disapproving than it had been in the early 1960s.[39] Since then many people have tasted the pleasures of the play that Richard Neville enjoyed, without perceiving such play as revolutionary, or even countercultural. One can choose to discount such changes as co-option and repressive tolerance, or one can choose to be glad that many aspects of our capitalist society have become more genuinely liberal.

9. *The Revolutionary Left and the Permissive Society*

Willie Thompson and Marcus Collins

It is no exaggeration to say that the twentieth century was dominated by the theme of revolution, and specifically political revolutions that were inspired by the Bolshevik Revolution of 1917. The effective silencing of this theme near the end of that century is truly one of the most startling developments of modern history. Though none of the twentieth-century revolutions occurred in the economically developed western states, the possibility arose on several occasions: in several states in the aftermath of the two world wars; in France and Spain in 1936; and for the last time in 1968–9, save for one final echo in Portugal in the mid-1970s.

Nevertheless a revolution of sorts *did* take place—a revolution in cultural norms in the 1960s and early 1970s associated with, though not directly provoked by, post-war consumer affluence.[1] The British version of this development was dubbed the 'permissive society' (the term appears to have become established around 1967, though it or similar phraseology had cropped up occasionally in earlier years)[2] involving a range of cultural shifts and legislative enactments focused mainly on matters of personal behaviour (though the removal of the gallows was rather more than that). In a sense it is still with us, as the cultural changes of the 1960s proved irreversible even in the much harsher political and economic climate of later decades.[3]

Our concern in this chapter is to examine the intersection of these two revolutionary movements—the political and the cultural—through the lens of British communist organisations. The groupings that we shall study are the Communist Party of Great Britain (CPGB);[4] the various antagonistic strands of the Trotskyist tradition; and the equally quarrelsome Maoists, who were new claimants to the Leninist heritage. All these organisations enjoyed a sudden efflorescence in tandem with the emergence of the permissive society.[5] The question is whether the revolutionaries drew sustenance from the permissive society and vice versa, or whether the two developments were related only in time.

This chapter investigates what the British revolutionaries made of their opportunities—their occasional successes and much more frequent failures—and considers why the cultural revolution in Britain never produced a political impact comparable to that in Continental Europe and the United States. Why, indeed, if the British revolutionary left was so sclerotic, did no other revolutionary movement arise to bypass it politically; and why did no part of it break with Leninist traditions and, in the words of the Black Panther, Bobby Seale, 'seize the time'? Was this on account of the character of the British polity or shortcomings in the revolutionary left itself—what Marxists liked to term the 'objective' and 'subjective' factors? The aim here is to explore the question, without expecting to produce any definitive answers.

The Revolutionary Groups

The revolutionary left in the UK, with around 50,000 members in its varied factions in the mid-1960s, was among the smallest and most fragmented in Europe.[6] Its internecine disputes need occasion no surprise if parallels are drawn to rival versions of particular religious faiths. Marxist organisations were *ipso facto* committed to theoretical interpretations of economic, social and political reality. Doctrinal differences soon became political ones which, if irresolvable through dialogue (as tended to be the case), resulted in splits and the formation of new organisations amid accusations of betrayal. However, in basic outlook and cultural style if not in particular political interpretations, the disputatious Leninists had more in common with each other than they shared with any other kind of organisation thanks to traditions dating back to the formation of the Bolshevik party and the early years of the Soviet state.

The Communist Party, though less closely supervised by Moscow than it had been before 1956, consoled itself for its political marginality with the successes of the Soviet state, whose potential still seemed far from exhausted.[7] Many members who appreciated the USSR's shortcomings nonetheless expected its political system to return to the original path laid down by the Russian Revolution.[8] The party was also expanding its influence in the trade union movement, much to the alarm of Harold Wilson. The Trotskyites (apart from the International Socialists or IS) likewise took comfort from the USSR's apparent economic success, however much they loathed its political system.[9] The Maoists ritually acknowledged the centrality of the workers' struggle, but concerned themselves principally with idolising the Great Helmsman and excoriating all other leftist groupings. All parts of the revolutionary left applauded national liberation movements in the Third World, though they interpreted their significance differently.

These organisations shared the theoretical premise best described as a 'labour metaphysic': the notion that the international working class was the bearer of a historical destiny to overthrow capitalism and replace it with a system of socialised production. Each regarded itself (however preposterous that might seem to outsiders) as the bearer of the most advanced working-class theoretical consciousness. And, in accordance with the Leninist tradition, each lionised the 'professional revolutionary': the theoretically informed and disciplined militant-activist who ate, drank and lived his or her commitment to the organisation's goals and whose time was devoted to attending meetings, peddling literature and participating in strikes and demonstrations in anticipation of the revolution to come. In retrospect, it might seem incredible that such ideas and organisations could ever be taken seriously in a country which had never possessed a mass communist party, but that would be to misjudge the political and cultural temper of the 1960s, especially following the French events of May 1968. For the revolutionaries, no less than for the counter-culture, the 1960s were years of hope.

Emerging Opportunities

It would be a severe failure in historical imagination to expect that revolutionary socialists instantly comprehended the meaning of the emergent cultural revolution. Their attention was directed elsewhere—above all, to the industrial workforce—so that, for the most part, the permissive society caught them unawares. While generally welcoming legislative and judicial liberalisation, they considered it a secondary issue that risked distracting them from the real business of revolutionaries. Yet permissiveness became an unavoidable issue in revolutionary left organisations thanks the successive waves of young people swelling their ranks in the 1960s.

The first batch came from a movement dominated by the young, the Campaign for Nuclear Disarmament (CND). The central motivation of CND supporters was their abhorrence of nuclear annihilation, but a great many other considerations played into their activism. The annual Aldermaston march[10] was a culturefest which brought together large numbers of young people eager to exchange ideas and to break with the political conventions of their elders. Aldermaston lacked many characteristics of later permissive movements. Its music was not rock but folk or hymn-like inspirational songs, drugs were conspicuous by their absence[11] and its critics were wrong to regard the march as a sort of walking brothel. Nevertheless, the combination of a burgeoning affluent society and the imminent threat of nuclear catastrophe was virtually designed to produce a *carpe diem* attitude among the young.

CND proved a marvellous recruiting ground and for a time transformed the fortunes of the Communist Party,[12] the Trotskyist Socialist Labour League (SLL),[13] and, to a lesser extent, the International Socialists. The hard-bitten traditionalists running these organisations were pleased enough with recruits of any sort, though their preference was not for the middle-class young people who formed a majority of the intake. Still, with the right approach these could be moulded and turned into activists. Closely aligned with CND was the New Left, whose principal spokespeople were originally E. P. Thompson and Stuart Hall. Starting out in the 1950s as a movement appealing to left-wing youth, its broad support fell away in the 1960s along with that of CND, leaving only its journal, the *New Left Review*, as an organ of Marxist theory.[14]

The large number of these young radicals who entered the Communist Party and its youth wing, the Young Communist League, diluted the cultural and stylistic rigidities of the organisation from the early 1960s onwards.[15] The first indication of the YCL's determination to engage with the emergent youth culture came in December 1963, when the Beatles appeared on the cover of its monthly paper *Challenge*. The paper sold marvellously on that occasion, and the same tactic was repeated (less successfully) a few months later with the Swinging Blue Jeans.[16] The YCL had ulterior motives in celebrating British bands, since their success appealed to the party's long-standing anti-Americanism. Many traditionalists nonetheless objected to this concession to commercialism, and absolutely loathed a 1967 recruiting leaflet entitled 'The Trend is Communism' that featured a mini-skirted young woman superimposed on concentric circles of garish purple and yellow. The leaflet proved to be very successful in winning recruits, but produced an irreconcilable division between those who wished to embrace the emergent youth scene and those who longed for the reassertion of Bolshevik certitudes.[17]

As the argument developed, the CP felt it necessary to address the issue theoretically, so that in March 1966 the YCL Secretary, Barney Davis, wrote an article in *Marxism Today* under the title 'British Youth—Progressive, Reactionary or Indifferent?' It focused almost exclusively upon class analysis and material circumstances. Though pop music did get a mention, attention was confined to protest music, while 'the drugs given to create artificial happiness [which] are taken by many young people' were interpreted as a simple reaction to anomie.[18] The writer worried that an opportunity was being missed: 'the harvest is there to be reaped [revealing phrase!]. Unfortunately at the moment many of the harvesters are in the wrong field and using the wrong tools.'[19]

The lesser groupings of the revolutionary left confronted similar opportunities and their responses illustrated the variety of positions available within the overall Leninist framework. Next in numbers to the CP were the Trotskyists of Gerry Healy's Socialist Labour League. Its youth organisation, the Young Socialists, attracted sufficient numbers of young people to make the organisation bigger than the SLL proper,[20] though they seldom stayed very long. Many did not even realise what they were joining, since the Young Socialists commonly held dances or rock concerts of a not identifiably political nature and counted in their recruitment figures everybody who attended.[21]

The SLL adopted a wholly instrumental attitude to the permissive society. Its focus was unwaveringly political in anticipation of the revolution (or fascist counter-revolution) just around the corner. 'Building the revolutionary leadership' was nearly its sole preoccupation and, if youth culture could contribute to that, all well and good. But a different lifestyle was expected of new recruits and those who took the apocalyptic rhetoric seriously soon became engaged in a frenetic round of meetings, demonstrations and paper sales. There was little difference between the Young Socialists' paper, *Keep Left*, and its senior counterpart, *The Newsletter*, even if it did on one occasion take a leaf out of *Challenge*'s book and include a photo of The Pretty Things on its front page.[22] Though *Keep Left* aimed to 'bring into active politics thousands of young people who had no previous contact with political parties,'[23] any casual young reader would have found much of it irrelevant if not incomprehensible. The same issue carried an article on pop groups headlined 'Unwitting Advocates of Idealism' (meaning philosophical idealism), which commented that

> The past year has witnessed a stream of discs expressing the frustrations felt by young people in a decaying society which offers them nothing...'My Generation' blames the older generation for the way youth is treated. But in fact it is capitalism which is responsible for problems of jobs, pay and facilities for youth ...

'The effect of all these songs', it claimed, was to 'divert the attention of youth away from a real struggle to overcome their problems.' Another issue devoted most of its space to a heavily footnoted polemic attacking an analysis of Trotsky published in a YCL journal—hardly an appropriate item in what was supposed to be a popular youth newspaper. For all its members' exertions, the SLL isolated itself through its rigidly traditionalist and monomaniacal postures and failed to win over a significant number of the young, though its hyper-activism made it for a time more numerically successful than its Trotsykist or neo-Trotskyist rivals.

The Maoists were a new element of the British revolutionary left in the late 1960s. Organisationally they were extremely fragmented and united only in their reverence for the Great Helmsman. They accordingly agreed on little about the permissive society save for their shared dislike of its libertarian manifestations. Even so, some did try to analyse the situation of British youth and to formulate an appropriate response. For example, the Maoist journal *The Marxist* ran a lengthy article in 1967 under the title 'Generation in Revolt?'[24] As might be expected, it focused almost entirely on analysing the class position of young people in Britain and estimating how this might be exploited to revolutionary ends, but did not altogether neglect questions of changing cultural norms:

> The cultural milieu inevitably reflects the rottenness at the heart of the system…The question is how to develop this [discontent] in a conscious revolutionary direction…the real task of changing society, of making revolution.

Revolutionary Politics and the Counterculture

The late 1960s and early 1970s spawned a second wave of youth activism of interest to the revolutionary left. It is important to keep in mind that the 'permissive society' did not mean only sex, lifestyle and the media ('the bed, the printed page and public entertainment', as the Marxist historian Eric Hobsbawm put it),[25] but also the collapse of deference to traditional adult authority and the defiance of controls over young people. Such issues allowed some elements of the revolutionary left to lead the mass movements they had always dreamed of, albeit neither on the scale seen in America and Continental Europe nor necessarily in the name of communism. Students formed the principal area of recruitment for the CP in this period, as for many other revolutionary left organisations. And, thanks to the party's organisational traditions, it exercised a decisive influence on election of Jack Straw and Charles Clarke to the presidency of the National Union of Students though the Broad Left network and eventually secured the election of a CP member, Digby Jacks, to the same position.[26]

The much smaller Trotskyist organisation, the International Marxist Group (IMG), capitalised most effectively on the student-led protests against the Vietnam War. During 1967 and 1968, its Vietnam Solidarity Campaign succeeded in mobilising ever-larger demonstrations, culminating in a monster rally in October 1968. Virtually all elements opposing the war felt able to participate in the VSC with the signal exception of the SLL, which forbade its members from taking orders from 'middle-class playboys' like Tariq Ali.[27] Its leader Gerry Healy could not bear to be upstaged by any Trotskyist competitor:

> VSC and its hangers-on are enemies of Marxist principles. Their 'October' campaign will be directed…towards confusing and misleading those who are seeking a road to revolutionary principles and a revolutionary leadership.[28]

The SLL thereby discredited and marginalised itself in the anti-war milieu, for no-one outside its own ranks took the justification seriously. The envy underlying its abstentionism was only too well understood.

IMG activists joined forces with the *New Left Review* in establishing the Revolutionary Socialist Students' Federation (RSSF) in June 1968, at the height of the anti-war campaign and student occupations. The RSSF aimed to implant 'revolutionary consciousness' into the spontaneity of student activism and won grudging support from the Maoists and the CP, which feared being outflanked. They needn't have worried, however, as the RSSF soon fragmented amid mutual recrimination. No more successful in the long term was the VSC's paper, the *Black Dwarf* which, though ostensibly ecumenical in its radicalism, soon mutated into the *Red Mole* and thereafter into openly Trotskyist successors. The IMG also won over the leading members of the *New Left Review* editorial board to a quasi-Trotskyist position after the *NLR*'s brief flirtation with Maoism at the height of the Chinese Cultural Revolution.[29]

The counterculture represented yet another permissive movement interacting with the revolutionary left. In some sense, it was a rival insofar as it offered an alternative Utopian vision to much the same target audience and using similar propagandistic techniques, most notably in its sanctification of Che Guevara. However, there was very little mention of the counterculture in the revolutionary left press of the late 1960s and what there was tended to be dismissive.[30] It was easy enough for communists to draw on their historical discourse and see in it no more than a derivative and frothy version of their old competitors, the anarchists. 'Shocking the bourgeois, is, alas, easier than overthrowing him', commented the CP member Eric Hobsbawm.[31]

Whatever their differences, revolutionary socialists all regarded themselves as Marxists, and Marx was very much a child of the Enlightenment. Rationalism—however crudely understood, and whatever bizarre conclusions might be reached—was therefore at the core of their identities. Consequently the counterculture, which appeared to disdain rationality, had to be ideological anathema.[32] Furthermore, while all Leninists despised 'bourgeois morality' as a matter of principle, they generally frowned on the hedonism associated with the Underground. Dedication, wholesome amusements and no more than minimal individuality, sartorial or otherwise, were the appropriate features of an idealised working class. The CP leadership sometimes attacked other groupings for their supposed moral laxity as well as their political shortcomings, although Trotskyist and Maoist leaders were for the most part every bit as puritanical.

It was therefore unsurprising that the *International Times* reported 'militant Marxist publications' to be 'quite virulently opposed to "freaks"'.[33] Yet, while that counterculture cannot be said ever to have been embraced by the Leninists, there was occasionally what might called a slantwise approach to it. Towards the end of the 1960s, the increasingly adventurous Young Communist League transformed *Challenge* into an Underground-style magazine modelled on *IT* and *Oz*, complete with sexually suggestive captions and photos of minimally clothed women. It was an approach that scandalised many in the YCL and the CP,[34] not to mention Trotskyists and Maoists. Although traditionalism temporarily reasserted itself in the YCL, this attempt to establish a link between revolutionary politics and the more far-reaching implications of the permissive society was a pointer to the liberalising trend within the CP over the following two decades.

A less antagonistic relationship to the counterculture also appears in writings by younger members of revolutionary left organisations in the late 1960s and early 1970s. The radical doctor David Widgery, who admitted to having never been 'a terribly orthodox International Socialist',[35] made a thoughtful, if largely individualised, effort to engage with the Underground. He adopted its styles, wrote extensively about it in various journals, participated in a prank with Richard Neville and even briefly edited *Oz* during its editors' imprisonment. Sheila Rowbotham's autobiography provides additional insights into the crossover between

London hippiedom and the revolutionary left. She was part of both cultures, whether taking advantage of the sexual revolution, trying to politicise working-class apprentices or involving herself in all manner of revolutionary left organisations. She joined the IS at the same time as having a Communist Party lover, while her main political endeavour was a collective dominated by IMG members and closely connected to the *New Left Review*. She was simultaneously struggling towards an articulated feminist outlook:

> Not only had I turned into a divided self, I was leading a double life during the hippie revolution...Part of me did not want to abandon reason...On the other hand the pull to float off once more into the irrational, where things just 'happened', was becoming irresistible.[36]

Identity Politics

Rowbotham's involvement in second-wave feminism, and Widgery's in the gay liberation movement, testified to the arrival of identity politics in Britain and, with it, a series of further dilemmas for the revolutionary left. To begin with feminism, all good socialists were formally committed to sexual equality (as it was then termed) and were perfectly satisfied with that. The CP had women's organisers and women's committees, but there was nothing necessarily feminist about those. Though the IS was later to claim that the women's movement in Britain originated with the Ford women machinists' strike in 1968 for equal pay and treatment,[37] a cynic might conclude that that was an *ex post facto* assessment governed by the organisation's labour metaphysic. The strike was reported in *Socialist Worker*, but not in any sense in feminist terms.[38] And, while *Black Dwarf* had proclaimed 1969 to be 'The Year of the Militant Woman', its commitment was in reality only gestural.

At the same time, the revolutionary left organisations found themselves having to deal with second-wave feminism. The Communist Party was prompt to applaud the growth of an autonomous women's movement and employed the concept of gender in theoretical discussions of feminism that began in earnest in 1972.[39] It also made significant efforts to appoint women to responsible positions in the organisation and, although this varied locally, to adapt its style of operation to take account of some of the criticisms made by feminists. Enlightenment had its limits, however, as when the CP repudiated *Red Rag*, a feminist journal established by some of its members which focused on sexual politics, advocated a 'feminist incomes policy' and printed comments such as 'I believe that the CP often blunts and diffuses the class struggle in Britain [and] is dominated by reformism.'[40] An 'apparent refusal to take what we were saying seriously' resulted in the majority of female editors resigning after only three issues from another periodical established mainly by Gramscian-influenced CP members.[41]

As for the Trotskyists, the IS and its successor, the Socialist Workers' Party (SWP), were too obsessed with the industrial struggle to embrace identity politics wholeheartedly. One woman member declared the women's liberation movement to be no 'fighting organisation' on the grounds that 'it puts the question of consciousness first, not the taking of power by the working class'.[42] The IMG mocked this attitude in an article entitled 'Tony Cliff's Nightmare—Feminism', commenting that the SWP leader was too 'fixated with the factory and the trade unions' to be able to 'appreciate the significance of the political campaigns waged by women against the state'.[43] Yet the IMG, even though it made elaborate arrangements for women's caucuses, did not use the concept of gender and ultimately identified women's oppression as an expression of class relations. A 1968 article entitled 'Don't Call US Birds!' that appeared in the IMG organ *International* accordingly denounced aspects of what would later be termed sexism while insisting that 'the one place that women are united with a common goal [is]...[on] *the factory floor*...always remembering *class* solidarity before *sex* solidarity'.

Gay liberation was if anything still harder for the revolutionary left to swallow. The Leninist left had long been hostile to homosexuality, in spite of attracting high-profile homosexual intellectuals. It was often identified with the public schools and the Nazi SA, or seen as being at best an unfortunate disability that would be rectified by the revolution. Like Sheila Rowbotham, Ann Tobin felt a close connection between sexual rebellion and revolutionary politics, but was disillusioned by her SLL comrades' lack of interest in, or understanding of, her developing lesbian identity in the early 1960s.[44]

Even so, no organisation dared to be confessedly homophobic by the 1970s. All acknowledged the right to a gay identity, though their actions told a different story. 'We were not allowed to set up our own group in IS nor were we allowed to belong to the major radical gay organisation in the country', recalled Bob Cant, because the IS was 'increasingly preoccupied with economic issues' and its leadership had 'not found the issue to cause any concern among the working-class members'.[45] Fellow IS member David Widgery could not interest the party newspaper in his review of Don Milligan's *The Politics of Homosexuality* (1973), leading him to comment that 'Sexual politics are taboo, obviously since machine-Leninism can't face the intimacy of their critique of hierarchy.'[46] The Communist Party appears to have been the only organisation to embrace gay politics as part of its Gramscian strategy of courting new social forces in the 1970s and 1980s.[47] The problem was that insufficient gay members could be found to constitute viable groups. There were only two interested individuals in 1980s' Scotland, though they nevertheless set up their own group and issued a periodical.

Culture and Revolution

The 1960s and 1970s witnessed a remarkable upsurge in the size and impact of the British revolutionary left. Its culture emerged into the public domain in an unprecedented fashion at the same time as what came to be termed the 'permissive society' was in the process of establishing itself. Permissiveness and its fallout surprised revolutionaries as much as anyone. They were in no way responsible for it, and much of what was involved contradicted their most cherished traditions. They responded by weighing its pros and cons in no very systematic manner and some, despite their own authoritarian disposition, were able to profit from the anti-authoritarian temper of the times.

Yet the permissive society's legacy to the revolutionary left was a relatively meagre one, all the more disappointing due to its initial promise. The answer to Barney Davis's question about youth—'Progressive, Reactionary or Indifferent?'—proved in the main to be 'Indifferent'. Tens of thousands had marched with CND and tens of thousands more participated in student protests and anti-Vietnam War rallies, but youthful rebellion proved too fragile a base on which to construct any revolutionary movement. Some on the revolutionary left –Sheila Rowbotham is a good example—found the permissive society attractive and answering to their needs, but traffic in the other direction was very limited. Attending a carnivalesque demonstration or occupying the vice-chancellor's office was one thing; attending endless committee meetings and trying to sell papers on cold streets to indifferent passers-by was quite another. A further obstacle was that so many of the cultural artefacts of the 1960s' generation originated in the United States. The revolutionary left, while applauding the black and student insurrectionaries across the Atlantic, almost unanimously detested American culture.

The failure of the revolutionary left to recruit larger numbers into their organisations owed much to the incompatibility between their internal culture and the character of the permissive society, not to mention the fact that political revolution was in any case impossible in mainland Britain.[48] The British scene, if not exactly demure, remained throughout much less confrontational and ferocious than that of Continental Europe or the USA, and this in a country which had done so much to give a lead to the ideology of 1960s' permissiveness. It is problematic to identify any principal reason why this should have been the case, but a number of considerations suggest themselves. Social and political relations were more tense elsewhere. The violent eruption of African-American discontent in the late 1960s had no British parallel[49] and the same went for the Vietnam draft, with all its implications for student protests. Across the Channel, memories of the Third Reich, Occupation and Resistance remained very recent ones, and Paris was, historically, the revolutionary city *par excellence.*

On the other side of the equation, the very success of permissiveness in Britain may have acted as a brake on revolution, even though it may not have looked that way at the time. Antagonism to the Wilson government was intense, yet the stream of liberalising legislation issuing from Westminster, the hype surrounding permissive icons and the usually accommodating attitude of college administrations to student protests may have done more to defuse than to fuel the rebellion desired by the revolutionary left. Matters would have been very different had Britain sent troops to Vietnam or deployed CRS-type police units against students, though how public opinion might have reacted is impossible to say.

For those who were involved, there nonetheless remains the feeling that a great opportunity may have been missed.[50] When new cultural phenomena erupted onto the scene, revolutionaries had to decide whether these were further expressions of capitalist decadence or what Martin Jacques termed 'a sign of developing but still immature rebellion'. Their publications of the period refer anxiously to the issue and, though some readers were never convinced, the balance tended to lean towards the latter interpretation.[51] What that meant, even among the most sympathetic of Leninists, was that the new ideas and practices were not to be taken on their own terms, but were to be exploited as a means of winning recruits to revolutionary organisations. Such an attitude prevailed across the whole spectrum of the revolutionary left, from the SLL's attitude to mods and rockers through the IMG's perception of student revolutionaries to the YCL's favourable reception of punk culture.[52]

The persistence of this orientation is in some senses a tribute to the ideological commitment of the Leninists and their sense of historic confidence that an enormous reservoir of support waited to be tapped if only they could get their message across. *Challenge* in the 1960s was fond of insisting that the best 'high' a person could get was not through drugs but communist political activity.[53] Certainly it was a very conceited outlook, but the Leninist culture was nothing if not conceited in this respect. There are of course more substantial reasons why the revolutionary left in over a century has failed to make any significant impact in the UK, yet such arrogance helps to explain why it made such a modest impact during this period. As traditional patterns of deference and subordination collapsed from the 1960s onwards, its various groups and factions were presented with unprecedented opportunities which they contrived to squander through a steadfast devotion to their own esoteric agendas.

10. *The International Context*

Arthur Marwick

Marcus Collins has provided us with a useful overview of the elements which go to make up the 'permissive society' and Britain's vanguard role in their development. In this chapter I shall argue that to understand the advent of permissiveness in Britain, and the quite complex relationships between what was happening there and elsewhere in the West, one has to grasp the international or transnational nature of what I have termed the Cultural Revolution of the Long Sixties (*c*.1957 to *c*.1974).[1] The origins of this 'revolution' lay in a unique convergence of a high proportion of young people in the various populations (a product of the wartime and post-war baby boom), their relative affluence, the release of the aspirations engendered by the war after the delays of reconstruction and austerity, the waning of the Cold War, and the arrival of causes worthy of noble protest (nuclear weapons, Algeria, Vietnam and the apparent persistence of Nazism in West Germany).

Whereas the post-war welfare state was something granted to peoples by governments, permissiveness was something created from within society. Its defining characteristics—reformed interpersonal relations, openness and honesty, emancipation from traditional prudishness and furtiveness in sexual matters and the freedom from, and rejection of, old authorities, conventions and taboos—did not affect simply a minority of pop stars, 'beautiful people', and their fellow travellers. They transformed the lives of majorities across all the Western countries, as permissive behaviour was publicised, legitimated and emulated, and moral and physical sanctions against it (fear of God, fear of pregnancy, fear of social ostracism) faded.

Since permissiveness was first and foremost a social phenomenon, the sources on which my study is based are not those of conventional political history. In addition to materials relating to various bodies associated with permissive causes, I have made extensive use of the letters, memoirs, and diaries in which people express their deeper feelings: some printed in newspapers or pamphlets, but most in archives yet to be thoroughly explored by other researchers. While oral interviews are important, I have not carried them out myself and would caution against preferring them to written archival materials. For example, there are some fantastically rich collections relating to the 1969 student protests at Cornell University in upstate New York, yet the 1999 book *Cornell '69* is very largely based on recently conducted oral interviews.[2] Letters and diaries written during the 1960s are almost always of far greater value than memories recorded thirty or forty years later.

Britain in Context

In 1991, I was conducting the American portion of my research for a comparative history of the 1960s in Western Europe and the United States. I happened to mention what I was doing in a casual conversation and got this response: 'Say, I never knew you guys had a sixties over there.' Perhaps the speaker was thinking of America in the 1960s as a time of extreme turmoil and violence, of civil war, of the 'unravelling' of American society.[3] Yet there was open violence, accompanied by fatalities, in France, West Germany and Italy, the violence continuing in the latter two countries in the form of brutal terrorism.[4] And, though there was less 'action' of this kind in Britain, perhaps there was more quiet 'permeation'. Foreigners commented extensively on what was happening in Britain, astonished that the country famous for Victorian stolidity and prudishness should in so many ways be taking the lead in breaking old taboos, establishing new sexual freedoms, and in fostering what Collins describes as an astonishing 'cultural efflorescence'. Compared with, above all, France and Italy, which both had vibrant indigenous popular cultures of their own—the most striking piece of evidence being the international success of the Italian song 'Volare'—Britain throughout the 1950s had a popular culture which was heavily dependent on, and derivative of,

American products. It was partly because British popular culture was such an empty vessel that, with the release of youthful and provincial energies, it could so readily be filled full and overflowing, invading America, and then, against more resistance, France, Italy and the rest of the European continent.[5]

Britain also had a reputation for being prudish and sexually repressed prior to the 1960s. Actually, we have to be careful not to take the mores of certain social groups in metropolitan Western Europe and the American east and west coasts as representative of whole societies. Yet, whereas Britain had looked to Paris for naughty novels and racy films until the late 1950s, its film industry thereafter outdid all others for explicitness.[6] Girls and boys everywhere could identify with the predatory Joe Lampton and the romantic Susan Brown who readily capitulates to him in *Room at the Top* of 1959, and even more so with the working-class Arthur and Doreen in *Saturday Night and Sunday Morning* (1960), who stage an elaborate and noisy charade to persuade Doreen's mother that Arthur has left the house before he creeps back to couple with Doreen on the couch. From student magazines and other sources it is apparent that permissive British films were greatly welcomed by young Americans eagerly jumping into the adult world of full sexual relations. Listen to this fascinating protest of two fifteen-year-old girls in Detroit to the general manager of the art house chain (whose policy was to admit only those over eighteen years) owning the cinema showing the British film *Georgy Girl* (1966):

> Let me assure that at the tender age of 15 we know, and have known for a long time, all about sex...It's an insult to our intellect that we are allowed to see the loud, fake Hollywood movies that are totally unrealistic, and harmful, as they give us a distorted picture of life. Your foreign films are very realistic, truthful and on the whole a great value to us.

On being telephoned, the mother of one of the girls said (in a neat demonstration of the generational cooperation examined later in this chapter) that she was perfectly happy for her daughter to see the film.[7]

It is important not to underestimate the continuing hold of Christian religion as a broad moral system in the Britain of the 1950s.[8] Equally important, however, was what I long ago referred to as 'secular anglicanism', which engendered a general tolerance and respect for individual rights in Britain that contrasted sharply with the bigotry and intolerance of Protestant denominations in the American Bible Belt and of Calvinism and the Catholic church in Continental Europe.[9] The greater informality of British religious practice meant that the long-term decline in religious observance was more evident here than in the other countries. Callum G. Brown has recently contested this view, arguing instead that the 'death' of Christian belief in Britain was a sudden affair intimately associated with the spread of permissiveness during the 'long sixties'.[10] Personally, I am not sure that he is totally convincing here, since the striking advent of permissiveness in Italy was not linked to a similar 'death' in religious belief.

What is strongly apparent in Britain is the way in which secular anglicanism developed into what I call 'measured judgement', a willingness on the part of legislators, the judiciary, and such influential people as film censor John Trevelyan and BBC head Hugh Carleton Greene, to accommodate and tolerate the changes in, and demands of, the wider society. Reactionary forces in politics, churches, universities, the police were much stronger in other countries, though this is not to say that measured judgement was a uniquely British phenomenon. In the case of West Germany, I am thinking of the politicians who amended the Emergency Laws so as to make them subject to Bundestag control, of the judges who insisted that the SDS files seized by the police in January 1967 must be returned, of justice minister Gustav Heinemann who, on Easter Sunday 1968, advocated a policy of tolerance towards protestors.[11] With respect to America, there is a wonderful piece of unwitting testimony in the autobiography of Tom Hayden, a leading figure in the radical socialist group SDS. Hayden wittingly makes the case that he and his fellow-protesters were basically right; unwittingly he brings out the existence of measured judgment deep within the 1960s American system (in contrast with the perversions of McCarthyism):

> It was remarkable that during the several years of political trials on conspiracy charges, the federal government failed to win against any of the sixty-five conspiracy defendants. Such defendants as the

> Harrisburg Seven, the Camden Seventeen, and the Gainesville Eight always managed to win, either before juries or appeals courts, a dramatic difference from the McCarthy era, only fifteen years before.[12]

The concept of due process in America, much like the ideals of Christian democracy and social democracy in Continental Europe, were instrumental in forestalling a concerted anti-permissive reaction.

Another important characteristic of Britain at this time was that it still had a more effective governmental system for getting legislation enacted and implemented than any other country except perhaps France under de Gaulle, Pompidou and Giscard d'Estaing. Compared with the immediate post-war period, both America and Italy were remarkably good at enacting, but still woeful at implementing, liberalising measures. In Britain, if we examine the words of the practitioners of measured judgement we find them again and again invoking the changes in attitudes and values in the wider society as their prime motivation.[13] We need not deny a certain primacy to Roy Jenkins—both as the backbench MP responsible for the reform of literary censorship in 1959 and the Home Secretary responsible for the 'civilised society' (or 'permissive') legislation of 1967–69—but it is clear that this legislation (though opposed by conservative elements) was congruent with aspirations being expressed in books and pamphlets and opinion surveys. Other countries had analogues of Jenkins, but Britain was the first to deal with the major issues of divorce, abortion, state-supplied contraceptives and homosexual acts by consenting adults in private (it is particularly worthy of note that these reforms were enacted by *private* members' bills).

Yet permissiveness, though a British coinage, was no British monopoly. Even where there was violent conflict, permissiveness permeated all sections of society. Abortion law reform was enacted in California and Colorado in 1967, and extended to five other states in 1968 and 1969. It was characteristic of a decision-making system different from that in Europe that the real culmination was the Supreme Court ruling in *Roe* v. *Wade*, announced on 22 January 1973, that abortions could be carried out legally.[14] Abortion reform came at the same time in West Germany, to France (in a strictly limited way) in 1975, and to Italy (in an even more tightly limited measure) in 1978. The most impressive sign of change within the depths of Italian society was the referendum held on 12 May 1974 by which Catholics sought to secure the overthrow of the 1968 law permitting divorce. The Catholic church, and almost all politicians, including left-wing ones, were quite sure that the Italian people would reject the very idea of divorce.[15] In fact, 59.1 per cent voted to endorse the divorce reform law and 40.9 per cent voted against: as these things go, an overwhelming victory.

Relations between Generations

In many ways the reforms most worthy of attention, and too often passed over, are the Representation of the People Act and the Family Law Reform Act of 1969, which lowered the age of legal majority and the voting age to eighteen. This brings me to another theme of this chapter: that there was no unique generation gap in the 1960s so that, apart from the rather contrived situations mentioned below, permissiveness was not a general source of conflict between the old and the young. By the end of the long sixties all Western countries had enthusiastically granted adulthood and the vote to young people. In the United States, the Voting Rights Act was passed in 1970, with the corresponding twenty-sixth amendment to the constitution coming the following year. Here is the senate committee report:

> The Committee is convinced that the time has come to extend the vote to eighteen-year-olds in all elections: because they are mature enough in every way to exercise the franchise; they have earned the right to vote by bearing the responsibilities of citizenship; and because our society has much to gain by bringing the force of their idealism and concern and energy into the constructive mechanism of elective government.[16]

West Germany, where measured judgement was strong despite the obvious disenchantment of some young people with the older generation, followed suit in 1972, with France and Italy joining them in 1974. New research that I have conducted on the American student movement in the archives of Cornell, Columbia, Berkeley, Stanford and UCLA casts further doubt on the notion of any clear-cut generational conflict.[17] I shall not repeat the broad coverage of my 1998 book, but shall concentrate on specific points brought out particularly sharply in my recent research. In all the universities I have studied, a majority of the academic staff was sympathetic to, or at least moderately tolerant of, changing student aspirations. Take, for example, the measured tone of a 1965 report submitted to the Cornell Board of Trustees by the young academic who chaired the Faculty Committee on Student Affairs. He began by noting that the Great Depression was 'sheer history' to the new generation of students, but that 'from their earliest years they have both been aware of atomic bombs and concerned about eventually securing college entrance'. He continued:

> (3) They have been exposed to an apparent 'freedom' in literature and the mass media that still seems strange to some of my generation.
> (4) They know more, expect more. The 'college level' teaching of 20 years ago bores them.
> (5) Overtly secure and affluent, they often have severe problems of knowing who they are, what they want, and where they are heading. Sometimes it is not clear whether their 'rebellion' is a demand for a greater freedom or for clearer guidance and a more challenging set of moral and intellectual examples...
> (7) They will not presently accept arbitrary authority.
> (8) Some of them see no sense in some traditional social rules and practices...[18]

University administrations for their part were not uniformly reactionary. Compared, say, to Columbia University, Cornell had a particularly liberal administration. Though somewhat pedantic, the president, James Perkins, was in many ways a model representative of measured judgment, deliberately instituting a scheme to bring black students into this upper-class Ivy League university. In contrast, Berkeley was part of the California state system and had a very conservative administration, hyper-sensitive to local populist sentiment.

Parents of student activists generally supported their children, as can be seen in the first major case of student unrest in 1960s' America.[19] Berkeley's Free Speech Movement (FSM) began as a protest against the university's prohibition against student organisations proselytising, raising funds, or recruiting, and culminated in the massive sit-in of 2 December 1964. Getting on for 800 students were arrested then and in the days that followed. Right away there emerged a theme that was to recur throughout the 1960s: the violence and the dishonesty of the police turned formerly respectful citizens into opponents of both police and university administrations, and strong supporters of their student offspring. One mother expressed her disillusionment upon realising that the Berkeley police had 'told me an out-and-out lie' when they denied that they were holding her daughter. In a letter to one of the lawyers organising a money-raising parents' defence committee for the arrested students, she wrote that 'I swallowed what I was told at each step until I realised I was actually being victimised by the very people I had spent my life teaching my children to trust and respect!'[20]

The letters of parents, neighbours, sympathetic lawyers, academics and the students themselves demonstrate a shared belief that Berkeley students were acting in support of their constitutional rights as American citizens. The Dean of Law wrote to the judge handling the case that:

> My work this past year with the student community, the campus administration and the entire faculty in its various groups has persuaded me that essentially all the FSM participants, even those whose leadership roles gained them considerable notoriety, conducted themselves seriously and honestly. I believe they subjectively acted in good faith, were to a fair degree driven to their subjective positions, and objectively were striving for legitimate ends.[21]

A mother who was herself a 1938 University of California graduate informed the parents' committee that both she and her own mother had twice written on her son's behalf to the judge, the president of the university and to the governor of California. She declared herself glad that her son had participated in the FSM and 'proud' of his and other students' courage, concluding that 'We must work to replace these administrators with people who will set a better example to our children.'[22] And, among the mass of letters which the defence committee encouraged students to write to the judge, was this statement by a female student:

> I participated in the sit-in demonstration in Sproul Hall on December 2 to protest certain university regulations which infringed my constitutional right to freedom of speech. I felt that I was justified in this action as, to the best of my knowledge, all previous attempts by students to negotiate with the administration in regard to this matter were unsuccessful as a result of the administration's indifference to the students' demands. I felt that the University was responding to outside pressures in passing the regulations in question and that students could only protest their rights through exerting a counterpressure in the form of a sit-in. I felt that I acted responsibly in choosing to participate in the sit-in, and, in fact, that I behaved in the *only* responsible way. Before arriving at the conviction that the students' demands were just, I listened to arguments on both sides carefully and read what responsible literature was available. I was well aware of the seriousness of the act of civil disobedience but felt that the nature of my grievance was of such importance that it justified and made obligatory my action....I was there on extremely urgent and legitimate business, to protest the abridgement of my constitutional rights. I refused to cooperate with the police officer who arrested me as I felt obliged to remain in the building until I had accomplished my aims.[23]

Although adults widely recognised, and generally tacitly accepted, that sexual mores were changing among young people, subsequent events at Berkeley tested their tolerance to destruction. Viewing sexuality as a revolutionary weapon, extreme student radicals deliberately violated every sexual taboo in order to incite reactionary elements into the sort of violent responses that, they believed, hasten the destruction of 'bourgeois society'. Accompanying such provocative behaviour was a fair measure of selfish male hedonism, gay and paedophile as well as straight, and a belligerent use of swear words (leading to the creation of Berkeley's 'Filthy Speech Movement').[24] The descent into the shouting of obscenities began in March 1965, sponsored by a ludicrous student publication, *Spider* (Sex, Politics, International communism, Drugs, Extremism, [opposition to] Religion), which advocated 'natural sexuality'. It is worth noting that it was not supported by the FSM steering committee, which declared that

> Only in the recent controversy over 'obscene' words can students be said not to have acted responsibly. The FSM did not initiate or support this controversy. We regret both that the students involved acted in an unfortunate manner and that the police and some administrators chose to escalate the issue and endanger campus peace rather than permit student interest in the subject to wane.[25]

There can be no doubt that gratuitous offensiveness and flagrant demonstrations of promiscuous behaviour antagonised hitherto tolerant adults at Berkeley and beyond.[26] Though many continued to maintain that the young people known to them were behaving responsibly, the forces of reaction in the police, in certain university administrations, in churches and in right-wing and racist movements used what they saw as the excessive sexual libertarianism of young people as an excuse for the violent suppression of all protest movements. White female students from the American North, taking part in the voter registration drives of 1963 in the South, would be constantly disturbed by phone calls from local whites asking 'how many nigger cocks y'all gotta suck 'fore ya can go to sleep at night?'[27] As such, the normalisation and naturalisation of sex, while permeating whole societies and bringing better lives to substantial majorities, nonetheless became a cause of confrontation and violence for certain powerful minorities.

In French universities, controversies over sexual expression centred on male access to female dormitories, and vice versa.[28] Though the issue became very closely associated with the student activism of May 1968 in France, recent brilliant work by Michael Seidman confirms my own contentions that, first, significant changes were already taking place well before 1968, and, second, that they had considerable support from adults.[29] Conflict on the issue broke out in 1964 at Anthony, Paris's original student residential area to the south of the city, where the administration had begun a policy of constructing lodges to control access to dormitories. Seidman notes that women students displayed strong but 'nuanced' opposition to the lodges, accepting their need on security grounds while objecting to 'what they considered to be outdated regulations that restricted their individual freedom.'[30] Beginning on 1 October 1965, there were massive student demonstrations and occupations against the building of the lodges. Police were brought in, and behaved in a violent fashion. Ultimately, three men and two women were expelled indefinitely from all university residences, and another man and woman were excluded for one year. Petitions, protests and letters declared their support of the protestors, who barricaded themselves into their residences, only to be met by more police brutality.

Then came the vital change: the director of the housing complex resigned and was replaced in January 1966 by Jacques Balland, a 36-year-old socialist and professor of history. He soon ended the 'Love War' at Anthony by allowing male and female students to visit each other's dormitories, a practice adopted in November 1967 by the directors of the other university dormitory complexes of the Paris region.[31] Contrary to a certain mythology about the origins of the events of May 1968, a highly permissive regime was instituted at the Nanterre campus to the west of Paris under the liberal and friendly Dean, Pierre Grappin.[32] This was entirely in keeping with the views of parents, who were much less concerned than officials with 'protecting' female students. According to Seidman, ninety per cent of parents gave formal permission for their daughters to receive male visitors as they chose.[33]

Whenever we talk about permissiveness in respect of France or Italy, we have to bear firmly in mind that at the beginning of the 1970s something like half a million backstreet abortions were being carried out in France, and perhaps getting on for twice as many in Italy. The confused, conservative, but changing condition of Italian public morality in the 'long sixties' can be judged from the reactions to two famous films, *La dolce vita* and *L'avventura* (both 1960). *L'avventura* was criticised for containing highly erotic scenes, though no one in it as much as began to take their clothes off. Meanwhile, *La dolce vita* had members of the audience at its Milan première shouting: 'It's contemptible, it's filth, it's lies.' Despite calls being made both by the Catholic church and in parliament for it to be seized and banned, the film broke box office records.

The generational shifts taking place in Italy were seen most starkly in contemporary surveys of girls and young women.[34] The most impressive of these was a study of attitudes to sex and marriage carried out in 1969 in Milan, Rome and Palermo among 528 young married women aged between 23 and 40 *and their mothers.* One has to be careful with some of the contrasts, of course: women in their fifties and sixties may express different attitudes about sex than they might have done when they were in their twenties or thirties. Nonetheless, the survey presents overwhelming evidence of the huge changes which have taken place during the 1960s—some of the younger women would have been married in the 1950s, but it is clear that the emancipation in their sexual attitudes came after rather than before marriage, that is to say well into the 1960s. Sixty-six per cent admitted that the question of sexual attraction was not relevant at the actual time of marriage. A twenty-nine-year-old Rome housewife said that she had not thought at all about sexual attractiveness at the time of her wedding; a thirty-three-year-old Milan housewife said that she had tried not to think about such things 'because I had received an education in which all of that was a sin'. The tragic nature of traditional Italian marriage and the phenomenal liberation achieved in the 1960s is brought out in the answers to the question of what most reinforces a marriage. Whereas satisfactory sexual relations appeared at the top of the daughters' list, being chosen by 22.3 per cent of them, the older women put them at the very bottom of theirs. In second place for daughters were 'communication and talking' (the choice of 20.5 per cent), but their mothers ranked them third from bottom. What the mothers thought most vital to success in a marriage was tolerance and patience on their own part.[35]

Of the 528 young wives, 478 said sex was fundamental to a woman's life; of the 528 mothers only 168 said the same, and 360 denied that sex had the importance attributed to it in the Italy of the late 1960s. Of the mothers, 67 per cent thought that sex was right only within marriage, while only 13.2 per cent of the daughters thought likewise. A forty-year-old Rome housewife, with a job as a white-collar worker, argued that if 'the union between husband and wife is not satisfying, it is human to search elsewhere'. A twenty-six-year-old housewife stated that 'Marriage is a bureaucratic fact, sexual attraction is an instinctive fact and thus perfectly legitimate.' Among the mothers, 70.4 per cent considered premarital sexual experience to be wrong, compared with only 18.5 per cent of the daughters. A thirty-two-year-old Milan housewife put it this way: 'If you arrive prepared there's no shock. Marriage is already very serious: having overcome the problem of sexual relations is a great help.' Of the 528 daughters, 149 had had affairs outside marriage, 48 from Milan, 76 from Rome and 26 in the Sicilian capital. An office worker of 28 declared belligerently that 'By his decision we stopped sexual relations for two years: without reason he had decided to neglect me, but I am young and have the right to a normal life, so I have a lover.'[36]

As the new feminist movement, which took its most radical forms in the United States, began to accelerate in the early 1970s, there were many statements that the much-vaunted sexual liberation had really only been liberation for men to exploit women. The contemporary evidence is that this was certainly not the view of young women in Italy.[37] Evidently the new opportunities and new freedoms were infinitely better than what had gone before.

Home Truths

In conclusion, families, while greatly changed in respect of the power accruing to both wives and young people, appear to have remained close during the 'cultural revolution', albeit less so in West Germany. Let me end by illustrating my argument with a comparison of the unpublished diary of a widowed Italian school teacher, Anna Avallone,[38] and the printed, limited-circulation memoir of Charlotte E. Keyes, the Jewish American wife of a Quaker university professor.[39] Avallone's son, Sergio, was coming to the end of his secondary schooling in 1967. Her diary details her distress over his insistence that teachers were authoritarian, his participation in the student protest movement and his ungracious and ill-mannered friends. The entry of 26 June records that she is very happy with Sergio's girlfriend, Giulia, save that she is also in the student movement, and, 'a new thing', she calls herself a 'feminist'. Avallone starts wondering if 'our way of thinking truly is too retrograde with respect to theirs; we think we can do good, make others happy by imposing our way of being happy; and thus, through too much love, we take from them their joy of living, remove their illusions, block their spontaneous activities, and spoil their dreams'. For the Italian August holiday, mother, son and girlfriend are together in the mountains. There is much talk of the late Pope, John XXIII, revealing that all are united in a kind of fundamental Catholicism.

In October 1967, Sergio goes to Turin University and finds lodgings with friends. Avallone is surprised to find that they are not as humble as she had expected, given all the talk about class equality and contempt for the bourgeoisie. Sergio takes part in an occupation and is arrested as one of the ringleaders, only to be released the next day. He continues to come and visit her on Saturdays and Sundays, but there seems to be nothing to say between them, 'still less when we discuss the inhibitions and disinhibitions of sex'. But this warm and profoundly honest document continues, 'I have to recognise that these kids are good; they will do anything for each other, they defend each other, they help each other.'

On 9 August 1968, she records what she calls 'confused thoughts': 'free love and sex have become the important topics of the day, self-fulfilment psychologically and physically, denial of any regulation and religion'. The first entry for the New Year (7 January 1969) reads in part:

> I am completely estranged from the student discussions, but I have listened attentively to the voices and the problems which are now at the basis of their life, and I have tried to understand; I must confess that I have understood that many of their ideas are concerned with group things which others, even if they should have taken a lead, have not tried to put into practice. Much more than political interventions and useless circulars, they need to be helped and encouraged. That our past and present respectability irritates them is now very clear, and responding to their demonstrations with violence is counter-productive and could produce very regrettable reactions.

But then the entry for 13 January relates that Avallone has received a letter from Sergio which is so painful that she is not able to transcribe it into the diary, though she quotes the gist:

> She is so bourgeois, she is an insurmountable obstacle to their idea of a new life. They are in different worlds: they want permanent revolution, continuous struggle, total absence of sexual inhibitions, suppression of all useless taboos.

Yet, in the same entry, she states that she is beginning to move towards Sergio's ideas. There is a full statement for 31 March: 'I have faith in Sergio and I gratefully appreciated Giulia's feminist ideas, because I began work when, in the family, a women who was not housewifely was thought badly of.' Earlier, she had been slightly scandalised on realising that Sergio and Giulia were sleeping together. However, on 24 August the young couple are married, Giulia wearing a mini skirt. This story of a mother's anger at her son and her reconciliation with, and developing understanding of, him and his girlfriend gives an insight into the deeper developments taking place beneath the surface of sloganising and fighting.

Charlotte E. Keyes's memoir is entitled *The Mother of a Draft-card Burner, a Young Man Already Imprisoned Four Times for His Beliefs, Tells of Her Own Agony—and Her Son's* and was printed by the New England Committee for Non-violent Action. In it, she recounts how, as 'respectable pacifists', she and her husband were stunned by the absolute pacifism of Gene, their son:

> He once told my husband and me, to our exasperation, 'Jail is my destiny', and he has indeed been imprisoned four times…What kind of odd-ball is our son…Is he a nut? Doesn't he think about his parents at all? How must we feel to have such a rebel for a son? Doesn't it humiliate us in our community—a university town, where my husband teaches? To be quite honest, we have run the gamut from shock, disagreement, anger to 'patient' (we always thought) explanation of why he was wrong, on to pride and finally to learning from him and changing our own lives…

Gene's parents thought it 'shocking' and 'preposterous' when he announced his intention to burn his draft card in public, but the memoir ends on a note of acceptance and reconciliation: 'As we have watched him grow and climb his high places, we no longer argue with him, no longer call him foolish. We stand by our son, and we learn from him.'

Not a typical American family, obviously. But the main point made by these two very different documents is one of great general validity and is supported in other collections of documents such as the correspondence between Cornell students and their parents during the unrest of 1969.[40] A critical element in the spread of permissiveness in all of its senses was that rather than being the symbol of the revolt of youth, it more often embodied a kind of collusion between the generations.

Notes and References

1. *Introduction: The Permissive Society and its Enemies*
Marcus Collins

1. Malcolm Bradbury, *The History Man*, London, 1975, p.23.
2. Examination of the models used to study permissiveness and the 1960s can be found in Tim Newburn, *Permission and Regulation: Law and Morals in Post-war Britain*, London, 1992, ch.1; Todd Gitlin, *The Sixties: Years of Hope, Days of Rage* [rev. edn], New York, 1993, p.421; Arthur Marwick, *The Sixties: Cultural Revolution in Britain, France, Italy and the United States, c.1958–74*, Oxford, 1998, pp.3–5; and *idem*, 'Introduction: Locating Key Texts amid the Distinctive Landscape of the Sixties', in Anthony Aldgate, James Chapman and Arthur Marwick (eds), *Windows on the Sixties: Exploring Key Texts of Media and Culture*, London, 2000.
3. Notable popular histories include Bernard Levin, *The Pendulum Years: Britain and the Sixties*, London, 1970; Jonathon Green, *All Dressed Up: The Sixties and the Counterculture*, London, 1999, xi; and Shawn Levy, *Ready, Steady, Go!: The Smashing Rise and Giddy Fall of Swinging London*, New York, 2002. For evocative memoirs, see Marianne Faithfull and David Dalton, *Faithfull*, London, 1994; and Michael Caine, *What's It All About?*, London, 1992.
4. For an example of this line of reasoning, see Digby Anderson, 'Introduction: At the End of Indulgence', in Digby Anderson (ed.), *Full Circle?: Bringing Up Children in the Post-Permissive Society*, London, 1988, p.10.
5. For examples of the apostrophisation of 'permissiveness' and its variants from each of the past three decades, see John Clarke et al., 'Subcultures, Cultures and Class', in Stuart Hall and Tony Jefferson (eds), *Resistance Through Rituals: Youth Subcultures in Post-war Britain*, London, 1975, pp.67, 72; Jeffrey Weeks, *Sex, Politics and Society: The Regulation of Sexuality since 1800*, London, 1981, pp.242, 252; and Newburn, *Permission and Regulation*, vii, p.48.
6. For the pejorative connotations of permissiveness in the United States, see Barbara Ehrenreich, 'Legacies of the 1960s: New Rights and New Lefts', in Barbara L. Tischler (ed.), *Sights on the Sixties*, New Brunswick, NJ, 1992, p.231. The term accordingly appears for the most part on conservative and fundamentalist sites on the internet. One quotes Jesus as having pronounced on 21 November 1977 that

'Permissiveness shall not be accepted by your God' (http://www.tldm.org/directives/d138.htm).

7. Tom McGrath in *IT*, no.10, 13 March 1967.
8. Ibid.
9. Douglas Rhymes, *No New Morality: Christian Personal Values and Sexual Morality*, London, 1964, pp.18–19.
10. Tom McGrath in *IT*, no.10, 13 March 1967; George Melly, *Revolt into Style: The Pop Arts in Britain*, London, 1970, p.11.
11. Tom McGrath in *IT*, no.10, 13 March 1967; Mick Farren and Edward Barker, *Watch Out Kids*, London, 1972, n.p.
12. Tom McGrath in *IT*, no.10, 13 March 1967; John A.T. Robinson, *Honest to God*, Philadelphia, 1963; Jonathan Aitken, *The Young Meteors*, London, 1967, p.297.
13. Tom McGrath in *IT*, no.10, 13 March 1967.
14. Richard Neville, *Play Power*, London, 1970; Charles Marowitz, *Burnt Bridges: A Souvenir of the Swinging Sixties and Beyond*, London, 1990, p.132.
15. Tom McGrath in *IT*, no.10, 13 March 1967.
16. E. Parkinson Smith and A. Graham Ikin, *Morality—Old and New*, Derby, 1964, p.6.
17. Edmund Leach, *A Runaway World?*, New York, 1968, p.56.
18. John Robinson, *Honest to God*, p.118. For changes in Anglican thinking during this period, see Jane Lewis and Patrick Wallis, 'Fault, Breakdown and the Church of England's Involvement in the 1969 Divorce Reform', *Twentieth-Century British History*, vol.11, no.3, 2000, p.317.
19. James Hemming, *Individual Morality*, London, 1969, p.67.
20. Bradbury, *History Man*, pp.23, 26–7.
21. Ibid., pp.7, 22, 26.
22. Ibid., p.37.
23. Ibid., pp.23, 72.
24. Ibid., p.124.
25. Ibid., pp.8, 32.
26. Tom McGrath in *IT*, no.10, 13 March 1967.
27. Bradbury, *History Man*, pp.28, 26.
28. Ibid., pp.49, 50.
29. Ibid., p.40.
30. Green, *All Dressed Up*, xi.
31. See M.L. Bush, *What is Love?: Richard Carlile's Philosophy of Sex*, London, 1998; J. Miriam Benn, *Predicaments of Love*, London, 1992; and Chris Nottingham, *The Pursuit of Serenity: Havelock Ellis and the New Politics*, Amsterdam, 1999.
32. Matthew Sweet, *Inventing the Victorians*, London, 2001, p.105; editorial in *The Adult*, vol.1, no.1, 1897, p.1.
33. Noel Annan, *Our Age: The Generation That Made Postwar Britain*, London, 1991; Virginia Nicholson, *Among the Bohemians: Experiments in Living, 1900–39*, New York, 2002; 'The Basis of the FPSI' (1933), in C.E.M. Joad (ed.), *Manifesto: The Book of the Federation of Progressive Societies and Individuals*, London, 1934, p.24.
34. Marcus Collins, *Modern Love: An Intimate History of Men and Women in Twentieth-Century Britain*, London, 2003, pp.42–8.
35. Paul B. Bull, *A Man's Guide to Courtship and Marriage*, London, 1932, viii.

36. The Church and Marriage: Evidence Presented to the Royal Commission on Marriage and Divorce, London, 1952, p.4.
37. Ross McKibbin, *Classes and Cultures: England, 1918–51*, Oxford, 1998, pp.424–6, 461–2. For Reithian puritanism at the BBC, see also D.L. LeMahieu, *A Culture for Democracy: Mass Communication and the Cultivated Mind in Britain between the Wars*, Oxford, 1988.
38. Public Morality Council, Minutes, 30 May 1940, London Metropolitan Archives, A/PMC/2.
39. Public Morality Council, Minutes, 27 October 1949, London Metropolitan Archives, A/PMC/3.
40. William Joynson-Hicks, Viscount Brentford, *Do We Need A Censor?*, London, 1929, p.20.
41. John Wolfenden, 'The Permissive Society', *Proceedings of the Royal Institution of Great Britain*, vol.46, 1973, p.28.
42. Liz Stanley, *Sex Surveyed, 1949–94*, London, 1995, pp.87, 98, 131.
43. C.E.M. Joad, *The Future of Morals*, London, 1936, p.75.
44. For the worldview of the Angry Young Men, see D.E. Cooper, 'Looking Back on Anger', in Vernon Bogdanor and Robert Skidelsky (eds), *The Age of Affluence, 1951–64*, London, 1970.
45. Marcus Collins, 'The Fall of the English Gentleman: The National Character in Decline, *c.*1918–1970', *Historical Research*, vol.75, no.187, 2002, pp.90–111; Hugh Thomas, 'The Establishment and Society', in Hugh Thomas (ed.), *The Establishment*, New York, 1959, p.19.
46. Robert Pitman in Kenneth Allsop and Robert Pitman, *A Question of Obscenity*, Northwood, 1960, viii; Lord Denning, *The Equality of Women*, Liverpool, 1960, p.3.
47. Colin Wilson, 'Beyond the Outsider', in Tom Maschler (ed.), *Declaration*, London, 1957, pp.20, 41; Kenneth Allsop in *A Question of Obscenity*, p.9; John Osborne, *Look Back in Anger*, London, 1957, p.31.
48. Kenneth Allsop, *The Angry Decade*, London, 1958, p.207; Alan McGlashen, 'Sex on These Islands', in Arthur Koestler (ed.), *Suicide of a Nation?*, London, 1963, p.210; E.M. Carstairs, *This Island Now*, London, 1962, p.45.
49. For an important reinterpretation of de-Christianisation, see Callum G. Brown, *The Death of Christian Britain: Understanding Secularisation, 1800–2000*, London, 2001. Brown sees the 1960s as an even more pivotal decade than I am suggesting here. He correspondingly places less importance on the permissive tendencies of secular intellectuals and Christian mutualists before the Second World War.
50. Archbishop of Canterbury Group, *Putting Asunder: A Divorce Law for Contemporary Society*, London, 1966, p.10.
51. *Final Report of the Committee on Procedure in Matrimonial Cases*, London, 1947, p.5; Scottish Law Commission, *Divorce: The Grounds Considered*, Edinburgh, 1967, p.4.
52. John Trevelyan, *What the Censor Saw*, London, 1973, p.231. For film and stage censorship, see Anthony Aldgate, 'Defining the Parameters of "Quality" Cinema for the "Permissive Society": The British Board of Film Censors and *This Sporting Life*', in *Windows on the Sixties*; and *idem*, *Censorship and the Permissive Society: British Cinema and Theatre, 1955–65*, Oxford, 1995.
53. Hugh Carleton Greene, *Third Floor Front: A View of Broadcasting in the Sixties*, London,

1969, pp.103, 136.

54. Alex Seago, *Burning the Box of Beautiful Things: The Development of a Postmodern Sensibility*, Oxford, 1995, p.23.
55. Colin MacInnes, *City of Spades*, London, 1957, p.69.
56. Bradbury, *History Man*, p.49.
57. John Selwyn Gummer, *The Permissive Society: Fact or Fantasy?*, London, 1971, p.56; John Wolfenden cited in Stuart Hall, 'Reformism and the Legislation of Consent', in National Deviancy Conference, *Permissiveness and Control: The Fate of the Sixties Legislation*, Basingstoke, 1980, p.9.
58. Francis Wyndham in David Bailey, *David Bailey's Box of Pin-ups*, London, 1965, n.p.
59. Twiggy, *An Autobiography*, London, 1975, p.21.
60. Mary Quant cited in John Crosby, 'London, The Most Exciting City in the World' (1965), in Ray Connolly (ed.), *In The Sixties*, London, 1995, p.79; Michael Caine cited in Aitken, *Young Meteors*, p.95.
61. Peter Evans in David Bailey and Peter Evans, *Goodbye Baby and Amen: A Saraband for the Sixties*, London, 1969, pp.7, 8.
62. Christopher Booker, *The Neophiliacs: The Revolution in English Life in the Fifties and Sixties*, London, 1969, p.298; Heather Cremonesi, 'Yeah, Yeah', in Frank Habicht, *Young London: Permissive Paradise*, London, 1969, xiv.
63. Melly, *Revolt*; Levin, *Pendulum Years*, p.83.
64. Julie Stephens, *Anti-Disciplinary Protest: Sixties Radicalism and Postmodernism*, Cambridge, 1998, pp.17–21.
65. David Alan Mellor and Laurent Gervereau, 'Introduction: Did the Sixties Really Happen?', in David Alan Mellor and Laurent Gervereau (eds), *The Sixties: Britain and France, 1962–73*, London, 1997; Marwick, *Sixties*, p.733. For the relationship between permissiveness and economic growth, see also Hall, 'Reformism', in *Permissiveness and Control*, p.39.
66. Jonathon Green, *Days in the Life: Voices from the English Underground, 1961–71*, London, 1988, viii.
67. David Widgery, *Preserving Disorder*, London, 1989, part I; Jeff Nuttall cited in Roger Hutchinson, *High Sixties: The Summers of Riot and Love*, Edinburgh, 1992, p.194.
68. Patricia Waugh, *Harvest of the Sixties: English Literature and Its Background, 1960 to 1990*, Oxford, 1995, p.210.
69. Leon Hunt, *British Low Culture: From Safari Suits to Sexploitation*, London, 1998, p.19; Joseph McAleer, *Passion's Fortune: The Story of Mills and Boon*, New York, 1999, p.288.
70. Nicholas Saunders, *Alternative London*, London, 1970; *idem*, *Alternative London* [rev. edn], London, 1972.
71. George McKay, *Senseless Acts of Beauty: Cultures of Resistance since the Sixties*, London, 1996. See also *idem* (ed.), *DIY Culture: Party and Protest in Nineties Britain*, London, 1998.
72. *Sunday Telegraph*, 5 June 1988.
73. NOP (1984), in *World Political Opinion and Social Surveys: Series One—British Opinion Polls, part I*, Reading, 1990, vol.173, p.13; *Sunday Telegraph*, 5 June 1988.
74. For example, see Anne Barlow et al., 'Just a Piece of Paper? Marriage and Cohabitation', in Alison Park et al. (eds), *British Social Attitudes: The Eighteenth Report*, London, 2001, p.33.
75. One Plus One, *Bulletin Plus*, vol.5, no.2, 2001, n.p.

76. For the Conservative Party's disarray over permissiveness, see Matthew Parris in *The Times*, 10 May 2003. Those who canonised Diana contrasted her modern ways with the fuddy-duddy attitudes and buttoned-up demeanour of her in-laws. Deep splits emerged in the Church of England over the appointment and subsequent resignation of a celibate homosexual, Jeffrey John, as Bishop of Reading in 2003.
77. Michael Jackson in *Guardian*, 5 July 1999.
78. Bradbury, *History Man*, pp.3, 5, 52.
79. Ibid., p.49.
80. Marwick, *Sixties*, pp.13, 194; Miriam Akhtar and Steve Humphries, *The Fifties and Sixties: A Lifestyle Revolution*, London, 2001, p.9.
81. Gummer, *Permissive Society*, p.92. For the left-wing study of subcultures, see esp. *Resistance Through Rituals*.
82. Marowitz, *Burnt Bridges*, pp.2, 3; Nik Cohn, *Yes, We Have No Bananas: Adventures in Other England*, London, 1999, x; Jim Haynes, *Thanks for Coming! An Autobiography*, London, 1984.
83. Sarah Thornton, *Club Cultures: Music, Media and Subcultural Capital*, Cambridge, 1995. See Pierre Bourdieu, *Distinction: A Social Critique of the Judgement of Taste*, London, 1986.
84. Widgery, *Preserving Disorder*, p.198.
85. Aitken, *Young Meteors*, pp.272–3; Booker, *Neophiliacs*, p.23.
86. Paul McCartney cited in Barry Miles, *Paul McCartney: Many Years from Now*, London, 1998, p.98.
87. Twiggy, *An Autobiography*, p.10; Fred Vermorel, *Fashion and Perversity: A Life of Vivienne Westwood and the Sixties Laid Bare*, London, 1996, pp.149–50.
88. Richard Hoggart, 'Proper Ferdinands?', in *The Permissive Society: The Guardian Inquiry*, London, 1969, p.79; Mark Davison and Ian Currie, *Surrey in the Sixties: Memories of a Swinging Decade*, Coulsdon, 1994; Dave Reeves (ed.), *Brummies: Swinging in the Sixties*, Birmingham, 1996.
89. Bradbury, *History Man*, p.4. For the significance of art colleges, see Simon Frith and Howard Horne, *Art into Pop*, London, 1987.
90. Angela Bartie, 'Godlessness and Dirt: Moral Controversies at the Edinburgh Festivals, 1963–7', unpublished paper delivered at the PCCBS Conference, Berkeley, CA, March 2004. Northern Ireland regularly ranked bottom among Western European countries on measures of permissiveness used in the World Values Survey conducted in the early 1990s. See Ronald Inglehart, Miguel Basañez and Alejandro Moreno, *Human Values and Beliefs: A Cross-cultural Sourcebook*, Ann Arbor, MI, 1998.
91. For the relationship between affluence and permissiveness, see Dick Hebdige, *Subculture: The Meaning of Style*, London, 1979; Colin Campbell, *The Romantic Ethic and the Spirit of Modern Consumerism*, Oxford, 1987; Frank Mort, *Cultures of Consumption: Masculinities and Social Space in Late Twentieth Century Britain*, London, 1996; and, for an American perspective, Thomas Frank, *The Conquest of Cool: Business Culture, Counterculture, and the Rise of Hip Consumerism*, Chicago, 1997.
92. Mary Quant, *Quant by Quant*, London, 1966, p.73.
93. Jeff Nuttall, *Bomb Culture*, London, 1968, p.210.
94. Marwick, *Sixties*, p.15.
95. Gordon Heald and Robert J. Wybrow, *The Gallup Survey of Britain*, London, 1986,

pp.229–30.

96. For class differences regarding divorce, see NOP (1984), in *World Political Opinion*, ser.1, pt.1, vol.173, p.13.
97. Judith Stacey, *Brave New Families: Stories of Domestic Upheaval in Late Twentieth-Century America* [rev. edn], Berkeley, CA, 1998, p.252.
98. Bradbury, *History Man*, pp.58, 84.
99. Juliet Mitchell, *Women's Estate*, Harmondsworth, 1971, p.140; Suzie Fleming, 'Women's Liberation', *Enough*, no.3, *c.*1971, p.10; Germaine Greer, *The Female Eunuch*, London, 1970, p.45.
100. Lucy Bland, 'Purity, Motherhood, Pleasure or Threat?: Definitions of Female Sexuality, 1900–1970s', in Sue Cartledge and Joanna Ryan (eds), *Sex and Love: New Thoughts on Old Contradictions*, London, 1983, p.28. For the most trenchant version of this argument, see Sheila Jeffreys, *Anticlimax: A Feminist Perspective on the Sexual Revolution*, London, 1990.
101. Beatrix Campbell, 'A Feminist Sexual Politics: Now You See It, Now You Don't', *Feminist Review*, no.5, 1980, p.2; Frank Musgrove, *Ecstasy and Holiness: Counter Culture and the Open Society*, London, 1974, p.29; NOP, *Report on Attitudes Towards Crime, Violence and Permissiveness in Society* (1970), in *World Political Opinion*, ser.1, pt.1, vol.129, x.
102. Simon Frith and Angela McRobbie, 'Rock and Sexuality', in Simon Frith and Andrew Goodman (eds), *On Record*, London, 1990, p.376.
103. Simon Frith, 'Afterthoughts', in *On Record*, p.422; Barbara Ehrenreich, Elizabeth Hess and Gloria Jacobs, *Re-Making Love: The Feminization of Sex*, London, 1986, ch.1; Angela McRobbie, *Feminism and Youth Culture*, Basingstoke, 1991, ch.7.
104. Women's Liberation Movement manifesto (1971), in Michelene Wandor (ed.), *The Body Politic: Writings from the Women's Liberation Movement in Britain, 1969–72*, London, 1972, p.2.
105. It is hard to reconcile women's conservatism in these matters with Anthony Giddens' contention that they pioneered the 'pure relationship' (Anthony Giddens's, *The Transformation of Intimacy: Sexuality, Love and Eroticism in Modern Societies*, Stanford, CA, 1992, p.2).
106. 39 per cent of men and 26 per cent of women approved, compared with disapproval rates of 40 per cent and 57 per cent respectively.
107. Kaye Wellings et al., *Sexual Behaviour in Britain: The National Survey of Sexual Attitudes and Lifestyles*, Harmondsworth, 1994, p.260.
108. Kerstin Hinds and Lindsey Jarvis, 'The Gender Gap', in Roger Jowell et al. (eds), *British Social Attitudes: The Seventeenth Report*, London, 2000, p.115. See also Collins, *Modern Love*, pp.214–16.
109. Bradbury, *History Man*, pp.50, 131, 229.
110. Mark Abrams, *The Teenage Consumer*, London, 1959; Jeffrey Richards, 'New Wave and Old Myths: British Cinema in the 1960s', in Bart Moore-Gilbert and John Seed (eds), *Cultural Revolution?: The Challenge of the Arts in the 1960s*, London, 1992, p.76; Lara Marks, *Sexual Chemistry: A History of the Contraceptive Pill*, New Haven, 2001, p.206.
111. Keith Richards (1967) cited in Levy, *Ready, Steady, Go!*, p.252; Bryan Wilson, 'The War of the Generations' (1964), in *The Youth Culture and the Universities*, London, 1970, p.97.

112. See Geoffrey Pearson, *Hooligan: A History of Respectable Fears*, Basingstoke, 1983.
113. Richard Weight, *Patriots: National Identity in Britain, 1940–2000*, Basingstoke, 2002, pp.393, 396.
114. For the humdrum ambitions of teenagers in this period, see Thelma Veness, *School Leavers: Their Aspirations and Expectations*, London, 1962; and Frank Musgrove, *Youth and the Social Order*, London, 1964, p.18.
115. Pearl Jephcott, *Time of One's Own: Leisure and Young People*, Edinburgh, 1967, p.88; E.M. Eppel and M. Eppel, *Adolescents and Morality*, London, 1966, p.213. See also Peter Willmott, *Adolescent Boys of East London*, London, 1966.
116. See Sylvia Ellis, '"A Demonstration of British Good Sense?": British Student Protest during the Vietnam War', in Gerard J. DeGroot (ed.), *Student Protest: The Sixties and After*, Harlow, 1998.
117. C.H. Whiteley and Winifred M. Whiteley, *The Permissive Morality*, London, 1964, p.57; John Barron Mays, *The Young Pretenders: A Study of Teenage Culture in Contemporary Society* [rev. edn], New York, 1967, p.32.
118. Smith and Ikin, *Morality*, p.5.
119. Lord Chancellor's Department, *Report of the Committee on the Age of Majority*, London, 1967, p.31.
120. Bradbury, *History Man*, pp.40, 218; Wolfenden, 'Permissive Society', pp.19, 26.
121. Bradbury, *History Man*, p.22; London Street Commune cited in Phil Cohen, *Rethinking The Youth Question: Education, Labour and Cultural Studies*, Durham, NC, 1999, p.23.
122. Wolfenden, 'Permissive Society', p.34.
123. Bradbury, *History Man*, pp.32, 69.
124. Paul Willis, *Profane Culture*, London, 1978, p.132.
125. Frank Parkin, *Middle-Class Radicalism: The Social Bases of the British Campaign for Nuclear Disarmament*, Manchester, 1968, p.34.
126. E.P. Thompson in *Universities and Left Review*, vol.1, no.1, 1957, p.35; editorial in *New Left Review*, no.1, 1960, p.1.
127. Stephens, *Anti-Disciplinary Protest*, p.4.
128. Bradbury, *History Man*, p.46; David McKie, 'The Quality of Life', in David McKie and Chris Cook (eds), *The Decade of Disillusion: British Politics in the Sixties*, Basingstoke, 1972, p.199.
129. Jack Straw cited by Michael Jones in *Sunday Times*, 21 March 1999; Tony Blair in *Observer*, 10 November 2002. See also Anthony Giddens, *The Third Way: The Renewal of Social Democracy*, Cambridge, 1998.
130. Editorial in *Daily Mail*, 26 June 2002; Carol Sarler in *Observer*, 2 February 2003.
131. Bradbury, *History Man*, p.138.
132. See Samuel Brittain, *Capitalism and the Permissive Society*, Basingstoke, 1973; and Steve Richards in *Independent on Sunday*, 17 June 2001.
133. Margaret Thatcher (1982) cited in Waugh, *Harvest*, p.67; Tim Collins cited by Matthew d'Ancona in *Sunday Telegraph*, 29 September 2002; William Hague cited by Jonathan Freedland in *Guardian*, 20 December 2000.
134. Margaret Thatcher (1982) cited in Waugh, *Harvest*, p.67; John Major cited in *Guardian*, 9 October 1993.
135. See David Leigh and Ed Vulliamy, *Sleaze: The Corruption of Parliament*, London, 1997;

and Andrew Grice in *Independent*, 10 October 2000.

136. Gillian Douglas, 'Family Law under the Thatcher Government', *Journal of Law and Society*, vol.17, no.4, 1990, p.422. See also Martin Durham, *Sex and Politics: The Family and Morality in the Thatcher Years*, Basingstoke, 1991.
137. Norman Tebbit in *The Times*, 23 November 1993.
138. See Roy Jenkins, *A Life at the Centre*, London, 1991, ch.9; and *idem*, *The Labour Case*, Harmondsworth, 1959, ch.9.
139. Kenneth Robinson in debate on Medical Termination of Pregnancy Bill, *Parliamentary Debates: House of Commons*, vol.634, col.855, 10 February 1961.
140. *Report from the Select Committee on Obscene Publications*, London, 1958, iv.
141. Alan Herbert, *A.P.H.: His Life and Times*, London, 1970, pp.238, 240.
142. Bradbury, *History Man*, pp.81, 98.
143. Mary Whitehouse, *Whatever Happened to Sex?*, Hove, 1977, p.188; editorial in *Daily Mail*, 14 June 2002.
144. Richard Hoggart, *The Uses of Literacy: Changing Patterns in English Mass Culture*, Fair Lawn, NJ, 1957, ch.7, p.146. See also *idem*, *The Way We Live Now*, London, 1995.
145. C.S. Lewis, *The Screwtape Letters*, London, 1942, p.126.
146. Pamela Hansford Johnson, *On Iniquity: Some Personal Reflections Arising Out of the Moors Murder Trial*, London, 1967, pp.17, 18, 40.
147. Whitehouse, *Whatever*, p.9; *idem* cited in Bart Moore-Gilbert and John Seed, 'Introduction', in *Cultural Revolution*, p.2.
148. T.R. Fyvel, *The Insecure Offenders: Rebellious Youth in the Welfare State*, London, 1961, p.179; Hansford Johnson, *On Iniquity*, p.113.
149. *Pornography: The Longford Report*, London, 1972, p.42; Gummer, *Permissive Society*, p.153.
150. *Come Together*, no.9, 1971; Leeds Revolutionary Feminist Group, 'Political Lesbianism: The Case Against Heterosexuality' (1979), in *Love Your Enemy?: The Debate between Heterosexual Feminism and Political Lesbianism*, London, 1981, p.6.
151. Philip Jenkins, *Intimate Enemies: Moral Panics in Contemporary Great Britain*, New York, 1992, p.130.
152. *Longford Report*, p.420.
153. Alan Travis, *Bound and Gagged: A Secret History of Obscenity in Britain*, London, 2000, p.231.
154. For reactions to the Longford Report, see Peter Stanford, *Lord Longford: A Life*, London, 1994, p.424.
155. Whitehouse, *Whatever*, pp.70, 193.
156. Ruth Wallsgrove (1977) cited in A.W.B. Simpson, *Pornography and Politics: The Williams Committee in Retrospect*, London, 1983, p.68.
157. *Come Together*, no.10, 1971; *Come Together*, no.9, 1971.
158. Debby Gregory in *London Women's Liberation Movement Newsletter*, no.155, 1980, n.p.
159. Fyvel, *Insecure Offenders*, p.114; Lynda Lee-Potter in *Daily Mail*, 20 March 2002.
160. Piers Paul Read in *Mail on Sunday*, 2 December 2001; Patrick Devlin, *The Enforcement of Morals*, London, 1959, p.12; John Capon, *And There Was Light: The Story of the Nationwide Festival of Light*, London, 1972, p.79.
161. Booker, *Neophiliacs*, appendix a; E.J. Mishan, *Making the World Safe for Pornography and Other Intellectual Fashions*, London, 1973, p.139.

162. Paul Johnson in *Daily Mail*, 15 September 2001.
163. Whitehouse, *Whatever*, p.198; Norman Tebbit in *The Times*, 23 November 1993.
164. Whiteley and Whiteley, *Permissive Morality*, pp.137, 138; Mervyn Griffith-Jones cited in C.H. Rolph (ed.), *The Trial of Lady Chatterley*, Harmondsworth, 1961, pp.16–17.
165. Gummer, *Permissive Society*, p.90.
166. Hansford Johnson, *On Iniquity*, p.139; William Barclay, *Ethics in a Permissive Society*, London, 1971, p.215; Arnold Lunn and Garth Lean, *The New Morality*, London, 1964, p.151.
167. Capon, *And There Was Light*, p.102.
168. *Longford Report*, p.415.
169. Evans in Bailey and Evans, *Goodbye Baby*, p.6.
170. The phrase is David Farber's; see David Farber (ed.), *The Sixties: From Memory to History*, Chapel Hill, NC, 1994. He is part of a generation of historians who have made the 1960s a more reputable subject in America than is yet the case in Britain.
171. Green, *All Dressed Up*, p.xiv.
172. Booker, *Neophiliacs*, p.12.
173. Paul Johnson, *Wake Up Britain!*, London, 1994, p.9; Digby Anderson, 'The Little Things That Matter: Trivia and the Maintenance of Social Order', in Digby Anderson (ed.), *Gentility Recalled: Mere Manners and the Making of Social Order*, London, 1996, p.28; L.H. Gann and Peter Duignan, 'The New Left and the Cultural Revolution of the 1960s: A Re-evaluation', *Hoover Essays*, no.10, 1995, n.p.; Gertrude Himmelfarb, *On Looking Into the Abyss: Untimely Thoughts on Culture and Society*, New York, 1994, p.106.
174. Michel Foucault, *The History of Sexuality, I: An Introduction*, London, 1979, parts I and II.
175. Ibid., part III.
176. Ibid., pp.7–8, 59.
177. Though Stuart Hall stated that the CCCS was 'never one school', there is a sufficient family resemblance between the writings discussed in this section to examine them together (Stuart Hall cited in Richard E. Lee, *Life and Times of Cultural Studies: The Politics and Transformation of the Structure of Knowledge*, Durham, NC, 2003, p.5). For the CCCS, see also Dennis Dworkin, *Cultural Marxism in Postwar Britain: History, the New Left, and the Origins of Cultural Studies*, Chapel Hill, NC, 1997, esp. ch.4.
178. Hall, 'Reformism', in *Permissiveness and Control*; Hebdige, *Subculture*.
179. Stanley Cohen, *Folk Devils and Moral Panics: The Creation of the Mods and the Rockers*, London, 1972; Jock Young, *The Drug Takers: The Social Meaning of Drug Use*, London, 1971, ch.6; Clarke et al., 'Subcultures', in *Resistance Through Rituals*, pp.64–5.
180. Ibid., p.40.
181. Hall, 'Reformism', in *Permissiveness and Control*, p.39; Clarke et al., 'Subcultures', in *Resistance Through Rituals*, p.65.
182. Foucault, *History of Sexuality*, p.101; Hebdige, *Subculture*, p.100; Stanley Cohen, *Folk Devils*, p.157.
183. Gertrude Himmelfarb, *One Nation, Two Cultures*, New York, 1999, p.15; Hall, 'Reformism', in *Permissiveness and Control*, p.6.
184. Gertrude Himmelfarb, *The De-Moralization of Society: From Victorian Virtues to Modern Values*, New York, 1995, p.248.

185. See ibid.; and Caroline Moore, 'Being a Gentleman: Manners, Independence and Integrity', in *Gentility Recalled*, p.60.
186 Himmelfarb, *De-Moralization*, pp.168, 262.
187. Peter Hitchens, *The Abolition of Britain: The British Cultural Revolution from Lady Chatterley to Tony Blair* [rev. edn], London, 2000, pp.xxi, 152, 344.
188. Himmelfarb, *De-Moralization*, pp.217–18.
189. Booker, *Neophiliacs*, p.308; Johnson, *Wake Up Britain!*, p.67; Hitchens, *Abolition of Britain*, p.230.
190. Himmelfarb, *One Nation*, pp.18, 26; Simon Heffer, 'Culture and Anarchy Revisited', 2003 talk on BBC Radio 4 (http://news.bbc.co.uk/1/hi/programmes/the_west-minster_hour/).
191. Dan Rebello, *1956 and All That: The Making of Modern British Drama*, London, 1999; Weeks, *Sex, Politics and Society*, ch.13; Stephen Heath, *The Sexual Fix*, Basingstoke, 1982; Nikolas Rose, *Governing the Soul: The Shaping of the Private Self*, London, 1990.
192. See Heffer, 'Culture and Anarchy'.
193. Foucault, *The History of Sexuality*, pp.65, 122.
194. Ibid., pp.28, 53, 55, 123.
195. Ibid., pp.22, 130, 131.
196. Ibid., p.116.
197. Ibid., pp.86, 93.
198. Phil Cohen, *Rethinking The Youth Question*, p.63; Hebdige, *Subculture*, p.44.
199. Hall, 'Reformism', in *Permissiveness and Control*, p.39.
200. Steven Box, 'Where Have All The Naughty Children Gone?'; John Clarke, 'Social Democratic Delinquents and Fabian Families'; and Nick Dorn, 'The Conservatism of the Cannabis Debate', all in *Permissiveness and Control*.
201. For a feminist critique of CCCS methodology by one of its members, see McRobbie, *Feminism and Youth Culture*.
202. Andrew Tolson, 'The Family in a "Permissive Society"', *Centre for Contemporary Cultural Studies Women Series Stencilled Paper*, no.30, 1975, n.p.; Stanley Cohen, *Folk Devils*, p.198; Hall, 'Reformism', in *Permissiveness and Control*, p.39; Clarke et al., 'Subcultures', in *Resistance Through Rituals*, p.67.
203. Stanley Cohen, *Folk Devils*; Hebdige, *Subculture*, p.3.
204. P.A.J. Waddington (1986) cited in Kenneth Thompson, *Moral Panics*, London, 1998, p.10.
205. Stanley Cohen, *Folk Devils*, p.143. For the mugging scare, see Stuart Hall et al., *Policing the Crisis: Mugging, the State and Law and Order*, Basingstoke, 1978. For a more extended critique of the literature on moral panics, see Angela McRobbie, *Postmodernism and Popular Culture*, London, 1994, ch.11.
206. Bradbury, *History Man*, p.73.

2. *Daring To Speak Whose Name? Queer Cultural Politics, 1920–1967*
Matt Houlbrook

1. Oscar Wilde to George Cecil Ives, cited in H. Montgomery Hyde, *The Other Love: An Historical and Contemporary Survey of Homosexuality in Britain*, London, 1970, p.2.
2. Arran cited in Antony Grey, *Quest for Justice: Towards Homosexual Emancipation*,

London, 1992, p.125.

3. See Mary Liddell, 'Give us back our Freedom', *Observer*, 12 January 2003. 'Lord Jenkins of Hillhead', *Guardian*, 6 January 2003. For wider discussions of the 'permissive society' see Tim Newburn, *Permission and Regulation: Law and Morals in Post-war Britain*, London, 1992; Cate Haste, *Rules of Desire: Sex in Britain, World War One to the Present*, London, 1992, pp.139–251; and Arthur Marwick, *The Sixties: Cultural Revolution in Britain, France, Italy and the United States, c.1958–c.1974*, Oxford, 1991.
4. Jeffrey Weeks, *Coming Out: Homosexual Politics in Britain from the Nineteenth Century to the Present*, London, 1977.
5. Chris Waters, 'Disorders of the Mind, Disorders of the Body Social: Peter Wildeblood and the Making of the Modern Homosexual', in Becky Conekin, Frank Mort, and Chris Waters (eds), *Moments of Modernity: Reconstructing Britain, 1945–1964*, London and New York, 1999, p.134. See also Weeks, *Coming Out*; Hyde, *Other Love*; Stephen Jeffrey-Poulter, *Queers, Peers and Commons: The Struggle for Gay Law Reform from the 1950s to the Present*, London, 1991; and Patrick Higgins, *Heterosexual Dictatorship: Male Homosexuality in Postwar Britain*, London, 1996.
6. For the continued salience of these distinctions, see Anna Marie Smith, *New Right Discourse on Race and Sexuality: Britain 1968–1990*, Cambridge, 1994.
7. 'West End Nest of Vice Smoked Out', *News of the World*, 5 March 1933.
8. I discuss this case in Matt Houlbrook, '"Lady Austin's Camp Boys": Constituting the Queer Subject in 1930s London', *Gender and History*, vol.14, no.1, 2002, pp.31–61.
9. Public Record Office [PRO]: CRIM 1 639: Austin S. and Others: Disorderly House / Conspiracy to Corrupt Morals: Depositions to Central Criminal Court 7 February 1933: PS 40 F Frederick Robbings: 49–50.
10. PRO: CRIM 1 639: Copy Depositions: SDDI F Frank Francis: 29.
11. Ibid., SDDI F Frank Francis: 29.
12. 'Alleged Scenes at West End Dances', *News of the World*, 26 February 1933.
13. PRO: CRIM 1 639: Copy Depositions: SDDI F Frank Francis: 29. See also the similar defence made in PRO: MEPO 3 758: Caravan Club: Disorderly House / Male Prostitutes: Minute 11a: 29 August 1934; 'Caravan Club Disclosures', *News of the World*, 28 October 1934.
14. George Ives, *The Continued Extension of the Criminal Law*, London, 1922; Anomaly, *The Invert and his Social Adjustment*, London, 1927. For this earlier work, see Havelock Ellis, *Studies in the Psychology of Sex, I: Sexual Inversion*, London, 1897; John Addington Symonds, *A Problem in Modern Ethics*, New York, 1971; and Edward Carpenter, *The Intermediate Sex: A Study of Some Transitional Types of Men and Women*, London, 1908.
15. Ives, *Continued Extension*, pp.21, 25.
16. Anomaly, *The Invert*, pp.7–8, 67.
17. Ibid., pp.72, 126, 138–9.
18. For the BSSSP, with which Carpenter, Ellis and Ives were all involved, and its discreet campaigning for law reform within elite circles through published pamphlets and meetings, see Weeks, *Coming Out*, pp.128–67; and Lesley Hall, '"Disinterested Enthusiasm for Sexual Misconduct": The British Society for the Study of Sex Psychology, 1913–47', *Journal of Contemporary History*, vol.30, no.4, October 1995, pp.665–86.
19. Anomaly, *The Invert*, pp.xi, xv, xxiii–xxiv.

20. See Matt Houlbrook, *Queer London: Perils and Pleasures in the Sexual Metropolis, 1918–57*, Chicago and London, 2005.
21. J.B. Lopian, 'Crime, Police and Punishment 1918–29: Metropolitan Experiences, Perceptions and Policies', University of Cambridge PhD Thesis, 1986, p.44.
22. See V.A.C. Gatrell, 'Crime, Authority and the Policeman State', in F.M.L. Thompson (ed.), *The Cambridge Social History of Britain, 1750–1950, iii: Social Agencies and Institutions*, Cambridge, 1993, pp.271–7.
23. See PRO: MEPO 3 2330: 1943; PRO: MEPO 3 989: Persons Frequenting Urinals Apparently for Improper Purposes: 1937–9; PRO: MEPO 3 987: 1935; PRO: MEPO 3 2331: Gross Indecency / Importuning: 1943; and "Conviction Quashed", *News of the World*, 13 February 1927.
24. Ives, *Continued Extension*, p.8.
25. PRO: MEPO 3 405: Francis Champain: Indecency: 1927: Attachment 35a: Confidential Street Offences Committee: Report of the Sub-committee. The best legal accounts of the case are 'Double Blue's Lapse', *News of the World*, 28 August 1927; 'Another Case Dismissed on Appeal', *Birmingham Daily Mail*, 21 September 1927; and 'Where Justice Erred', *News of the World*, 25 September 1927. For Joynson-Hicks's referral of the case, see PRO: HO 45 12633: Appointment of Commission to Consider the Law and Practice in Relation to Soliciting etc.: Section 483171 / 85: 18 October 1927.
26. PRO: MEPO 3 405: Minute 4a: Mr J. Chester to the Commissioner of Police: 27 September 1927.
27. 'Wrecked his Career', *News of the World*, 15 May 1932. The men represented by Curtis-Bennett included a respected author, a public school games master, an independent gentleman, an ex-army officer and solicitor's clerk and an ex-army major and stockbroker. See PRO: MEPO 3 994: Mitford B.: Minute 9a: Mr Kendal to Brig. James Whitehead: 14 November 1936; 'Two Men Acquitted', *News of the World*, 8 May 1932; 'Gave Notice of Appeal', *News of the World*, 18 June 1922; 'Ex-Officer to Appeal', *News of the World*, 28 March 1926; and 'Jury Upholds the Honour of Major', *News of the World*, 19 February 1933.
28. For the 'good character' defence, see 'Hyde Park Arrest', *News of the World*, 8 January 1922; 'Artist Arrested', *News of the World*, 20 June 1926; 'Dismissed the Charge', *News of the World*, 21 March 1926; and 'Gave Notice of Appeal', *News of the World*, 18 June 1922.
29. 'Major in the Dock', *News of the World*, 17 April 1927; 'Veteran Major's Sin', *News of the World*, 29 May 1927.
30. 'Conviction to Stand', *News of the World*, 21 September 1930.
31. 'Vicar in Custody', *News of the World*, 24 September 1944.
32. Judge Cecil Whitely (Recorder of London), 'The Problem of the Moral Pervert', *Medical Press*, 15 July 1932; Whitely, 'The Problem of the Moral Pervert', *Journal of the Institute of Hygiene*, April 1933.
33. Chris Waters, 'Edward Glover, the Institute for the Scientific Treatment of Delinquency and the Question of Homosexual Law Reform in Mid Twentieth-Century Britain' (unpublished paper); Laura Doan, *Fashioning Sapphism: The Origins of a Modern English Lesbian Subculture*, New York, 2001, p.48.
34. PRO: HO 144 22298: Criticism of Elderly Judge's Treatment of Homosexual

Offences: Section 430931 / 1: John B.: 28 February 1922.

35. Waters, 'Edward Glover'. Such judicial critiques increasingly influenced the policy positions of organisations like the National Vigilance Association. Fawcett Library [FL]: NVA: Executive Minutes, vol.11, box 195: 28 June 1932; FL: NVA: Executive Minutes Book, vol.10, box 196: 26 November 1935.
36. These continuities were reinforced by the personal and institutional ties between the BSSSP and men like Norman Haire and Edward Glover and the ISTD. See Chris Waters, 'Havelock Ellis, Sigmund Freud and the State: Discourses of Homosexual Identity in Interwar Britain', in Lucy Bland and Laura Doan (eds), *Sexology in Culture: Labelling Bodies and Desires*, Cambridge, 1998, pp.165–79.
37. See, for example, Pat Thane, 'Population Politics in Postwar British Culture', in Conekin et al., *Moments of Modernity*, pp.114–33; Newburn, *Permission and Regulation*, p.164; and Waters, 'Disorders of the Mind', pp.137–8.
38. See, for example, 'Severity Misplaced', *Observer*, 21 October 1956; Waters, 'Disorders of the Mind', pp.140–3; and National Sound Archive [NSA]: C456 93 01: C.H. Rolfe.
39. For the debates over Wolfenden's appointment, see Higgins, *Heterosexual Dictatorship*, pp.3–12; and John Wolfenden, *Turning Points*, London, 1976, pp.129–46. The committee's papers are contained in PRO: HO 345 1–20: The Departmental Committee on Homosexual Offences and Prostitution: 1954–57.
40. Frank Mort, 'Mapping Sexual London: The Wolfenden Committee on Homosexual Offences and Prostitution: 1954–7', *New Formations*, vol.37, 1999, pp.92–113.
41. PRO: HO 345 2: Correspondence: Undated and unsigned memo.
42. Ibid., J.A. Newsom: 22 August 1956. W. Conwy Roberts, 8 August 1955.
43. Ibid., G.H. Macmillan: 1 July 1955.
44. Ibid., Anatole James: 30 May 1955.
45. Ibid., Roberts: 28 June 1955.
46. PRO: HO 345 14: CHP TRANS 32: Two Witnesses Called by the Chairman: 28 July 1955: 32.
47. NSA: C456 89 01: Patrick Trevor-Roper.
48. PRO: HO 345 2: Correspondence: Undated and unsigned memo.
49. Leslie Moran, *The Homosexual(ity) of Law*, London and New York, 1996, pp.102–7; Mort, 'Mapping Sexual London', pp.108–9.
50. PRO: HO 345 2: Correspondence: Roberts 15 December 1954.
51. NSA: C456 89 01: Patrick Trevor-Roper.
52. PRO: HO 345 4: Correspondence: Chairman's comments on Roberts's memo.
53. Wildeblood's circumstances were more complex, since he volunteered to give evidence whilst serving an eighteen-month prison sentence for gross indecency. See Peter Wildeblood, *Against the Law*, London, 1955.
54. Mort, 'Mapping Sexual London', p.109.
55. Wildeblood, *Against the Law*, p.7.
56. For Trevor-Roper and Winter's use of medical discourses, see: PRO: HO 345 8: CHP 53; and PRO: HO 345 8: CHP 70: Memorandum submitted by Mr C.W.
57. Wildeblood, *Against the Law*, p.175.
58. PRO: HO 345 13: CHP TRANS 24: Peter Wildeblood: 24 May 1955: 1892 11, 1896 12. See also PRO: HO 345 8: CHP 69: Memorandum submitted by witness

from 28 July 1954.

59. PRO: HO 345 8: CHP 51: Memorandum submitted by Peter Wildeblood.
60. PRO: HO 345 14: CHP TRANS 32: 2612 12; PRO: HO 345 15: CHP TRANS 24: 1854 1.
61. PRO: HO 345 8: CHP 54; CHP 51.
62. PRO: HO 345 14: CHP TRANS 32: 2619 16.
63. PRO: HO 345 14: CHP TRANS 32: 2622 18.
64. Wildeblood, *Against the Law*, p.13.
65. Ibid., p.17.
66. PRO: HO 345 14: CHP TRANS 32: 2597 5–6.
67. Ibid., 2619 16.
68. PRO: HO 345 8: CHP 53. For such notions of respectability, see Martin Francis, 'Tears, Tantrums, and Bared Teeth: The Emotional Economy of Three Conservative Prime Ministers, 1951–1963', *Journal of British Studies*, vol.41, no.1, 2002, pp.354–87; and Marcus Collins, 'The Fall of the English Gentleman: The National Character in Decline, *c.*1918–1970', *Historical Research*, vol.75, no.187, 2002, pp.90–111.
69. Wildeblood, *Against the Law*, p.175.
70. Compare Wildeblood's public statements with press reports of his trial: 'All Day Hearing of Montagu Case', *News of the World*, 24 January 1954; PRO: HO 345 8: CHP 51; PRO: HO 345 13: CHP TRANS 24. There are similar gaps between Trevor-Roper's testimony and his later recollections. See NSA: C456 89 01: Patrick Trevor-Roper; PRO: HO 345 8: CHP 53; and PRO: HO 345 14: CHP TRANS 32.
71. PRO: HO 345 14: CHP TRANS 32: 2600 7.
72. PRO: HO 345 8: CHP 51; PRO: HO 345 14: CHP TRANS 32: 2600 7.
73. PRO: HO 345 14: CHP TRANS 32: 2600 7.
74. PRO: HO 345 1: *Report of the Departmental Committee on Homosexual Offences and Prostitution*, London, 1957, pp.9, 10, 12, 24, 44.
75. See Gordon Westwood, *Society and the Homosexual*, London, 1952; *idem*, *A Minority: A Report on the Life of the Male Homosexual in Great Britain*, London, 1960; Peter Wildeblood, *A Way of Life*, London, 1956; Mary Renault, *The Charioteer*, London, 1953; Angus Wilson, *Hemlock and After*, London, 1952; and Rodney Garland, *The Heart in Exile*, London, 1953. For *Victim*, see John Hill, *Sex, Class and Realism: British Cinema, 1956–1963*, London, 1997, pp.90–4.
76. Homosexual Law Reform Society, *Homosexuals and the Law*, London, 1959. Grey, *Quest for Justice*, passim. PRO: HO 291 125: Leo Abse's bill to Amend the Law re Homosexual Offences: 1960–1964.
77. PRO: HO 291 123: General notes on Homosexual Offences and Prostitution: 1957–1958; PRO: FD 23 1893: Homosexuality: 1958–1962; PRO: HO 291 125: Leo Abse's bill to Amend the Law re Homosexual Offences: 1960–1964; PRO: PREM 13 1563: Law Relating to Homosexual Offences: 1965–1967; PRO: HO 291 129: Sexual Offences Bill: 1966–1967. PRO: HO 291 130: Suggestion for Extending Provision Requiring DPP's Consent etc.: 1967.
78. On this point, see the memoirs of two men who most certainly did not meet the demands of respectability: Tom Driberg, *Ruling Passions*, London, 1977; and Quentin Crisp, *The Naked Civil Servant*, London, 1968, p.207.

79. David Bell and Jon Binnie, *The Sexual Citizen: Queer Politics and Beyond*, Cambridge, 2000, pp.2–3.
80. Newburn, *Permission and Regulation*, p.62.
81. Higgins, *Heterosexual Dictatorship*, p.3.
82. Weeks, *Coming Out*, p.156.

3. Little By Little? Arena Three and Lesbian Politics in the 1960s
Alison Oram

1. From an oral history account by Jackie Forster, who was involved with *Arena Three* in its later years, in Suzanne Neild and Rosalind Pearson (eds), *Women Like Us*, London, 1992, p.93. My thanks to Lesley Hall for her commentary on the original conference paper as well as a later draft; to Carol Smith, Annmarie Turnbull and Anna Clark for their feedback; and to Marcus Collins for his detailed editorial comments.
2. The MRG changed its name to the Minorities Research Trust in 1967 and nominally separated from the magazine (*Arena Three*, vol.4, no.6, June 1967). For clarity I shall refer to the organisation throughout as the MRG.
3. For Dusty Springfield, see Patricia Juliana Smith, '"You Don't Have to Say You Love Me": The Camp Masquerades of Dusty Springfield', in Patricia Juliana Smith (ed.), *The Queer Sixties*, New York, 1999.
4. However, Wilson notes that they had prepared the ground for the emergence of these more militant groups (Elizabeth Wilson, *Only Halfway to Paradise: Women in Postwar Britain, 1945–1968*, London, 1980, p.9). John D'Emilio describes a similar attitude among US gay liberationists in his *Sexual Politics, Sexual Communities: The Making of a Homosexual Minority in the United States, 1940–1970*, Chicago, 1983. Thanks to Carol Smith for discussing the views of GLF members in the early 1970s.
5. Jeffrey Weeks, *Coming Out: Homosexual Politics in Britain from the Nineteenth Century to the Present*, London, 1977, pp.169–71, 177–9; Lillian Faderman, *Surpassing the Love of Men: Friendship and Love Between Women from the Renaissance to the Present*, London, 1981, pp.378–82.
6. Weeks, *Coming Out*, pp.179–80.
7. Martin Meeker, 'Behind the Mask of Respectability: Reconsidering the Mattachine Society and Male Homophile Practice, 1950s and 1960s', *Journal of the History of Sexuality*, vol.10, no.1, 2001, pp.78–116; Jennifer Terry, *An American Obsession: Science, Medicine and Homosexuality in Modern Society*, Chicago, 1999, ch.12; Leila J. Rupp, *A Desired Past: A Short History of Same-Sex Love in America*, Chicago, 1999, pp.159–69. In fact D'Emilio's *Sexual Politics* made this argument about American homophile groups as long ago as 1983, though it made a distinction between the cautious activities they pursued in the 1950s and their more militant tactics in the 1960s (pre-Stonewall) which the more recent studies have challenged.
8. Emily Hamer, *Britannia's Glory: A History of Twentieth-Century Lesbians*, London, 1996, ch.9; Jill Gardiner, *From The Closet To The Screen: Women at the Gateways Club, 1945–85*, London, 2003, chs.5–6. Rebecca Jennings also discusses *Arena Three* in her unpublished PhD thesis, 'Lesbian Identities in Britain, 1945–1970: Personal Testimonies and the Construction of Post-war Lesbian History', Manchester University, 2003. For oral history accounts by MRG women, see Ceri Ager, Jackie Forster and Diana

Chapman in Neild and Pearson, *Women Like Us*; and Diana Chapman in Hall Carpenter Archives Lesbian Oral History Group, *Inventing Ourselves: Lesbian Life Stories*, London, 1989.

9. *Arena Three*, vol.6, no.12, December 1969.
10. Hall's classic lesbian novel, *The Well of Loneliness*, was banned for obscenity in 1928 but became legally available in Britain in 1949. For changing medical views of lesbianism, see Alison Oram and Annmarie Turnbull, *The Lesbian History Sourcebook: Love and Sex between Women in Britain from 1780 to 1970*, London, 2001, ch.7.
11. Wilson, *Only Halfway to Paradise*, pp.104–9.
12. *Towards a Quaker View of Sex*, London, 1964, pp.39–40.
13. Elizabeth Wilson, 'Memoirs of an anti-heroine', in Bob Cant and Susan Hemmings (eds), *Radical Records: Thirty Years of Lesbian and Gay History*, London, 1988, p.50.
14. Antony Grey, *Quest for Justice: Towards Homosexual Emancipation*, London, 1992, p.69; Oram and Turnbull, *Lesbian History Sourcebook*, p.204.
15. See Maureen Duffy, *The Microcosm*, London, 1966, for a description of the Gateways club. For Soho coffee bars, see Tony Parker, *Five Women*, London, 1965, pp.95–7. For west London clubs, see Gardiner, *From The Closet*. For Manchester, see Alkarim Jivani, *It's Not Unusual: A History of Lesbian and Gay Britain in the Twentieth Century*, London, 1997, pp.131–7. For Brighton, see Brighton Ourstory Project, *Daring Hearts: Lesbian and Gay Lives of 50s and 60s Brighton*, Brighton, 1992.
16. Grey, *Quest for Justice*, pp.135–6; Gardiner, *From The Closet*, p.96.
17. Dilys Rowe, 'A Quick Look at Lesbians', *The Twentieth Century*, Winter 1962–3, pp.67–72.
18. Though it was described by one patronising detractor as 'a naïve schoolgirlish magazine' (Nicholas Saunders, *Alternative London*, London, 1970, p.146). My thanks to Marcus Collins for this reference.
19. In the early years MRG discussed the idea of founding a permanent club or meeting place.
20. The breakaway group also wanted to establish more transparent financial management of MRG, which Langley rebuffed (Gardiner, *From The Closet*, p.122; Hamer, *Britannia's Glory*, pp.181–2). Kenric and MRG are often lumped together in the historiography as having similar aims (see Weeks, *Coming Out*, p.179 and H. Montgomery Hyde, *The Other Love: An Historical and Contemporary Survey of Homosexuality in Britain*, London, 1970, pp.285–6), but this split demonstrates the more far-reaching objectives of MRG and *Arena Three*.
21. This and the other aims of the MRG were listed in all issues of *Arena Three*.
22. Alberto Melucci, *Nomads of the Present: Social Movements and Individual Needs in Contemporary Society*, London, 1989; Nickie Charles, *Feminism, the State and Social Policy*, Basingstoke, 2000, ch.2; Alan Scott, *Ideology and the New Social Movements*, London, 1990, ch.1. Millie Thayer usefully discusses differences between lesbian groups using NSM theory in 'Identity, Revolution and Democracy: Lesbian Movements in Central America', *Social Problems*, vol.44, no.3, August 1997, pp.386–407.
23. Weeks, *Coming Out*, p.169.
24. Hamer, *Britannia's Glory*, pp.179–80; Gardiner, *From The Closet*, pp.97–101.
25. Charlotte Wolff, *Love Between Women*, London, 1971, pp.18–19, 72–5. Subscribers to *Arena Three* (a larger group than membership of MRG) totalled over 600 in 1965,

and were reported as being around 450 in 1970 (*Arena Three*, vol.7, no.6, July 1970; Hamer, *Britannia's Glory*, p.183).

26. Its founders were five professional women and a survey of its readers in 1966 showed that they were mainly teachers, nurses and office workers. Very few were manual workers (Hyde, *The Other Love*, pp.284–5). The desire for normality and acceptance, as against the asserting of a visible lesbian identity, was also reflected in a key debate on dress codes remembered by members many years later. Was it acceptable to wear 'natty gent's suiting' to meetings held in public places as part of an unashamed lesbian identity? Some were strongly against this, arguing that it was both more self-accepting and strategic to be discreet and dress like 'normal' women. See Diana Chapman's accounts in Hall Carpenter Archives, *Inventing Ourselves*, p.55; and Neild and Pearson, *Women Like Us*, pp.40, 101. See also Hamer, *Britannia's Glory*, pp.173–4.
27. Diana Chapman in Hall Carpenter Archives, *Inventing Ourselves*, pp.53–4.
28. Meeker has similarly argued that respectability was a strategy for the Mattachine Society in the 1950s (Meeker, 'Reconsidering the Mattachine Society', p.81).
29. See Melucci, *Nomads of the Present*, chs 2–3 for NSMs' aim of constructing a collective identity. See Thayer, 'Lesbian Movements in Central America' for discussion of a similar process in the lesbian movement in Costa Rica.
30. John Keane and Paul Mier, 'Preface', in Melucci, *Nomads of the Present*.
31. For NSMs' concern with symbolic and cultural practices, see Melucci, *Nomads of the Present*; Nick Crossley, 'Working Utopias and Social Movements: An Investigation Using Case Study Materials from Radical Mental Health Movements in Britain', *Sociology*, vol.33, no.4, November 1999; and Charles, *Feminism, the State and Social Policy*, pp.31–3.
32. Chris Waters, 'Havelock Ellis, Sigmund Freud and the State: Discourses of Homosexual Identity in Interwar Britain', in Lucy Bland and Laura Doan (eds), *Sexology in Culture: Labelling Bodies and Desires*, Cambridge, 1998; *idem*, 'Disorders of the Mind, Disorders of the Body Social: Peter Wildeblood and the Making of the Modern Homosexual', in Becky Conekin, Frank Mort and Chris Waters (eds), *Moments of Modernity: Reconstructing Britain, 1945–1964*, London, 1999.
33. The medical literature on lesbianism has yet to be thoroughly researched for the UK, but see Oram and Turnbull, *Lesbian History Sourcebook*, ch.3. The topic is very neglected compared to the USA, on which see Terry, *An American Obsession*. I would like to thank Chris Waters for discussing my interpretations of this literature.
34. Contemporary doctors commented on the lack of research. See A. Winner, 'Homosexuality in Women', *Medical Press*, vol.218, no.5652, 3 September 1947; and W.L. Neustatter, 'Homosexuality: The Medical Aspects', in J. Tudor Rees and Harley V. Usill (eds), *They Stand Apart: A Critical Survey of the Problems of Homosexuality*, London, 1955.
35. Winner, 'Homosexuality in Women'; 'Medica' [Joan Malleson], *Any Wife or Any Husband*, London, 1950, pp.123–31; British Medical Association, *Homosexuality and Prostitution*, London, 1955, pp.16–19, 48–9; Eustace Chesser, *Odd Man Out: Homosexuality in Men and Women*, London, 1959; Anthony Storr, *Sexual Deviation*, Harmondsworth, 1964, ch.7.
36. BMA, *Homosexuality and Prostitution*, p.18.

37. Chesser, *Odd Man Out*, chs 7–8. Also see Malleson, *Any Wife*; Storr, *Sexual Deviation*; and an American text first published in Britain in 1957, Frank S. Caprio, *Female Homosexuality*, London, 1957. For motherhood avoidance, see Eustace Chesser, *Sexual Behaviour: Normal and Abnormal*, London, 1949, pp.ix, 164–71. There is little commentary on the development of post-war psychoanalytic theory on lesbianism in Britain but see Noreen O'Connor and Joanna Ryan, *Wild Desires and Mistaken Identities: Lesbianism and Psychoanalysis*, London, 1993, pp.192–3.
38. For aversion therapy and lesbians, see M.J. MacCullough and M.P. Feldman, 'Aversion Therapy in Management of 43 Homosexuals', *British Medical Journal*, vol.2, 3 June 1967, pp.594–7; and Gardiner, *From The Closet*, p.42. Luchia Fitzgerald in Jivani, *It's Not Unusual*, pp.126–7, describes narrowly avoiding a lobotomy.
39. Gardiner, *From The Closet*, pp.43–4.
40. Hamer, *Britannia's Glory*, p.177.
41. Diana Chapman in Hall Carpenter Archives, *Inventing Ourselves*, pp.49–50.
42. The latter, to be examined by a graphologist who would also provide individual interpretation, elicited 56 sample letters (*Arena Three*, vol.6, nos.10/11, October/November 1969; *Arena Three*, vol.7, no.1, January 1970). It was reported that most of the analysed 'handwritings' showed much stress and anxiety in relation to social situations, and a considerable incidence of loneliness although the tone of the report was sympathetic (*Arena Three*, vol.7, no.4, April 1970).
43. *Arena Three*, vol.8, no.6, June 1971. This report on the formation of the Federation of Homophile Organisations emphasised the need for more trained counsellors.
44. See for example *Arena Three*, vol.4, no.6, June 1967; *Arena Three*, vol.7, no.6, July 1970. These articles were by 'a well-known psychotherapist' writing under a pseudonym.
45. *Arena Three*, vol.1, no.1, January 1964, p.4; *Arena Three*, vol.3, no.1, January 1966, p.8.
46. *Arena Three*, vol.1, no.1, 1964, p.3. The article 'The Public Image', was by Hilary Benno, a *nom de plume* of Esme Langley.
47. Letter from S.W. of Penzance in *Arena Three*, vol.1, no.6, June 1964, p.13. Also see *Arena Three*, vol.2, no.12, December 1965, p.22; and *Arena Three*, vol.3, no.1, January 1966, p.2.
48. *Arena Three*, vol.1, no.5, May 1964, p.9; *Arena Three*, vol.5, no.1, January 1968, p.3.
49. *Arena Three*, vol.3, no.5, June 1966, p.2. Also see *Arena Three*, vol.5, no.1, January 1968 for an article on medical views of homosexuality which quoted the positive views of a British doctor. The Hooker report of 1970, commissioned by the American ONE Institute, was reviewed favourably in *Arena Three*, vol.7, no.10, October 1970.
50. In the same way homosexual groups in the USA also tried to reshape scientific perspectives and achieve public acceptance through participating in research projects during the 1950s and 1960s (Terry, *An American Obsession*, pp.353–6; Meeker, 'Reconsidering the Mattachine Society', pp.93–4, 99).
51. *Arena Three*, vol.1, no.4, April 1964, pp.9, 11.
52. *Arena Three*, vol.2, no.4, April 1965.
53. Terry suggests a similar context for US groups (Terry, *An American Obsession*, pp.19, 355–6).
54. *Arena Three*, vol.2, no.11, November 1965. The research was published as E. Bene,

'On the Genesis of Female Homosexuality', *British Journal of Psychiatry*, vol.111, no.478, September 1965, pp.815–21.

55. *Arena Three*, vol.3, no.5, June 1966.
56. *Arena Three*, vol.2, no.8, August 1965, p.9.
57. Reported in *Arena Three*, vol.6, no.1, January 1969, pp.10–12. The research was based on 123 lesbians (MRG and Kenric members) and a similar number of married heterosexual women, and published as F.E. Kenyon, 'Physique and Physical Health of Female Homosexuals', *Journal of Neurology, Neurosurgery and Psychiatry*, vol.31, 1968, pp.487–9; and *idem*, 'Studies in Female Homosexuality IV: Social and Psychiatric Aspects', *British Journal of Psychiatry*, vol.114, no.516, November 1968, pp.1337–50.
58. *Arena Three*, vol.6, no.2, February 1969, p.5.
59. *Arena Three*, vol.6, no.4, April 1969, p.3.
60. *Arena Three*, vol.7, no.1, January 1970, p.5; J. Hopkins, 'The Lesbian Personality', *British Journal of Psychiatry*, vol.115, no.529, December 1969, pp.1433–6. Dr Charlotte Wolff also solicited volunteers in 1968 for a book about female homosexuality, later published as *Love Between Women* (*Arena Three*, vol.5, no.5, May 1968).
61. *Arena Three*, vol.7, nos.11/12, November/December 1970, pp.10–11.
62. Terry, *An American Obsession*, pp.17–18, 23, ch.12; Meeker, 'Reconsidering the Mattachine Society', p.99.
63. *Arena Three*, vol.6, no.1, January 1969, pp.10–12.
64. See Smith, *The Queer Sixties*; and Sandra McDermott, *Studies in Female Sexuality*, London, 1970. For the filming of *Sister George*, see Gardiner, *From The Closet To The Screen*, ch.7.
65. *Arena Three*, vol.6, nos.10/11, October/November 1969, pp.6–7; *Arena Three*, vol.7, no.2, February 1970; *Arena Three*, vol.7, no.3, March 1970, p.11. See also *Arena Three*, vol.7, no.4, April 1970 for a report of a Gay Lib conference in Los Angeles.
66. Diana Chapman in Hall Carpenter Archives, *Inventing Ourselves*, p.57.
67. Weeks, *Sex, Politics and Society*, pp.285–6.
68. Lisa Power, *No Bath But Plenty of Bubbles: An Oral History of the Gay Liberation Front, 1970–73*, London, 1995, ch.8; Aubrey Walter (ed.), *Come Together: The Years of Gay Liberation, 1970–3*, London, 1980, pp.47, 52–4.
69. The *Observer*, *Sunday Times*, *Daily Telegraph*, *Daily Mail* and *Guardian* all refused to advertise *Arena Three* at this point, but the *Sunday Telegraph* did carry the ad.
70. *Arena Three*, vol.7, no.7, July 1970, p.6. Also see ibid., p.2.
71. *Arena Three*, vol.7, nos.11/12, November/December 1970, p.17; *Arena Three*, vol.8, no.4, April (actually June) 1971, pp.10–11. *Arena Three*'s advertising manager at the time was Jackie Forster. She was later to found *Sappho*, which continued much of the work of the MRT and *Arena Three*.
72. *Arena Three*, vol.7, no.1, January 1970, pp.6–7.
73. *Arena Three*, vol.7, no.3, March 1970, pp.3–5; *Arena Three*, vol.7, no.2, February 1970, p.5; *Arena Three*, vol.7, no.5, May/June 1970, p.11; *Arena Three*, vol.7, no.6, July 1970, pp.7–9; *Arena Three*, vol.7, nos.11/12, November/December 1970, p.6.
74. This is clear in the published correspondence with Kenric (*Arena Three*, vol.8, no.1, January 1971, p.14). The new editorial group began to build bridges with Kenric at this time.

75. *Arena Three*, vol.7, nos.8/9, September 1970, pp.7–10; *Arena Three*, vol.8, no.1, January 1971, p.16; *Arena Three*, vol.8, no.3, March 1971, p.16. See also Hamer, *Britannia's Glory*, p.184.
76. *Arena Three*, vol.8, no.2, February 1971, pp.12, 16. *Arena Three* also endorsed the gay liberation criticism of David Reuben's book, *Everything You Always Wanted to Know About Sex* for its negative representation of homosexuality—see 'Outspeak', *Arena Three*, vol.8, no.2, February 1971, p.13. *Arena Three* published appeals from GLF groups for more women members (*Arena Three*, vol.8, no.3, March 1971, p.14), and reported their activities in most 1971 issues.
77. *Arena Three*, vol.8, no.6, June 1971, pp.10–11. The Federation was short-lived, bogged down, according to Antony Grey, by its ponderous constitution and the caution of other affiliated groups (Grey, *Quest for Justice*, pp.181–2).
78. *Arena Three*, vol.8, no.3, March 1971, p.12. Announcement of the weekly GLF dance at Middle Earth, Covent Garden, *Arena Three*, vol.8, no.5, May 1971, p.6.
79. The documentary was broadcast on 9 February 1971. See Gardiner, *From The Closet*, pp.111–13 for a discussion of the impact of the film.
80. *Arena Three*, vol.8, no.5, May 1971, p.12.
81. *Arena Three*, vol.8, no.2, February 1971, p.2.
82. Power, *No Bath*, p.307. This gender split occurred somewhat later outside London—for example, in Lancaster and the north-east in early 1974 (information from Carol Smith).
83. *Arena Three*, vol.7, no.5, May/June 1970, p.10; *Arena Three*, vol.8, no.1, January 1971, pp.10–11; *Arena Three*, vol.8, no.2, February 1971, p.18; *Arena Three*, vol.8, no.3, March 1971, p.12.
84. *Arena Three*, vol.8, no.3, March 1971, p.7.
85. Although 2,000 copies were now being printed, sales had not increased sufficiently to cover the costs of the new-style magazine. *Arena Three*, vol.8, no.1, January 1971, p.18; *Arena Three*, vol.8, no.7–12, Summer 1971. For *Sappho*, founded in 1972, see accounts by Diana Chapman in Hall Carpenter Archives, *Inventing Ourselves*, p.56; Jackie Forster in Angela Stewart-Park and Jules Cassidy, *We're Here: Conversations with Lesbian Women*, London, 1977, p.57; Jackie Forster, Ceri Ager and others in Neild and Pearson, *Women Like Us*, pp.41, 93–6.
86. *Arena Three*, vol.2, no.2, February 1965, p.13.

4. Homosexuality, Permissiveness and Morality in France and Britain, 1954–82 **Julian Jackson**

1. 'Marc Daniel' (aka Michel Duchein), *Arcadie*, no.148, April 1966.
2. 'The Collinson Column', *Quorum*, vol.2, no.7, *c*.1974, Hall Carpenter Archives [henceforth HCA], Journals 26.
3. John D'Emilio, *Sexual Politics, Sexual Communities: The Making of a Homosexual Minority in the United States, 1940–1970*, Chicago and London, 1983; Martin Meeker, 'Behind the Mask of Respectability: Reconsidering the Mattachine Society and Male Homophile Practice, 1950s and 1960s', *Journal of the History of Sexuality*, vol.10, no.1, 2001, pp.78–116; Hubert Kennedy, *The Ideal Gay Man: The Story of Der Kreis*, New

York, 1999.

4. See Jacques Girard, *Le Mouvement homosexuel en France, 1945–80*, Paris, 1981; Frédéric Martel, *The Pink and the Black: Homosexuals in France since 1968*, Stanford, CA, 2000; Florence Tamagne, *Histoire de l'homosexualité en Europe: Berlin, Londres, Paris, 1919–39*, Paris, 2000; Jeffrey Merrick and Michael Sibalis (eds), *Homosexuality in French History and Culture*, New York, 2001.
5. Michael Sibalis, 'Gay Paris' in David Higgs (ed.), *Queer Sites: Gay Urban History since 1600*, London, 1999, p.29.
6. Michel Foucault, *Histoire de la sexualité, i: Le Volonté de savoir*, Paris, 1976.
7. Michael Sibalis, 'Homophobia, Vichy France and the "Crime of Homosexuality": The Origins of the Ordinance of 6 August 1942', *GLQ*, vol.8, no.3, 2002, pp.301–18.
8. Jean-Paul Sartre, 'Qu'est qu'un collaborateur?', in *Situations iii*, Paris, 1949, pp.43–61.
9. Daniel Guérin, *Shakespeare et Gide en correctionnelle*, Paris, 1959, pp.93–121.
10. Arcadie was the name of a movement and of the review published by that movement. When referring to the review alone, the name will be italicised.
11. Marcel Jouhandeau, *Carnets de l'écrivain*, Paris, 1957, pp.274–5.
12. 'Allocution Prononcée lors de la présentation des voeux au club', 8 January 1965. Mimeographed circular in my possession [henceforth these circulars in my possession will be referenced: JTJ].
13. Olivier Jablonski, 'The Birth of a French Homosexual Press in the 1950s', in Merrick and Sibalis, *Homosexuality in French Culture*, pp.239–40.
14. *Arcadie*, no.21, November 1955; *Arcadie*, no.22, December 1955. See also the dossier on this affair in the archives of the ICSE in Amsterdam.
15. The letter of 20 July 1960 was attached to the circular of March 1965 [JTJ].
16. 'Contre l'homophilie', *Juventus*, no.4, September 1959.
17. For an excellent overview of the French press in this period, see Jablonski, 'The Birth of a French Homosexual Press'.
18. *Arcadie*, no.96, December 1961.
19. *Arcadie*, nos.115–16, July-August 1963.
20. *Arcadie*, no.40, April 1957.
21. Circular, June 1956 [JTJ].
22. 'Lettre personnelle', December 1965 [JTJ].
23. 'Serge Talbot', *Arcadie*, no.48, December 1957.
24. 'Lettre personnelle', December 1961 [JTJ].
25. *Arcadie*, no.46, June 1958.
26. *Arcadie*, no.3, March 1954.
27. Circular, February 1959 [JTJ].
28. *Arcadie*, no.63, March 1959.
29. René Guyon, 'Les droits humains et le deni de liberté sexuelle', *Arcadie*, no.2, February 1954.
30. *Arcadie*, no.3, March 1954.
31. 'Marc Daniel' (aka Michel Duchein), *Arcadie*, no.100, April 1962.
32. 'Robert Amar', *Arcadie*, no.75, March 1960.
33. *Arcadie*, no.94, November 1961.

34. André Baudry to Paul Mirguet, November 1960, reproduced in 'Lettre personnelle', December 1962 [JTJ].
35. 'A-C. Desmon', *Arcadie*, no.82, October 1960.
36. Circular, December 1964 [JTJ].
37. 'Lettre personnelle', December 1958 [JTJ].
38. Armand Jammot, *Les Homosexuels aux Dossiers de l'Ecran*, Paris, 1975.
39. 'Lettre personnelle', December 1965 [JTJ].
40. Jean Le Bitoux, 'Le Groupe de libération homosexuelle (1975–1978)', *La Revue h*, nos.5–6 (1998), pp.43–52.
41. Interview with Michel Duchein.
42. See Guy Hocquenghem and Jean-Louis Bory, *Comment nous appelez-vous déja?*, Paris, 1977.
43. 'Serge Talbot', *Arcadie*, no.48, December 1957.
44. 'A-C. Desmon', *Arcadie*, no.202, October 1970.
45. See the CUARH's newspaper, *Homophonies*, founded in November 1980.
46. *Gai pied*, no.38, May 1982.
47. On the HLRS see Jeffrey Weeks, *Coming Out: Homosexual Politics in Britain from the Nineteenth Century to the Present*, London, 1977, pp.168–82; Stephen Jeffery-Poulter, *Peers, Queers and Commons: The Struggle for Gay Law Reform from 1950 to the Present*, London, 1991, pp.38–41, 49–50, 85–88; Antony Grey, *Quest for Justice: Towards Homosexual Emancipation*, London, 1992; and Patrick Higgins, *Heterosexual Dictatorship: Male Homosexuality in Postwar Britain*, London, 1996, pp.124–7, 142–4.
48. Antony Grey, *Speaking Out: Writings on Sex, Law, Politics and Society, 1954–95*, London, 1997, pp.218; see also the interview with Grey in *Man and Society*, no.17, February 1973.
49. Grey, *Speaking Out*, p.223.
50. HCA Albany Trust 7/28b, Abse to Grey, 10 March 1967.
51. Grey, *Speaking Out*, p.126.
52. 'Sex, Morality and Happiness', *Man and Society*, no.11, 1969–70.
53. Grey, *Speaking Out*, p.66.
54. See HCA Albany Trust [henceforth AT] 7/3.
55. HCA AT 10/33: Antony Grey, 'Social Organisation for Homosexuals', 2 May 1968.
56. HCA AT 7/29: Arran to Grey, 9 February 1967.
57. HCA AT 7/29: Grey to Arran, 20 February 1967.
58. HCA AT 7/29: 'Note on Arran Intervention on *World at One*'.
59. HCA AT 7/60: Grey to Horsfall, 15 December 1969.
60. Bob Cant and Susan Hemmings, *Radical Records: Thirty Years of Lesbian and Gay History*, London, 1988, pp.15–33.
61. HCA CHE 2/1: Minutes of EC, 5 March 1972.
62. Aubrey Walter (ed.), *Come Together: The Years of Gay Liberation, 1970–3*, London, 1980; Lisa Power, *No Bath But Plenty of Bubbles*, London, 1995.
63. *New Statesman*, January 1971; 'Homophile Liberation', *Man and Society*, no.14, Winter 1973–4.
64. Jeffrey Weeks quoted in Power, *No Bath*, p.30; Walter, *Come Together*, p.16.
65. Antony Grey quoted in Power, *No Bath*, p.11.
66. HCA CHE 5/3: Roger Baker to Alan Horsfall, 7 January 1971.

67. HCA CHE 4/1: 'Gay Lib in London', *Bulletin*, December 1970.
68. HCA CHE 5/4: Paul Temperton to Nick Stanley, 21 June 1971.
69. HCA CHE 5/3: Temperton to Ryle (14/771); HCA CHE 4/1: 'CHE-GLF Rap in Birmingham', *Bulletin*, July 1971; HCA CHE 2/1: Minutes of EC, 17 July 1971.
70. HCA CHE 4/1: 'The Reuben Book Scandal', *Bulletin*, October 1971.
71. HCA CHE 4/1, *Bulletin*, February 1972.
72. HCA CHE 4/1: 'CHE Action Getting under Way', *Bulletin*, February 1972.
73. HCA CHE 4/1, *Bulletin*, October 1971.
74. *Gay News*, no.48, June 1974.
75. Grey, *Quest for Justice*, p.138; *Man and Society*, no.10, Winter 1966; *Gay News*, no.44, 16 May 1974.
76. 'Marc Daniel' (aka Michel Duchein), 'Les Leçons d'un défaite', *Arcadie*, no.50, February 1958; see also his 'Homosexualité et politique électorale en Californie', *Arcadie*, no.76, April 1960.
77. *Quorum*, vol.2, no.7, *c.*1974.
78. See Martel, *The Pink and the Black*, for a controversial denunciation of the dangers of homosexual 'communitarianism' by a gay writer.
79. 'Marc Daniel' (aka Michel Duchein), *Arcadie*, no.129, September 1964.
80. *Libération*, 12 July 1982. The article was signed DE, 'Didier Eribon', but Eribon has subsequently revealed that Foucault was its author.
81. On Foucault and Arcadie, see Didier Eribon, *Michel Foucault et ses contemporains*, Paris, 1994, pp.274–81.

5. *Beatniks, Moral Crusaders, Delinquent Teenagers and Hippies: Accounting for the Counterculture*
Colin Campbell

1. Although the counterculture took somewhat different forms between (and within) North America and Western Europe, its central ingredients included a rejection of all hierarchy, bureaucracy and established forms of authority, coupled with a dismissal of what were perceived to be the values and attitudes of the older generation. In their place, counterculturalists generally sought to construct an 'alternative' society embracing communal events, drug-use, sexual activity, and to a lesser extent, mysticism and meditation. An Underground press, in addition to the crucial role played by rock music, and especially such leading figures as Bob Dylan and the Beatles, helped to bind these various ingredients together. For first-hand accounts of 'the Underground' (as it was called in the UK), see Jeff Nuttall, *Bomb Culture*, London, 1970; and Richard Neville, *Play Power*, London, 1970. For a flavour of the counterculture in the USA, see Abbie Hoffman (aka 'Free'), *Revolution for the Hell of It*, New York, 1968; and Tom Wolfe, *The Electric Kool-Acid Test*, New York, 1968.
2. Most of the material cited is drawn from either the United States or the United Kingdom. For evidence that the cultural revolution was indeed far more widespread than this, especially throughout Europe, see Arthur Marwick, *The Sixties: Cultural Revolution in Britain, France, Italy and the United States, c. 1958–74*, Oxford, 1998.
3. Daniel A. Foss and Ralph W. Larkin distinguish four phases of the movement, covering the period 1950 through to 1970. These they call 'The Old Left' (1950–65);

'The Hippies' (1965–7); 'The New Left' (1967–9), and 'The Woodstock Aquarian Phase' (1969–70). See Daniel A. Foss and Ralph W. Larkin, 'From "The Gates of Eden" to "Day of the Locust"', *Theory and Society*, vol.3, no.1, 1976, pp.45–64. Quite when the counterculture could be said to have ended—or indeed if it has ended even now—are issues that cannot be dealt with in detail here. Several writers have argued that the effects of the 1960s are still being felt today, either in the continuing influence of the 'boomer generation' (see Annie Gottlieb, *Do You Believe in Magic? The Second Coming of the 60s Generation*, New York, 1987), or in continuing 'countercultural' groups such as the New Age Travellers (see Kevin Hetherington, *New Age Travellers: Vanloads of Uproarious Humanity*, London, 2000). Several commentators have noted that the New Age Movement is in fact a direct continuation of the countercultural movement of the 1960s, for which see Paul Heelas, *The New Age Movement: The Celebration of the Self and the Sacralization of Modernity*, Oxford, 1996; and Wouter J. Hanegraaff, *New Age Religion and Western Culture: Esotericism in the Mirror of Secular Thought*, Leiden, 1996.

4. See the discussion in Colin Campbell, *The Romantic Ethic and the Spirit of Modern Consumerism*, Oxford, 1987, pp.195ff.
5. Paul O'Neil, 'The Only Rebellion Around' (1959), in Thomas Parkinson (ed.), *A Casebook On The Beat*, New York, 1961, p.244.
6. See Francis J. Rigney and L. Douglas Smith, *The Real Bohemia: A Sociological and Psychological Study of the 'Beats'*, New York, 1961.
7. Paul McCartney cited in Marwick, *Sixties*, p.59.
8. Beatniks existed in France too, but there the parallel movement among the disaffiliated young was generally known as 'café existentialism', this being the philosophy that had most affinities with Beat attitudes. See Marwick, *Sixties*, p.33.
9. William Burroughs cited in Ann Charters (ed.), *The Beats: Literary Bohemians in Postwar America*, Detroit, MI, 1983, xiii. See also David Matza on the essential differences between political radicalism and bohemianism (David Matza, 'Subterranean Traditions of Youth', *Annals of the American Academy of Political and Social Science*, no.338, 1961, pp.102–18). For an analysis of the Beat movement as 'cultural politics', see Jerold M. Starr, *Cultural Politics: Radical Movements in Modern History*, New York, 1985.
10. Gene Feldman and Max Gartenberg (eds), *The Beat Generation and The Angry Young Men*, New York, 1958, p.17.
11. O'Neil, 'The Only Rebellion Around', p.233.
12. John Barron Mays, *The Young Pretenders: A Study of Teenage Culture in Contemporary Society*, London, 1965, p.230.
13. John Osborne, *Look Back in Anger*, London, 1957, p.34.
14. Ibid., p.89.
15. Feldman and Gartenberg, *The Beat Generation*, p.15.
16. Paul Goodman, *Growing Up Absurd: Problems of Youth in the Organized System*, London, 1961, p.15.
17. Ibid., p.114.
18. Ibid., p.169.
19. Though not all CND supporters were young, John Minnion and Philip Bolsover report that those under 21 accounted for some 40 per cent of participants in the

Aldermaston march of Easter 1959 and that the proportion of young people climbed still higher in later marches (John Minnion and Philip Bolsover [eds], *The CND Story: The First 25 Years of CND in the Words of the People Involved*, London, 1983, p.27). The theologian Kenneth Leech noted a 1959 survey which indicated that nine out of ten young people supported CND 'for moral reasons' (Kenneth Leech, *Youthquake: Spirituality and the Growth of a Counter-Culture*, London, 1976, p.15). For material on CND, see Frank Parkin, *Middle-Class Radicalism: The Social Bases of the British Campaign for Nuclear Disarmament*, Manchester, 1968; Peggy Duff, *Left, Left, Left: A Personal Account of Six Protest Campaigns, 1945–65*, London, 1971; John Mattausch, *A Commitment to Campaign: A Sociological Study of CND*, Manchester, 1989; and Richard Taylor and Colin Pritchard, *The Protest Makers: The British Nuclear Disarmament Movement of 1958–1965, Twenty Years On*, Oxford, 1980. The anti-apartheid movement was also an important cause for this section of young people in the UK.

20. Parkin, *Middle-Class Radicalism*, p.105. For a historical study of unilateralists' moral stance, see Meredith Veldman, *Fantasy, the Bomb and the Greening of Britain: Romantic Protest 1945–1980*, Cambridge, 1994.
21. David Burner, *Making Peace with the 60s*, Princeton, NJ, 1996, p.41.
22. This emphasis on an essentially moral response was very marked even in the writings of those who were consciously striving to create a new political movement. Thus the New Left veterans who contributed to *Out of Apathy* stressed the importance of 'moral intuition' and the role that 'the moral imagination' could play in human history (Robin Archer et al. (eds), *Out of Apathy: Voices of the New Left, Thirty Years On*, London, 1989, p.6).
23. Mays, *The Young Pretenders*, p.32. In the USA there were some 22 million teenagers in 1964 and their numbers were increasing three times faster than the overall population, reaching what one demographer called a 'critical mass…as fissionable as any nuclear pile' (Grace Palladino, *Teenagers: An American History*, New York, 1996, p.195).
24. See Mike Brake, *The Sociology of Youth Culture and Youth Subcultures: Sex and Drugs and Rock 'n' Roll?*, London, 1980.
25. Kenneth Hudson, *The Language of the Teenage Revolution: The Dictionary Defeated*, London, 1983, pp.1–2.
26. Similarly, there had been youth 'gangs' before, although these had been largely a response to poverty and hence the emphasis had been on the material rewards of criminal activity rather than on the need to assert a distinctive, non-adult cultural style.
27. Paul Jacobs and Saul Landau, *The New Radicals: A Report with Documents*, Harmondsworth, 1967, p.70.
28. Sherri Cavan, *Hippies of the Haight*, St Louis, MO, 1972, p.177.
29. Richard Mills, *Young Outsiders: A Study of Alternative Communities*, London, 1973, p.51.
30. These differences were often obscured by left-wing writers who tended to idolise working-class 'rebels', imputing an inchoate political consciousness and radical motivation to actions that were expressive of little more than boredom and a desire to shock combined with a peer group ethic which stressed 'macho' values. See for example Stuart Hall's assertion that 'young working-class people' were instinctively 'radical' (Stuart Hall, 'Politics of Adolescence?', *Universities and Left Review*, no.6, 1959, p.3. For an account of the real, and essentially apolitical, stance of 'young

working-class people' see Matza, 'Subterranean Traditions').

31. See below for a discussion of their reaction to Dylan's 'apostasy'. In the 1950s it was automatic, as Anthony Scaduto puts it, that 'The folkies [the folk singers and their followers] sneered at rock' (Anthony Scaduto, *Bob Dylan* [rev. edn], London, 1973, p.29).
32. Tuli Kupferberg cited in Bruce Cook, *The Beat Generation*, New York, 1971, p.225.
33. It is important to recognise that this rapprochement was in many ways more apparent than real, for much still separated middle-class and working-class youth. In particular there were crucial features of the teenage-delinquent subculture that played little part in the lives of either Beat-bohemians or moral crusaders. The central role accorded to violence, in the male version of this subculture at least, is an obvious case in point, the majority of the latter being self-declared pacifists. At the same time, the two middle-class groups did not share the chauvinism, the homophobia, or the racism of the typical rocker, while the delinquents did not share middle-class students' relative indifference to wealth or the acquisition of status-signifying consumer goods.
34. For an account of the evolution of the protest song, see R. Serge Denisoff, 'The Evolution of the American Protest Song', in R. Serge Denisoff and Richard A. Peterson (eds), *The Sound of Social Change*, New York, 1972.
35. Hudson, *Language of the Teenage Revolution*, p.28.
36. George Melly, *Revolt into Style: The Pop Arts in Britain*, London, 1970, p.36.
37. Music writer Charlie Gillett estimates that the changeover from rock 'n' roll to rock music occurred sometime between 1958—which is when he judged rock 'n' roll proper to have petered out—and 1964, which is when rock music proper came into existence (Charlie Gillett, *The Sound of The City: The Rise of Rock and Roll*, New York, 1970, p.1).
38. Paul Willis, *Profane Culture*, London, 1978, p.164.
39. Arnold Shaw, *The Rock Revolution*, London, 1969, p.2.
40. See Edward Lee, *Music of the People: A Study of Popular Music in Great Britain*, London, 1970, p.197.
41. Denisoff, 'Evolution', p.124.
42. See Scaduto, *Bob Dylan*, p.213; and Gillett, *Sound of The City*, p.326.
43. According to Arnold Shaw, members of the audience actually threw things at the stage (Shaw, *Rock Revolution*, p.54).
44. Ibid., p.188. Emphases in original.
45. Palladino, *Teenagers*, p.195.
46. Lois Rather, *Bohemians to Hippies: Waves of Rebellion*, Oakland, CA, 1977, p.112.

Mark Jones

6. Down the Rabbit Hole: Permissiveness and Paedophilia in the 1960s

1. Eustace Chesser, *Is Chastity Outmoded?*, London, 1960.
2. This phrase was in Carstairs's draft of his talk, and was widely quoted in the press, but was not in the broadcast version. The talks were published as G.M. Carstairs, *This Island Now*, London, 1963.
3. John A.T. Robinson, *Honest to God*, London, 1963, p.105.

4. Paul Johnson, 'The Menace of Beatlism' (1964), in Hanif Kureishi and Jon Savage (eds), *The Faber Book of Pop*, London, 1995, p.197. The reason for this apparent indolence might have been revealed elsewhere: 'John [Lennon] said that they have been told that girls masturbate when they are on stage' (Michael Braun, *'Love Me Do!': The Beatles' Progress*, Harmondsworth, 1965, p.32).
5. Mary Whitehouse, *Who Does She Think She Is?* (rev. edn), London, 1972, pp.138–9.
6. Peter Laurie, *The Teenage Revolution*, London, 1965, pp.151, 152.
7. Tony Palmer, *The Trials of Oz*, London, 1971, p.185.
8. See the relevant discussions in John Sutherland, *Offensive Literature: Decensorship in Britain, 1960–1982*, London, 1982: on IT, pp.104–7; *The Little Red Schoolbook*, pp.111–16; *Oz*, pp.117–26; and *Nasty Tales*, pp.132–4.
9. Vladimir Nabokov, *Lolita*, London, 1959 (orig. Paris, 1955).
10. See Harry Hendrick, *Child Welfare: England 1872–1989*, London, 1994, pp.242–57.
11. Dianne Doubtfire, *Lust for Innocence*, London, 1964 (orig. London, 1960). Doubtfire wrote a number of other crime novels in the 1960s, children's books in the 1970s, and writers' guides in the 1980s.
12. Ibid., pp.52, 75.
13. Ibid., pp.87–8.
14. Ibid., p.112.
15. Pamela Hansford Johnson, *On Iniquity: Some Personal Reflections Arising Out of the Moors Murder Trial*, London, 1967.
16. Emlyn Williams, *Beyond Belief: A Chronicle of Murder and Its Detection*, London, 1967.
17. Peter Loughran, *The Train Ride*, New York, 1968 (orig. London, 1966). Loughran did not publish another book until two horror novels appeared in the 1980s. The protagonist of *The Third Beast*, London, 1987, commits several murders to revenge the killing of his thirteen-year-old niece.
18. Loughran, *The Train Ride*, pp.120–1.
19. Ibid., p.123.
20. Marianne Sinclair, *Watcher in the Park*, London, 1971 (orig. London, 1968). Sinclair wrote an earlier novel in which an adolescent girl is sexually abused—*Paradox Lost*, London, 1963—and has published several books on film, including *Hollywood Lolita: A Study of the Nymphet Syndrome in the Movies*, London, 1988.
21. Sinclair, *Watcher*, p.13.
22. Ibid., p.26.
23. Ibid., p.69.
24. Ibid., p.86.
25. Ibid., p.139.
26. Leslie Thomas, *His Lordship*, London, 1972 (orig. London, 1970), p.143.
27. Ibid.
28. Kenneth C. Barnes, *He and She*, London, 1958, p.121.
29. John James, *The Facts of Sex*, London, 1969, p.31. I am indebted to Hera Cook for this reference.
30. John London, *Seductions*, London, 1970 (orig. New York, 1969), p.13.
31. Ibid., p.17.
32. Tina Chad Christian, *Baby Love*, London, 1969 (orig. London, 1968), back cover. *Baby Love* was filmed by Alistair Reid in 1969. Luci is fifteen in the film.

33. Christian, *Baby Love*, p.54.
34. Ibid., p.132.
35. Ibid., p.81.
36. John Farris, *Harrison High*, London, 1961 (orig. New York, 1959), back cover.
37. For 'child-women' in 1960s soft-core pornography, see Marcus Collins, *Modern Love: An Intimate History of Men and Women in Twentieth-Century Britain*, London, 2003, pp.151–2.
38. 'In the course of several marketing reviews by our international Publishing Group, it became fairly clear that there had developed in recent years an interesting social phenomenon, that is, a substantial interest by a substantial number of men-at-large in what could be loosely termed the "schoolgirl"' (Gunilla Jorgens in *Schoolgirl Sex*, London, 1971, n.p.).
39. Jason Douglas in ibid., n.p.
40. See Tim Tate, *Child Pornography: An Investigation*, London, 1990, pp.33–69.
41. The Who, 'Fiddle About' (John Entwhistle), *Tommy*, Track, 1969; Jethro Tull, 'Aqualung' (Ian Anderson), *Aqualung*, Reprise, 1971; John's Children, 'Sarah Crazy Child' (Marc Bolan), b-side of 'Come And Play With Me In The Garden', Track, 1967; Donovan, 'Mellow Yellow' (Donovan Leitch), Epic, 1966 (also on *Mellow Yellow*, Epic, 1967); Donovan, 'Superlungs My Supergirl' (Donovan Leitch), *Barabajagal*, Epic, 1969; Van Morrison, 'Cyprus Avenue' (Van Morrison), *Astral Weeks*, Warner Brothers, 1968; Blind Faith, *Blind Faith*, Polydor, 1969.
42. The Rolling Stones: 'Family' (Mick Jagger/Keith Richards), *Metamorphosis*, Decca, 1975 (recorded in 1968); 'Cocksucker Blues' (Jagger/Richards), *The Rest of the Best*, Teldec, 1984 (aka 'Schoolboy Blues', recorded in 1970); 'Stray Cat Blues' (Jagger/Richards), Beggars Banquet, Decca, 1968. It should be noted that 'Stray Cat Blues' does not specify the gender of the child and some commentators believe it to be a boy, and that in live performances of the period the age is changed from fifteen to thirteen, as can be heard in the version on *Get Yer Ya-Ya's Out*, Decca, 1970.
43. Guy Peellaert and Nik Cohn, *Rock Dreams*, London, 1974, n.p.; The Rolling Stones, *It's Only Rock* 'n' *Roll*, Rolling Stones Records, 1974.
44. William Bloom, *A Canterbury Tale: A Game for Children*, London, 1973 (orig. London, 1971), back cover. Ellipses in original. Kelvin is actually seventeen at the novel's opening, and Jenny is thirteen. Bloom is now a writer on holistic spirituality and health.
45. Bloom, *A Canterbury Tale*, p.59.
46. Richard Neville, *Play Power*, London, 1971 (orig. London, 1970), p.60.
47. *Pornography: The Longford Report*, London, 1972, p.313.
48. Germaine Greer, 'Seduction is a four-letter word' (1973), in *The Madwoman's Underclothes: Essays and Occasional Writings 1968–1985*, London, 1986, p.154.
49. Valida Davila, 'A Child's Sexual Bill of Rights', in Jeanne Paslé-Green and Jim Haynes (eds), *Hello I Love You! A Collection of Voices*, Paris, 1975 (orig. Paris, 1974), p.29.
50. Tom O'Carroll, *Paedophilia: The Radical Case*, London, 1980, pp.207–17. For a survey of attempts by paedophile rights campaigners to gain support within gay, lesbian, feminist and socialist movements, see Sheila Jeffreys, *Anticlimax: A Feminist Perspective on the Sexual Revolution*, London, 1990, pp.188–210.
51. There is no mention of child sexual abuse in David Holbrook's otherwise compre-

hensive attack on permissiveness, *Sex and Dehumanization in Art, Thought and Life in Our Time*, London, 1972, or of child pornography in *idem* (ed.), *The Case Against Pornography*, London, 1972.

52. '[I]f "maturity" is to be measured by our ability to ignore what may be happening between a man and a child in a dark alley then Heaven save us from it.' (Whitehouse, *Who Does She Think She Is?*, p.102). It is the only reference to paedophilia in the book.
53. Mary Whitehouse, *Whatever Happened to Sex?*, London, 1978 (orig. Hove, 1977), p.73.
54. Ian McEwan, 'Butterflies', in *First Love, Last Rites*, London, 1975; *idem*, 'In Between the Sheets', in *In Between the Sheets*, London, 1978.
55. *Straw Dogs*, dir. Sam Peckinpah, 1971. Adapted from Gordon M. Williams, *The Siege of Trencher's Farm*, London, 1969.
56. The film makes some significant changes to Williams's novel, most particularly in the characters of Henry Niles and his victim, Janice Heddon. In the original, Niles is a convicted, escaped, multiple child murderer, and Janice is an eight-year-old mentally disabled child; in the film it is suggested that he has only once before molested a child, and she is a flirtatious teenager, who attempts to seduce Sumner and makes sexual advances to Niles.
57. *Get Carter*, dir. Mike Hodges, 1971. Adapted from Ted Lewis, *Jack's Return Home*, London, 1970.
58. *The Offence*, dir. Sidney Lumet, 1973. Adapted from a 1968 stage play by John Hopkins, *This Story of Yours*, Harmondsworth, 1969.
59. Jack Sargeant, introduction to Peter Whitehead, *Baby Doll*, London, 1996, n.p.
60. Sargeant refers to '[I]conography which is also strangely reminiscent of John Tenniel's of the child Alice in Lewis Carrol's [sic] *Alice in Wonderland*', and Sinclair to 'the masked child who is not a child' (Whitehead, *Baby Doll*, n.p).
61. Whitehead's 1960's films include *Wholly Communion* (1965), which documented the International Poetry Incarnation at the Royal Albert Hall; *Charlie is My Darling* (1966), following the Rolling Stones during a tour of Ireland; *Tonite Let's All Make Love in London* (1967), featuring Pink Floyd and assorted other swingers and heads; *Benefit of the Doubt* (1967), about the Peter Brook/Royal Shakespeare Company production of *US*; and *The Fall* (1968), including footage of the Columbia University student protests within a fictional self-dramatisation.
62. *Daddy*, dir. Peter Whitehead and Niki De Saint Phalle, 1973. Co-director De Saint Phalle was abused by her father when she was eleven (Niki De Saint Phalle, *Mon Secret*, Paris, 1994; *idem*, *Traces: An Autobiography Remembering 1930–1949*, New York, 2000).
63. Peter Whitehead, *Nora and…*, London, 1990.
64. The phrase and its tripartite concept of late 1960s reality is J. G. Ballard's, from an interview with Brendan Hennessy in *Transatlantic Review*, no.39, 1971, pp.62–3.
65. Peter Whitehead, *Tonite Let's All Make Love in London*, Pytchley, 1999.
66. Gordon Burn, *Alma Cogan: A Novel*, London, 1991; Simon Mawer, *The Fall*, London, 2003; David Peace, *Nineteen Seventy-Four*, London, 1999.
67. Nicci French, *The Memory Game*, London, 1997.

7. *Rupert Bare: Art, Obscenity and the Oz Trial* Gerry Carlin

1. Cited in John Sutherland, *Offensive Literature: Decensorship in Britain, 1960–1982*, London, 1982, pp.120–1. Editor Richard Neville was no stranger to obscenity charges—the earlier Sydney edition of *Oz* had been found guilty of obscenity in late 1963. See Neville, *Hippie Hippie Shake*, London, 1996, ch.2.
2. The defence's insistence that the trial had 'nothing to do with obscenity' was proclaimed on a Friends of *Oz*/Independence Day Carnival poster that appeared in June 1971.
3. Barry Miles, *In the Sixties*, London, 2002, p.139; *idem* cited in Jonathon Green, *Days in the Life: Voices From the English Underground, 1961–71*, London, 1988, p.145.
4. Beth Bailey, 'Sex as a Weapon: Underground Comix and the Paradox of Liberation', in Peter Braunstein and Michael William Doyle (eds), *Imagine Nation: The American Counterculture of the 1960s and '70s*, New York and London, 2002, p.306. On the precariousness of the hippie sense of a 'symbolically shared' community, see Paul Willis, *Profane Culture*, London, 1978, pp.111–14. The internationalism of the Underground press would be ensured by organisations such as the Underground Press Syndicate and Liberation News Service, which allowed material to be freely circulated between Europe and the US; see Richard Neville, *Play Power*, London, 1970, pp.151–3.
5. Warren Hague, 'Love, Peace, Acid, Beads, Crashpads, Lightshows, Arts Labs, Karma, Incense, Grateful Dead & Far Out!', *Oz*, no.42, May/June 1972, p.54.
6. *IT*, no.56, 9–22 May 1969 had run a similarly worded editorial after a police raid on its offices: 'If you want revolution—sexual freedom, freedom of thought, freedom to discover who you really are—in short, if you want a new world and won't settle for less, then these journals are your only overt communications media.'
7. The call for young editors appears in *Oz*, no.26, February/March 1970, p.46. Incidentally, the response to this call suggests that *Oz* already had a young readership, and wasn't necessarily trying to acquire one through a 'kids' edition.
8. Richard Neville cited in Tony Palmer, *The Trials of Oz*, London, 1971, p.35. See also 'A Draft Charter of Children's Rights', *Oz*, no.36, July 1971, pp.26–7.
9. Images from Crumb's pen were pretty ubiquitous in *Oz* and, as I mention later, the British 'Adult Comix' *Nasty Tales* would face similar obscenity charges over a reproduced Crumb drawing two years after the *Oz* trial.
10. 'Eggs Ackley Among the Vulture Demonesses' is reprinted in Gary Groth (ed.), *The Complete Crumb Comics Volume 6*, Seattle, 1991, pp.8–22.
11. The cartoon appears in *Oz*, no.28, May 1970, pp.14–15. The fact that Rupert is having sex with a 'vulture demoness' isn't apparent in the *Oz* montage and didn't arise as an issue at the trial. The prosecution *did* assume, however illogically, that one of the Rupert captions referring to 'Gypsy Granny' did describe the (faceless) female in question, and suggested that Rupert was having sex with an elderly woman. See Palmer, *The Trials of Oz*, p.92.
12. Roger Lewis, *Outlaws of America: The Underground Press and Its Context—Notes On a Cultural Revolution*, Harmondsworth, 1972, p.47. On comics in the British Underground, see esp. David Huxley, *Nasty Tales: Sex, Drugs, Rock 'n' Roll and Violence in*

the British Underground, Manchester, 2001; and Robert Dickinson, *Imprinting the Sticks: The Alternative Press Beyond London*, Aldershot, 1997, ch.3.

13. Oscar Wilde cited in Adam Parfrey, *Modernism and the Theater of Censorship*, New York and Oxford, 1996, p.8. See also H. Montgomery Hyde, *The Trials of Oscar Wilde*, New York, 1973, p.201.
14. There are interesting parallels here with slightly later debates around the issue of American pop music. Progressive and influential intellectuals like Richard Hoggart, Raymond Williams and E.P. Thompson warned against the colonisation and erasure of indigenous popular culture by such American imports, citing native working-class venues like the music hall and the pub as the true sites of indigenous creativity and value. On this opposition, see Robert Hewison, *Too Much: Art and Society in the Sixties, 1960–75*, London, 1986, ch.1. For an extended treatment of the comics campaign, see Martin Barker, *A Haunt of Fears: The Strange History of the British Horror Comics Campaign*, London and Sydney, 1984.
15. See Miles, *In the Sixties*, pp.301–2; and Alan Travis, *Bound and Gagged: A Secret History of Obscenity in Britain*, London, 2000, pp.233–4.
16. Mary Whitehouse, *Whatever Happened to Sex?*, London, 1978, pp.233, 235; Ross McWhirter cited in Michael Tracey and David Morrison, *Whitehouse*, Basingstoke, 1979, p.137.
17. See Roger Hutchinson, *High Sixties: The Summers of Riot and Love*, Edinburgh, 1992, p.146. Inspector Luff is cited in Jim Anderson's unpublished memoir of the trial; many thanks to Jonathon Green for this material. Ironically, one major by-product of the *Oz* and other underground obscenity trials would be to expose the corruption in the obscene publications squad itself. See for example Travis, *Bound and Gagged*, ch. 9.
18. Palmer, *The Trials of Oz*, p.134.
19. Neville, *Play Power*, p.19.
20. Mary Whitehouse cited in Tracey and Morrison, *Whitehouse*, p.89.
21. John Trevelyan, *What the Censor Saw*, London, 1973, pp.180–231.
22. John Wolfenden, 'The Permissive Society', *Proceedings of the Royal Institution of Great Britain*, vol.46, 1973, pp.27, 33–4.
23. Pierre Bourdieu, *Distinction: A Social Critique of the Judgement of Taste*, London, 1986, pp.365–71.
24. Neville, *Play Power*, p.158.
25. See '*Oz* Sucks…', *Oz*, no.28, May 1970, pp.30–2; and Palmer, *The Trials of Oz*, pp.54–8.
26. Cited in Neville, *Hippie Hippie Shake*, p.292. The *Suck* ad appears in *Oz*, no.28, May 1970, p.28.
27. Palmer, *The Trials of Oz*, pp.170–1. After the trial, Neville would specifically condemn this separation when he wrote: 'Future Underground Press trials are bound to be nasty, brutish and short. Expert witnesses are virtually *persona non grata* and the publication in question can no longer be taken "as a whole". Rupert Bear can now be isolated and stamped upon without the surrounding textual terrain being taken into account' (Richard Neville, 'Letter From Our Founder', *Oz*, no.39, December 1971, pp.2–3).
28. On the role of 'Pop' art and design in this breakdown of traditional cultural distinctions, see Alex Seago, *Burning the Box of Beautiful Things: The Development of a Postmodern*

Sensibility, Oxford and New York, 1995.

29. See Neville, *Hippie Hippie Shake*, p.127. The next issue of *Oz* would ironically advertise the 'artistic' form of *Oz*, no.16 by calling it 'The worst-selling, most praised *Oz* ever' (*Oz*, no.17, December 1968, p.3).
30. See Rosalind Krauss, 'The Photographic Conditions of Surrealism', in *The Originality of the Avant-Garde and Other Modernist Myths*, Cambridge, MA and London, 1986.
31. Norbert Lynton, 'Saints and Jesters', in *The Permissive Society: The Guardian Enquiry*, London, 1969, pp.109, 110.
32. Jeff Nuttall, *Bomb Culture*, London, 1968, esp. section III.
33. Marcel Duchamp, 'The Creative Act', reprinted in Calvin Tomkins, *Duchamp: A Biography*, London, 1997, pp.509–10.
34. Vivian Berger cited in Palmer, *The Trials of Oz*, p.71.
35. On the ironic historical distance achieved by the period's 'retrochic' styles, see Raphael Samuel, *Theatres of Memory, i: Past and Present in Contemporary Culture*, London, 1994, p.95. On the role of *bricolage* in subcultural expression, see Dick Hebdige, *Subculture: The Meaning of Style*, London, 1979. In an early paper, Stuart Hall makes an interesting distinction between American and British psychedelic fashion, suggesting that while American youth culture is driven by middle-class aspirations to dress *down* and identify with 'the poor', British youth culture 'is still, primarily, the preserve of working-class kids' whose aspirations to flamboyant stylishness represent 'the "soul-movements" of a previously deprived group'. See Hall, 'The Hippies: An American "Moment"', *Centre for Contemporary Cultural Studies Stencilled Occasional Paper*, Birmingham, 1968, p.5.
36. Simon Frith and Howard Horne suggest that 'Reading Blake's *Sgt. Pepper* sleeve—name the faces, spot the cannabis, decode the lyrics—was like reading the underground press' (*Art Into Pop*, London and New York, 1989, p.57). Jeff Nuttall makes the point about certain arrangements of characters being culturally 'disallowed' when discussing the extended catalogue of artists and thinkers that constitute Adrian Henri's poem 'Me' in Nuttall, *Bomb Culture*, pp.132–3. For a discussion of 'historical pastiche' with specific reference to the Beatles, see Bob Neaverson, *The Beatles Movies*, London and Washington, DC, 1997, pp.85–6.
37. George Melly, *Revolt into Style: The Pop Arts in Britain*, Harmondsworth, 1970, pp.8–9.
38. See for example Simon Reynolds, 'Return to Eden: Innocence, Indolence and Pastoralism in Psychedelic Music, 1966–96', in Antonio Melechi (ed.), *Psychedelia Britannica: Hallucinogenic Drugs in Britain*, London, 1997.
39. Jon Savage, 'The Psychedelic 100', in James Henke and Parke Puterbaugh (eds), *I Want To Take You Higher: The Psychedelic Era, 1965–1969*, San Francisco, 1997, p.195. Similar scepticism about childhood emerged in American psychedelia, where the Jefferson Airplane's tribute to Lewis Carroll's Alice books, 'White Rabbit', suggests that the magical transformations that pervade the childhood imagination are forbidden in the grey adult world.
40. See Neville, *Hippie Hippie Shake*, p.343, and Palmer, *The Trials of Oz*, pp.168–9.
41. Palmer, *The Trials of Oz*, pp.92, 234. Neville paraphrases Lawrence's own pleas for *Chatterley* as 'an honest, healthy book' which wants 'men and women to be able to think sex, fully, completely, honestly and cleanly'; see D.H. Lawrence, 'À Propos of

Lady Chatterley's Lover', in *A Selection from Phoenix*, Harmondsworth, 1971, pp.329–30. Such entreaties were a key feature of the Chatterley defence; see C.H. Rolph, *The Trial of Lady Chatterley: Regina* v. *Penguin Books Limited*, Harmondsworth, 1961, pp.175–205.

42. Palmer, *The Trials of Oz*, p.194; editorial from the *Daily Mirror* cited in ibid., p.234.
43. *Oz*, no.27, April 1970, pp.24–5. These and other photographs had already appeared in 'The Virgin Forest: Photographs by Thomas Weir', *Avant-Garde*, no.10, January 1970, pp.10–17.
44. Charles Shaar Murray, 'Brown Shoes Don't Make It', *Oz*, no.28, May 1970, p.22. Murray would later become an established music journalist and author.
45. Herbert Marcuse, *One Dimensional Man*, London, 1968, p.71. Marcuse would define repressive desublimation as the 'flattening out' of all radical challenges to the dominant culture through 'their wholesale incorporation into the established order, through their reproduction and display on a massive scale' (p.58). On the influence of Marcuse, see Hewison, *Too Much*, pp.136–8.
46. *Oz*, no.24, October/November 1969. The Crumb cartoon is reproduced from *Snatch Comics*, no.1, 1968, the same issue that *Nasty Tales* would later plunder. The phrase 'Jail Bait of the Month' would resurface in *Oz*, no.28 on a photograph of an actual schoolgirl (p.7), and the prosecution would pick up on this promotion of sex 'below the age of consent' (Palmer, *The Trials of Oz*, p.192).
47. David Widgery, 'What Went Wrong', *Oz*, no.48, Winter 1973, pp.8–9, 66.
48. See Nigel Fountain, *Underground: The London Alternative Press, 1966–74*, London and New York, 1988, p.144; and Marsha Rowe, 'Up From Down Under', in Sara Maitland, *Very Heaven: Looking Back at the 1960s*, London, 1988, p.163.
49. Aubrey Walter (ed.), *Come Together: The Years of Gay Liberation, 1970–3*, London, 1980, pp.114–16.
50. Frith and Horne, *Art Into Pop*, p.55.
51. Marsha Rowe (ed.), *Spare Rib Reader*, Harmondsworth, 1982, p.13.

8. *'Questioning and Dancing on the Table': The Ludic Liberalism of Richard Neville*
Rychard Carrington

1. For a commentary upon the *Oz* trial, see Gerry Carlin's chapter in this volume.
2. Both of these comments appear on the cover of the paperback edition of Richard Neville, *Play Power*, London, 1971.
3. Angela Carter, 'Truly, It Felt Like Year One', in Sarah Maitland (ed.), *Very Heaven: Looking Back at the 1960s*, London, 1988, p.212; Jonathon Green, *All Dressed Up: The Sixties and the Counterculture*, London, 1998, p.360.
4. Julie Stephens, *Anti-Disciplinary Protest: Sixties Radicalism and Postmodernism*, Cambridge, 1998, p.80.
5. E-mail to the author, 6 June 2001; Neville cited in Nigel Fountain, *Underground: The London Alternative Press, 1966–74*, London, 1988, p.57.
6. Herbert Marcuse, 'Repressive Tolerance', in Robert Paul Wolff, Barrington Moore, Jr and Herbert Marcuse, *A Critique of Pure Tolerance*, Boston, 1965, pp.81–117.
7. David Steigerwald, *The Sixties and the End of Modern America*, New York, 1995, p.135.

8. Ibid., p.136; Abbie Hoffman (aka 'Free'), *Revolution for the Hell of It*, New York, 1968, esp. pp.65–6.
9. Richard Neville, *Hippie Hippie Shake*, London, 1995, p.86.
10. E-mail to the author, 6 June 2001.
11. Neville, *Hippie Hippie Shake*, pp.86–7.
12. Ibid., p.95.
13. Neville cited in Fountain, *Underground*, p.57.
14. R.D. Laing, *The Politics of Experience and The Bird of Paradise*, Harmondsworth, 1967, p.15.
15. See Tony Palmer, *The Trials of Oz*, London, 1971.
16. This relationship has been well explored in an American context by Thomas Frank in *The Conquest of Cool: Business Culture, Counterculture and the Rise of Hip Consumerism*, Chicago, 1997.
17. Neville cited in Green, *All Dressed Up*, p.137.
18. Ferrier cited in Neville, *Hippie Hippie Shake*, p.205.
19. Neville cited in Carol Sarler, 'A Moral Issue', *Sunday Times Magazine*, 9 June 1991.
20. Richard Neville, 'Nowhere to Go' (1972), in *Out of My Mind*, London, 1996, p.5.
21. *Idem*, *Play Power*, pp.207, 18, 70; *idem*, *Hippie Hippie Shake*, p.83.
22. *Idem*, *Play Power*, p.228.
23. Kenneth Tynan, 'A Few Million Spermatozoa', *Observer*, 22 February 1970.
24. Clive James, 'Cuter Than A Cub Koala: Richard Neville's *Play Power*' (1970), in *The Metropolitan Critic: Non-Fiction, 1968–73* [rev. edn], London, 1994, pp.204–5.
25. Richard Neville, 'All Of God's Children Got De Clap', *Oz*, no.31, December 1970.
26. Neville, *Play Power*, p.227.
27. Neville cited in Palmer, *The Trials of Oz*, p.224.
28. For the Angry Brigade, see Tom Vague, *Anarchy in the UK: The Angry Brigade*, Edinburgh, 1997; and Gordon Carr, *The Angry Brigade: The Cause and the Case*, London, 1975.
29. Neville cited in Fountain, *Underground*, p.126. Despite his later criticism of the second-wave feminism, Neville wrote a review castigating *Cosmopolitan* in the first issue of *Spare Rib* in 1972. Jeffrey Weeks describes a similar relationship between the Underground and the Gay Liberation Movement (Jeffrey Weeks, *Coming Out: Homosexual Politics in Britain from the Nineteenth Century to the Present* [rev. edn], London, pp.187–8).
30. Neville, *Out of My Mind*, p.4.
31. Neville cited in Jonathon Green, *Days in the Life: Voices from the English Underground, 1961–1971*, London, 1988, p.341.
32. Neville cited in Green, *Days in the Life*, p.341.
33. Richard Neville, 'From Utopia to Bloomingdales' (1976), in *Out of My Mind*, p.19.
34. Mortimer cited in Palmer, *The Trials of Oz*, p.202.
35. Arthur Marwick, *The Sixties: Cultural Revolution in Britain, France, Italy and the United States, c.1958–c.1974*, Oxford, 1998, p.13.
36. Ibid., p.13.
37. Roy Jenkins, *The Labour Case*, Harmondsworth, 1959, p.135.
38. Neville cited in Green, *Days in the Life*, p.128.
39. Hard statistical evidence that changes in the cultural landscape were matched by

changes of attitude in the population at large is hard to come by, especially for the years preceding Social and Community Planning Research's annual *British Social Attitudes* reports, first published in 1984. Some evidence for a marked increase in 'permissive' attitudes is provided in Christie Davies, *Permissive Britain: Social Change in the Sixties and Seventies*, London, 1975.

9. *The Revolutionary Left and the Permissive Society*
Willie Thompson and Marcus Collins

1. See Arthur Marwick, *The Sixties: Cultural Revolution in Britain, France, Italy and the United States, c.1958–c.1974*, Oxford, 1998.
2. Alan McGlashen wrote in 1963 (admittedly of the interwar period) that 'English youth…plunged gaily enough into the sexually permissive society which was thus created', while Geoffrey Gorer used the word 'permissiveness' in the sense of morality in 1955 (Alan McGlashen, 'Sex on These Islands', in Arthur Koestler (ed.), *Suicide of a Nation?*, London, 1963, pp.205–6; Geoffrey Gorer, *Exploring English Character*, London, 1955, p.95).
3. The same has been largely true elsewhere apart from one major reversal in the US—the reintroduction of executions (on an informally racially discriminatory basis).
4. For the Communist Party during this period, see John Callaghan, *Cold War, Crisis and Conflict: The History of the Communist Party of Great Britain, 1951–68*, London, 2003.
5. The CPGB, though it declined in overall numbers, in other respects shared in the growth of the revolutionary left at this time.
6. See John Callaghan, *The Far Left in British Politics*, Oxford, 1987.
7. Western commentators at the time, with the initial Soviet successes in the space race seeming to give substance to Khrushchev's extravagant prognostications, frequently conceded the superiority of the Soviet-style planned economy.
8. The renowned biographer of Trotsky and Stalin, Isaac Deutscher, held this view and was respected widely on the left.
9. The IS distinguished itself with its theory that communist regimes were not 'degenerate workers' states' (the orthodox Trotskyist position) but a form of 'state capitalism'.
10. Many other large demonstrations also occurred—those from 1961 at the US naval base in the Holy Loch were especially important.
11. On drugs, see Jonathon Green, *All Dressed Up: The Sixties and the Counterculture*, London, 1998, pp.173–201; and Marwick, *Sixties*, pp.78, 480ff. The initial Communist Party attitude to drugs was very hostile and occasional attempts in the earlier 1960s to propose the legalisation of cannabis were always overwhelmingly defeated at its congresses.
12. It was around this point that the YCL reached its peak of approximately 5000 members. Yet Mike Waite, author of the most comprehensive account of the YCL, comments that 'The goals and outlooks formed by participants in youth subcultures seemed anarchistic, individualistic and just too new when set against the enduring traditional concerns of the left' (Mike Waite, 'Young People and Formal Political Activity: A Case Study: Young People and Communist Politics in Britain,

1920–1991: Aspects of the History of the Young Communist League', University of Lancaster MPhil Thesis, 1992, p.335).

13. The SLL was dictatorially led by the sinister Gerry Healy, who regarded all Trotskyites not aligned with him as heretics and renegades.
14. The New Left has been discussed extensively in print. For the original New Left, see e.g. Lin Chun, *The British New Left*, Edinburgh, 1993; and Michael Kenny, *The First New Left: British Intellectuals after Stalin*, London, 1995. For the *New Left Review* after 1963, see Duncan Thompson, 'Pessimism of the Intellect?', *Socialist History*, no.20, 2001, pp.19–39.
15. In Glasgow, a major CP stronghold with 2000 members, the leadership were very nervous about the impetuosity of the YCL, but tolerated it so long as its political orthodoxy remained unquestioned.
16. This initiative aroused some vociferous objections. It was excused on the grounds that the band had given an interview to the paper.
17. The leaflet is used as part of the cover illustration of the recently published final volume of the CP's history, Geoff Andrews, *Endgames and New Times: The Final Years of British Communism 1964–1991*, London, 2004.
18. Not long afterwards, however, even leading YCLers and young party members were experimenting with cannabis and LSD. One was even a pusher, though he was never caught (personal record).
19. Barney Davis, 'British Youth—Progressive, Reactionary or Indifferent?', *Marxism Today*, April 1966, pp.76–82.
20. Precise numbers are difficult to estimate—the figures were kept highly secret. If the experience of the Young Communist League is anything to go by, the YS itself would probably not have known exactly how many members it had, but it is reckoned to have been between two and four thousand at its height. For example, see Tony Whelan's IMG pamphlet, *The Credibility Gap: The Politics of the SLL*, London, 1970, p.12.
21. Tariq Ali, *The Coming British Revolution*, London, 1972, p.127.
22. *Keep Left*, March 1966. That the group was scheduled to play at a YS dance provided the pretext for the picture.
23. *Keep Left*, October 1964.
24. Mike Faulkner, 'Generation in Revolt', *The Marxist*, no.4, May-June 1967, pp.19–32.
25. Eric Hobsbawm, 'Revolution and Sex' (1969), in *Revolutionaries*, London, 1973, p.218.
26. The Broad Left was the successor to the Radical Student Alliance, largely initiated by communist students and rather inaccurately dismissed by some commentators.
27. In his memoirs, Tariq Ali recounts how he was won over to the IMG (*Street Fighting Years: An Autobiography of the Sixties*, London, 1987, pp.163–86). See also Sylvia Ellis, '"A Demonstration of British Good Sense?": British Student Protest during the Vietnam War', in Gerard J. DeGroot (ed.), *Student Protest: The Sixties and After*, Harlow, 1998.
28. *The Newsletter*, vol.12, no.581 (sic), 27 August 1968.
29. These shifts can be followed in the changing emphasis of the journal's contents at that time.
30. At the time I was engaged in writing hostile reviews of New Left volumes in the CP

daily, *Morning Star* [WT].

31. Hobsbawm, *Revolutionaries*, p.219.
32. Hobsbawm commented, 'Wilhelm Reich, the apostle of orgasm, did indeed start out, as the New Left reminds us, as a revolutionary marxist-cum-freudian…But can we be really surprised that such a man ended by concentrating his interest on orgasm rather than organization?', ibid., p.219.
33. *International Times*, no.78, 24 April-7 May 1970.
34. Waite, 'Young Communist League', pp.276–80.
35. David Widgery, *Preserving Disorder*, London, 1989, p.xiii.
36. Sheila Rowbotham, *Promise of a Dream: Remembering the Sixties*, London, 2000, p.160 ff.
37. Nora Carlin, 'Robbing Peta to Pay Pauline', *Socialist Review*, 17 October-14 November 1981, p.27.
38. 21 September 1968. It is reproduced in David Widgery's *The Left in Britain 1956–68*, Harmondsworth, 1976, pp.297–9.
39. Rosemary Small, 'Marxism and the Family', *Marxism Today*, December 1972, pp.361–5; Irene Brennan, 'Discussion Paper on Marxism and the Family', *Marxism Today*, January 1973 (an 'official' statement); Judith Hunt, 'Women and Liberation' *Marxism Today*, November 1975, pp.326–36.
40. Sue O'Sullivan, *Red Rag*, no.11, Autumn 1976, p.29. (O'Sullivan considered herself 'a marxist-leninist feminist').
41. 'Women's Editorial', *Politics and Power*, vol.3, 1981, p.2.
42. Kathy Ennis, 'Women's Consciousness', *International Socialism*, no.68, April 1974, pp.27–8.
43. Valerie Coultas, 'Tony Cliff's Nightmare—Feminism', *International*, vol.6, no.4, November 1981, p.13.
44. Ann Tobin, 'Somewhere over the Rainbow', in Bob Cant and Susan Hemming (eds), *Radical Records: Thirty Years of Lesbian and Gay History*, London, 1988, pp.250–1.
45. Bob Cant, 'Normal Channels', in Cant and Hemming, *Radical Records*, p.208. David Widgery, reminiscing on his naiveté, wrote of the prevailing assumption that 'after the revolution there won't be any problem because we'll all be heterosexual' (cited in Green, *All Dressed Up*, p.392).
46. Widgery, *Preserving Disorder*, p.51.
47. In the 1980s, for example, the *Marxism Today* editorial board made a point of having its bimonthly meeting lunch breaks in the restaurant of a gay centre.
48. In respect of public alienation from the state, the situation on the mainland differed of course dramatically from that prevailing in Northern Ireland.
49. Michael Defreitas (Michael X) in the UK was no more than a sinister caricature of Malcolm X. In 1968 the YCL saw nothing incongruous in having a white individual (WT) write on Black Power in its theoretical journal.
50. That feeling might be reinforced by the relative success of the Scottish Socialist Party since 1997—occurring moreover in the dog-days of Leninism.
51. Martin Jacques, 'Trends in Youth Culture: Some Aspects', *Marxism Today*, September 1973, p.274.
52 Waite, 'Young Communist League', pp.353 ff.
53. Ibid., p.340.

10. The International Context
Arthur Marwick

1. Arthur Marwick, *Class: Image and Reality in Britain, France, and the United States,* c. *1930 to the present* (rev edn.), 1990, pp.290–307; *idem, Beauty in History: Society, Politics and Personal Appearance, c. 1500 to the Present,* 1988, pp.343–57; *idem, The Sixties: Cultural Revolution in Britain, France, Italy and the United States,* c.*1958–74*, Oxford, 1998, pp.3–22.
2. Donald Alexander Downs, *Cornell '69: Liberalism and the Crisis of the American University*, Ithaca, NY, 1999.
3. The classic account in this vein is Allen J. Matusow's *The Unraveling of America: A History of Liberalism in the 1960s*, New York, 1984. The classic response is W.J. Rorabaugh's *Berkeley at War: The 1960s*, Oxford, 1989, p.x, in which he states that that 'it was only centralised authority which was in decline. At the local level, those on the bottom saw less a disintegration of society than a rebirth of community spirit and individual liberty.'
4. Much of the extreme violence in the non-British countries was due to adherence to 'The Great Marxisant Fallacy'. Capitalism was not in a state of crisis; the working class, while ready to act when prices rose above wages, was generally contented with the broad rise in living standards, and could always be appeased with wage adjustments; and there was no dialectical process by which existing 'bourgeois' society would be readily replaced by an 'alternative' society. The philosopher Herbert Marcuse told student meetings in West Berlin in 1967 that students would form the revolutionary vanguard leading the underclass of racial minorities and the dispossessed: heady stuff for students, but nonsense. Activists believed they could provoke a final crisis in which existing regimes would collapse, while drop-outs and hippies believed that if they opted out of bourgeois society, that society would collapse by itself. On the other side, the forces of what was inaccurately called 'law and order' believed or affected to believe that there genuinely was a threat—that those declaiming their Marxisant predictions really would make serious, well-planned (such planning as there was, was pathetic) attempts at revolution. Actually, there was never any possibility of revolution.
5. Marwick, *Sixties*, pp.455–79.
6. See Anthony Aldgate, *Censorship and the Permissive Society: British Cinema and Theatre, 1955–1965*, Oxford, 1995.
7. Cited in the Memphis State University student magazine, *Tiger Rag*, 6 December 1966. The issues of this magazine, based at a very small conservative university, provide good evidence of the spread of permissiveness.
8. Callum G. Brown, *The Death of Christian Britain: Understanding Secularisation 1800–2000*, London, 2001, pp.170–5.
9. Arthur Marwick, *British Society Since 1945* (rev. edn), Harmondsworth, 1996, pp.10, 14, 150, 151, 260, 285, 331, 375, 395, 462, 470.
10. Brown, *Death of Christian Britain*, pp.176–80.
11. Klaus Hildebrand, *Von Erhard zur Großen Koalition, 1963–1969*, Stuttgart, 1984; Karl Dietrich Bracher, Wolfgang Jäger and Werner Link, *Republik im Wandel, 1969–1974: Die Ära Brandt*, Stuttgart, 1986, pp.127–55; Wolfgang Jäger and Werner Link,

Republik im Wander, 1974–1982: Die Ära Schmidt, Stuttgart, 1987, pp.58–60, 118, 186–91.

12. Tom Hayden, *Reunion: A Memoir*, New York, 1988, p.452.
13. Marwick, *Sixties*, pp.79, 94.
14. David J. Garrow, *Liberty and Sexuality: The Right to Privacy and the Making of Roe v. Wade*, New York, 1994, pp.354–88.
15. A key document in this regard is an article by the veteran Socialist leader Pietro Nenni in *Epoca*, 25 May 1974.
16. Cited in Harold W. Chase, 'Twenty-Sixth Amendment', *Dictionary of American History*, 1976, vii, p.133.
17. Here is a select list of particularly useful collections not already listed in the Note on Sources, at the end of my *Sixties*, pp.859–61.

    Bancroft Library: Free Speech Movement Participant Papers, BANC MSS 99/162c (very useful on the 'Filthy Speech Movement', parents' defence committees, and the massive range of letters about student actions and motivations. Even richer here, are the papers of a leading lawyer defending the students: Malcolm Burnstein Papers, BANC MSS 99/249c. The Papers of Charles R. Gary, BANC MSS 2001/66c, concentrate mainly on Black activists such as Angela Davis.

    Green Library, Stanford Hoover Institution Archives: stronger on the 'enemies' of the permissive society than on the protagonists of permissiveness and protest. Very useful on the latter are the New Left Collection, the Joseph Dunbacher papers, and the Kenneth G. Fuller papers. Wonderfully revealing on the former are the Elizabeth Churchill Brown papers, the Robert B. Dresser papers, and the Don Mulford papers.

    UCLA Special Collections: the Vietnam Conflict Collection of rare pamphlets and other printed ephemera is of wider social significance than might be thought (see Charlotte Keyes's memoir below).

    Cornell University Rare Books and Manuscripts: in 1997 I scarcely did more than note the incredible richness of the Challenge to Governance Project records from 1969–70 (47/5/1309), practically unique in its collection of letters from students to parents and parents to students. These can now be magnificently amplified by the James Perkins papers (3/10/1022), containing torrents of abusive and supportive letters from parents, outsiders, and students, and by the similar John Marsham papers (41/1/1207), Marsham being the editor of the newspaper sent out to all Cornell graduates.

    Columbia Rare Book and Manuscript Library: MsCOLL/Diamond-Sigismund. Diamond was Columbia professor of sociology who was not a reactionary, but who, unlike many of his colleagues took a detached view of student 'revolutionary' and 'countercultural' demands.

    Fondazione Archivio Diaristico Nazionale, Pieve S. Stefano (AR), Italy: I gathered the richest fruits here in 1991, the more recent acquisitions being mainly rather contrived memoirs rather than authentic diaries. However, useful diaries and memoirs for 1960s' attitudes are: Rosario Amodeo (00504), Mario d'Andrea, Nino Faggioti (03729), Cino Ghigi (005721) and Franco Mancuso (02172).
18. Cornell University, Perkins Papers 3/10/1022, box 1, folder 1, 'Board of Trustees 1963–5': paper for board meeting by Robin M. Williams, Jr, Chairman Faculty

Committee on Student Affairs, 26 April 1965.

19. The United States is often also given primacy in regard to the student activism that was such a distinctive feature of the long sixties. In fact, what happened at Berkeley in 1964 had been preceded by fairly violent student demonstrations in France, Italy and West Germany (in favour of better conditions and against, say, the Algerian war or the entry of neo-fascists into government). But then politically-motivated student activism, springing in part out of the early civil rights and voter enrolment campaigns, was pretty new in America.
20. BANC MSS 99/249c, box 1.27: letter of 16 December 1964.
21. BANC MSS 99/249c, box 2.11: letter from Dean of Law to Judge Crittenden, 12 July 1965.
22. BANC MSS 99/249c, box 2.7: undated letter (December 1964?) to chairman of Parents' Committee.
23. BANC MSS 99/249c, box 4.1: undated letter (July 1965?) to Crittenden.
24. See Bancroft Library sources cited in Marwick, *Sixties*, pp.725–7.
25. BANC MSS 99/162c, cartons 1.1, 1.7, 1.10, 1.21. Cornell had an obscene words episode of its own, for which see Cornell University, Perkins Papers 3/10/1022, box 9, folders 42–4.
26. BANC MSS 99/162c, carton 1; conversation with Elena Danielson, curator Hoover Archives and Berkeley student in the late 1960s, 2001.
27. Sally Belfrage, *Freedom Summer*, New York, 1965, p.65.
28. For controversies over mixed dormitories in the United States, see *Tiger Rag*, which from September 1966 to February 1967 reported on the issue not only at Memphis State University but at campuses across the United States.
29. Michael Seidman, 'The Pre-May 1968 Sexual Revolution', *Contemporary French Civilization*, vol.25, no.1, 2001, pp.20–41.
30. Ibid., p.45.
31. Ibid., pp.28–9.
32. Ibid., p.35.
33. Ibid., p.33.
34. Lieta Harrison, *L'Iniziazione: come le adolescenti italiani diventano donne*, Milan, 1966, pp.1, 39–132.
35. *Idem, La donna sposata: mille moglie accusano*, Milan, 1972, pp.17–79, 207–32.
36. Ibid.
37. This comes through very clearly in the contemporary interviews printed in Romolo Gobbi, *Il '68 alla rovescia*, Milan, 1988.
38. Fondazione Archivio Diaristico Nazionale, Pieve S. Stefano, Anna Avallone, 'Il mio sessantotto: ricordi di una "madre" a "insegnate"'.
39. Charlotte E. Keyes, *The Mother of a Draft-card Burner, a Young Man Already Imprisoned Four Times for His Beliefs, Tells of Her Own Agony—and Her Son's*, Voluntown, CN, n.d. A copy can be found in Department of Special Collections, UCLA Library, Vietnam Conflict Collection, box 7, folder 7.
40. See Cornell University, Challenge to Governance Project records, 1969–70 (47/5/1309).

Select Bibliography on Permissiveness and the 1960s

Social Theory

Beck, Ulrich and Elisabeth Beck-Gernscheim. *The Normal Chaos of Love*, Cambridge, 1995.

Bourdieu, Pierre. *Distinction: A Social Critique of the Judgement of Taste*, London, 1986.

Foucault, Michel. *The History of Sexuality*, vol.i, New York, 1990.

Giddens, Anthony. *Modernity and Self-Identity: Self and Society in the Late Modern Age*, Stanford, CA, 1991.

Giddens, Anthony. *The Transformation of Intimacy: Sexuality, Love and Eroticism in Modern Societies*, Stanford, CA, 1992.

Habermas, Jürgen. *Legitimation Crisis*, Cambridge, 1988.

Jameson, Fredric. *Postmodernism, or the Cultural Logic of Late Capitalism*, Durham, NC, 1991.

The 1960s

Akhtar, Miriam and Steve Humphries. *The Fifties and Sixties: A Lifestyle Revolution*, London, 2001.

Annan, Noel. *Our Age: The Generation That Made Postwar Britain*, London, 1991.

Booker, Christopher. *The Neophiliacs: The Revolution in English Life in the Fifties and Sixties*, London, 1969.

Conekin, Becky, Frank Mort and Chris Waters (eds). *Moments of Modernity: Reconstructing Britain, 1945–64*, London, 1999.

Davies, Christie. *Permissive Britain: Social Change in the Sixties and Seventies*, London, 1975.

Donnelly, Mark. *Sixties Britain: Culture, Society and Politics*, Harlow, 2005.

Gardiner, Juliet. *From the Bomb to the Beatles: The Changing Face of Postwar Britain, 1945–65*, London, 1999.

Hutchinson, Roger. *High Sixties: The Summers of Riot and Love*, Edinburgh, 1992.

Hylton, Stuart. *Magical History Tour: The 1960s Revisited*, Stroud, 2000.
Levin, Bernard. *The Pendulum Years: Britain and the Sixties*, London, 1970.
Miles, Barry. *In the Sixties*, London, 2002.
Sandbrook, Dominic. *Never Had It So Good: A History of Britain from Suez to the Beatles*, London, 2005.

Victorianism

Barret-DuCrocq, Françoise. *Love in the Time of Victoria*, Harmondsworth, 1991.
Bland, Lucy. *Banishing the Beast: English Feminism and Sexual Morality, 1885–1914*, Harmondsworth, 1995.
Collini, Stefan. *Public Moralists: Political Thought and Intellectual Life in Britain, 1850–1930*, Oxford, 1991.
Gay, Peter. *The Bourgeois Experience: Victoria to Freud*, v vols, New York, 1984–98.
Jeffreys, Sheila (ed.). *The Sexuality Debates*, London, 1987.
Marcus, Steven. *The Other Victorians: A Study of Sexuality and Pornography in Mid Nineteenth-Century England*, New York, 1966.
Mason, Michael. *The Making of Victorian Sexual Attitudes*, Oxford, 1994.
Mason, Michael. *The Making of Victorian Sexuality*, Oxford, 1994.
Pedersen, Susan and Peter Mandler (eds). *After the Victorians: Private Conscience and Public Duty in Modern Britain*, London, 1994.
Petrow, Stefan. *Policing Morals: The Metropolitan Police and the Home Office, 1870–1914*, Oxford, 1994.
Roberts, Elizabeth. *A Woman's Place: An Oral History of Working-Class Women, 1890–1940*, Oxford, 1984.
Searle, G.R. *Morality and the Market in Victorian Britain*, Oxford, 1998.
Walkowitz, Judith. *City of Dreadful Delight: Narratives of Sexual Danger in Late Victorian London*, Chicago, 1992.

Bohemianism

Bell, Quentin. *Bloomsbury*, London, 1968.
Brandon, Ruth. *The New Women and the Old Men: Love, Sex and the Woman Question*, London, 1990.
Bush, M.L. *What is Love?: Richard Carlile's Philosophy of Sex*, London, 1998.
Carpenter, Edward. *Love's Coming of Age* (rev. edn), London, 1913.
Ellis, Havelock. *Studies in the Psychology of Sex*, ii vols, New York, 1942.
Ellman, Richard. *Oscar Wilde*, Harmondsworth, 1989.
Hall, Lesley A. '"Disinterested Enthusiasm for Sexual Misconduct": The British Society for the Study of Sex Psychology, 1913–47', *Journal of Contemporary History*, vol.30, no.4, 1995, pp.665–87.
Heilmann, Ann (ed.). *The Late Victorian Marriage Question*, v vols, London, 1998.

Jackson, Holbrook. *The Eighteen Nineties: A Review of Art and Ideas at the Close of the Nineteenth Century*, London, 1913.

Neill, A.S. *That Dreadful School*, London, 1937.

Nicholson, Virginia. *Among the Bohemians: Experiments in Living, 1900–39*, New York, 2002.

Nottingham, Chris. *The Pursuit of Serenity: Havelock Ellis and the New Politics*, Amsterdam, 1999.

Russell, Bertrand. *Marriage and Morals*, London, 1929.

Showalter, Elaine. *Sexual Anarchy: Gender and Culture at the Fin de Siècle*, New York, 1990.

Thomas, Matthew. *Anarchist Ideas and Countercultures in Britain, 1880–1914: Revolutions in Everyday Life*, Aldershot, 2005.

Wells, H.G. *Socialism and the Family*, London, 1906.

Culture

Aldgate, Anthony, James Chapman and Arthur Marwick (eds). *Windows on the Sixties: Exploring Key Texts of Media and Culture*, London, 2000.

Appleyard, Bryan. *The Pleasures of Peace: Art and Imagination in Postwar Britain*, London, 1989.

Carpenter, Humphrey. *That Was Satire That Was: The Satire Boom of the 1960s*, London, 2000.

Davies, Alistair and Alan Sinfield (eds). *British Culture of the Postwar*, London, 2000.

Hewison, Robert. *Too Much: Art and Society in the Sixties, 1960–75*, London, 1986.

Hunt, Leon. *British Low Culture: From Safari Suits to Sexploitation*, London, 1998.

Laing, Stuart. *Representations of Working-Class Life, 1957–64*, Basingstoke, 1986.

LeMahieu, D.L. *A Culture for Democracy: Mass Communication and the Cultivated Mind in Britain between the Wars*, Oxford, 1988.

Marwick, Arthur. *Culture in Britain since 1945*, Oxford, 1991.

Melly, George. *Revolt into Style: The Pop Arts in Britain*, London, 1970.

Moore-Gilbert, Bart and John Seed (eds). *Cultural Revolution?: The Challenge of the Arts in the 1960s*, London, 1992.

Moore-Gilbert, Bart (ed.). *The Arts in the 1970s: Cultural Closure?*, London, 1994.

Nehring, Neil. *Flowers in the Dustbin: Culture, Anarchy and Postwar England*, Ann Arbor, MI, 1993.

Rose, Jonathan. *The Intellectual Life of the British Working Classes*, New Haven, CT, 2001.

Samuel, Raphael. *Theatres of Memory, vol. i: Past and Present in Contemporary Culture*, London, 1994.

Veldman, Meredith. *Fantasy, the Bomb and the Greening of Britain: Romantic Protest, 1945–80*, Cambridge, 1994.

Music

Beatles, The. *The Beatles Anthology*, London, 2000.
Bromell, Nick. *Tomorrow Never Knows: Rock and Psychedelics in the 1960s*, Chicago, 2001.
Chapman, Robert. *Selling The Sixties: The Pirates and Pop Music Radio*, London, 1992.
Davis, Stephen. *Old Gods Almost Dead: The 40-Year Odyssey of the Rolling Stones*, London, 2001.
Faithfull, Marianne and David Dalton. *Faithfull*, London, 1994.
Frith, Simon and Howard Horne. *Art into Pop*, London, 1987.
Frith, Simon. *The Sociology of Rock*, London, 1978.
Inglis, Ian (ed.). *The Beatles, Popular Music and Society*, Basingstoke, 2000.
MacDonald, Ian. *Revolution in the Head: The Beatles' Records and the Sixties* (rev. edn), London, 2005.
Miles, Barry. *Paul McCartney: Many Years from Now*, London, 1998.
Oldham, Andrew Loog. *Stoned*, London, 2000.
Reynolds, Simon and Joy Press. *The Sex Revolts: Gender, Rebellion and Rock 'n' Roll*, Cambridge, MA, 1995.
Savage, Jon. *England's Dreaming: Sex Pistols and Punk Rock*, London, 1991.
Stark, Steven D. *Meet the Beatles: A Cultural History of the Band that Shook Youth, Gender and the World*, New York, 2005.
Whiteley, Sheila. *The Space Between the Notes: Rock and the Counter-Culture*, London, 1992.

Cinema

Dickinson, Margaret (ed.). *Rogue Reels: Oppositional Film in Britain, 1945–90*, Berkeley, CA, 1999.
Durgnat, Raymond. *A Mirror for England: British Movies from Austerity to Affluence, London*, 1970.
Harper, Sue and Vincent Porter. *British Cinema of the 1950s: The Decline of Deference*, Oxford, 2003.
Hill, John. *Sex, Class and Realism: British Cinema, 1956–63*, London, 1986.
McGillivray, David. *Doing Rude Things: The History of the British Sex Film, 1957–81*, London, 1992.
Murphy, Robert. *Sixties British Cinema*, London, 1992.

Television

Chapman, Graham et al. *Monty Python's Flying Circus: Just the Words*, ii vols, London, 1989.

Chapman, James. *Saints and Avengers: British Adventure Series of the 1960s*, London, 2002.

Cook, Jim (ed.). *Television Sitcom*, London, 1981.

Corner, John (ed.). *Popular Television in Britain: Studies in Cultural History*, London, 1991.

Greene, Hugh. *Third Floor Front: A View of Broadcasting in the Sixties*, London, 1969.

Sendall, Bernard. *Independent Television in Britain, ii: Expansion and Change, 1958–68*, London, 1983.

Fashion and Design

de la Haye, Amy. *The Cutting Edge: 50 Years of British Fashion, 1947–97*, Woodstock, NY, 1997.

Fogg, Marnie. *Boutique: A 60s Cultural Phenomenon*, London, 2003.

Harris, Jennifer, Sarah Hyde and Greg Smith. *1966 and All That: Design and the Consumer in Britain, 1960–9*, London, 1986.

Jackson, Lesley. *The Sixties: Decade of Design Revolution*, London, 1998.

Quant, Mary. *Quant by Quant*, London, 1966.

Twiggy. *An Autobiography*, London, 1975.

Vermorel, Fred. *Fashion and Perversity: A Life of Vivienne Westwood and the Sixties Laid Bare*, London, 1996.

The Visual and Performing Arts

Bailey, David and Peter Evans. *Goodbye Baby and Amen: A Saraband for the Sixties*, London, 1969.

Bailey, David. *David Bailey's Box of Pin-ups*, London, 1965.

Mellor, David. *The Sixties Art Scene in London*, London, 1993.

Rebello, Dan. *1956 and All That: The Making of Modern British Drama*, London, 1999.

Seago, Alex. *Burning the Box of Beautiful Things: The Development of a Postmodern Sensibility*, Oxford, 1995.

Tynan, Kenneth. *A View of the English Stage*, London, 1984.

Walker, John A. *Left Shift: Radical Art in 1970s Britain*, London, 2002.

Literature and the Press

Bennett, Tony and Janet Woollacott. *Bond and Beyond: The Political Career of a Popular Hero*, London, 1987.

Bingham, Adrian. *Gender, Modernity and the Popular Press in Interwar Britain*, Oxford, 2004.

Bradbury, Malcolm. *The Modern British Novel*, London, 1993.

Dickinson, Robert. *Imprinting the Sticks: The Alternative Press beyond London*, Aldershot, 1997.
Ferguson, Marjorie. *Forever Feminine: Women's Magazines and the Cult of Femininity*, London, 1983.
Freeman, Gillian. *The Undergrowth of Literature*, London, 1967.
Marnham, Patrick. *The Private Eye Story*, London, 1982.
McAleer, Joseph. *Passion's Fortune: The Story of Mills and Boon*, New York, 1999.
Ritchie, Harry. *Success Stories: Literature and the Media in England, 1950–9*, London, 1988.
Sutherland, John. *Bestsellers: Popular Fiction of the 1970s*, London, 1981.
Waugh, Patricia, *Harvest of the Sixties: English Literature and Its Background, 1960 to 1990*, Oxford, 1995.

Social Commentary

Connolly, Cyril. 'Post-War England' (1946), in *idem*, *Ideas and Places*, London, 1953.
Bracewell, Michael. *The Nineties: When Surface Was Depth*, London, 2002.
Carstairs, E.M. *This Island Now*, London, 1962.
Guardian. *The Permissive Society: The Guardian Inquiry*, London, 1969.
Hoggart, Richard. *The Uses of Literacy: Changing Patterns in English Mass Culture*, Fair Lawn, NJ, 1957.
Leach, Edmund. *A Runaway World?*, New York, 1968.
Maschler, Tom (ed.). *Declaration*, London, 1957.
Osborne, John. *Damn You, England: Collected Prose*, London, 1994.
Raban, Jonathan. *Soft City*, London, 1974.
Sampson, Anthony. *Anatomy of Britain*, New York, 1962.

Surveys and Polls

Abrams, Mark, David Gerard and Noel Timms (eds). *Values and Social Change in Britain*, Basingstoke, 1985.
British Social Attitudes, 1984–.
Gorer, Geoffrey. *Exploring English Character*, London, 1955.
Gorer, Geoffrey. *Sex and Marriage in England Today*, London, 1971.
Heald, Gordon and Robert J. Wybrow. *The Gallup Survey of Britain*, London, 1986.
ICM Research. *Relationships Poll*, London, 1990.
Jacobs, Eric and Robert Worcester. *Typically British? The Prudential MORI Guide*, London, 1991.
Jacobs, Eric and Robert Worcester. *We British: Britain under the MORIscope*, London, 1990.
Jowell, Roger, Sharon Witherspoon and Lindsay Brook (eds). *British Social*

Attitudes—Cumulative Sourcebook: The First Six Surveys, Aldershot, 1991.

World Political Opinion and Social Surveys: Series One—British Opinion Polls, part i, Reading, 1990.

Gender and the Family

Bourke, Joanna. *Working-Class Cultures in Britain, 1890–1960: Gender, Class and Ethnicity*, London, 1994.

Collins, Marcus. *Modern Love: An Intimate History of Men and Women in Twentieth-Century Britain*, London, 2003.

Fletcher, Ronald. *Britain in the Sixties: The Family and Marriage*, Harmondsworth, 1962.

Gavron, Hannah. *The Captive Wife: Conflicts of Housebound Mothers*, London, 1966.

Hakim, Catherine. *Female Heterogeneity and the Polarisation of Women's Employment*, London, 1996.

Jamieson, Lynn. *Intimacy: Personal Relationships in Modern Societies*, Cambridge, 1998.

Laing, R.D. *The Politics of the Family and Other Essays*, London, 1971.

Lewis, Jane. *The End of Marriage? Individualism and Intimate Relations*, Cheltenham, 2001.

Maitland, Sara (ed.). *Very Heaven: Looking Back at the 1960s*, London, 1988.

Mort, Frank. 'Social and Symbolic Fathers and Sons in Postwar Britain', *Journal of British Studies*, vol.38, no.3, 1999, pp.353–85.

Roberts, Elizabeth. *Women and Families: An Oral History*, Oxford, 1995.

Slater, Eliot and Moya Woodside. *Patterns of Marriage: A Study of Marriage Relationships in the Urban Working Classes*, London, 1951.

Smart, Carol. *The Ties That Bind: Marriage and the Reproduction of Patriarchal Relations*, London, 1984.

Steedman, Carolyn. *Landscape for a Good Woman: A Story of Two Lives*, New Brunswick, NJ, 1987.

Weeks, Jeffrey, Brian Heaphy and Catherine Donovan. *Same-Sex Intimacies: Families of Choice and Other Life Experiments*, London, 2001.

Wilson, Elizabeth. *Only Halfway to Paradise: Women in Postwar Britain, 1945–68*, London, 1980.

Young, Michael and Peter Willmott. *Family and Kinship in East London*, London, 1957.

Young, Michael and Peter Willmott. *The Symmetrical Family: A Study of Work and Leisure in the London Region*, London, 1973.

Zweininger-Bargielowska, Ina (ed.). *Women in Twentieth-Century Britain*, Harlow, 2001.

Sexuality

Berridge, Virginia. *AIDS in the UK: The Making of a Policy, 1981–94*, Oxford, 1996.
Chesser, Eustace. *Is Chastity Outmoded?*, London, 1960.
Hall, Lesley A. *Sex, Gender and Social Change in Britain since 1880*, Basingstoke, 2000.
Jeffreys, Sheila. *Anticlimax: A Feminist Perspective on the Sexual Revolution*, London, 1990.
Jenkins, Philip. *Intimate Enemies: Moral Panics in Contemporary Great Britain*, New York, 1992.
Johnson, Anne M. et al. *Sexual Attitudes and Lifestyles*, Oxford, 1994.
McLaren, Angus. *Twentieth-Century Sexuality*, Oxford, 1999.
Plummer, Kenneth. *Telling Sexual Stories: Power, Change and Social Worlds*, London, 1995.
Porter, Roy and Lesley Hall. *The Facts of Life: The Creation of Sexual Knowledge in Britain, 1650–1950*, New Haven, CT, 1995.
Stanley, Liz. *Sex Surveyed, 1949–94*, London, 1995.
Weeks, Jeffrey. *Invented Moralities: Sexual Values in an Age of Uncertainty*, Cambridge, 1995.
Weeks, Jeffrey. *Sex, Politics and Society: The Regulation of Sexuality since 1800* (rev. edn), London, 1989.
Weeks, Jeffrey. *Sexuality and Its Discontents: Meanings, Myths and Modern Sexualities*, London, 1985.
Wellings, Kaye et al. *Sexual Behaviour in Britain: The National Survey of Sexual Attitudes and Lifestyles*, Harmondsworth, 1994.
Wilson, John. *Logic and Sexual Morality*, Harmondsworth, 1965.

Heterosexuality

Collins, Marcus. 'The Pornography of Permissiveness: Men's Sexuality and Women's Emancipation in Mid Twentieth-Century Britain', *History Workshop Journal*, no.47, 1999, pp.99–120.
Comfort, Alex. *The Joy of Sex: A Cordon Bleu Guide to Lovemaking*, New York, 1972.
Cook, Hera. *The Long Sexual Revolution: English Women, Sex and Contraception, 1800–1975*, Oxford, 2004.
Fisher, Kate. *Birth Control, Sex and Marriage in Britain, 1918–60*, Oxford, 2006.
Hall, Lesley A. *Hidden Anxieties: Male Sexuality, 1900–39*, Cambridge, 1991.
Heath, Stephen. *The Sexual Fix*, London, 1982.
Marks, Lara. *Sexual Chemistry: A History of the Contraceptive Pill*, New Haven, CT, 2001.
Stopes, Marie Carmichael. *Married Love: A New Contribution to the Solution of Sex Difficulties*, London, 1918.

Szreter, Simon. 'Victorian Britain, 1837–1963: Towards a Social History of Sexuality', *Journal of Victorian Culture*, vol.1, no.1, 1996, pp.136–49.
Szreter, Simon. *Fertility, Class and Gender in Britain, 1860–1940*, Cambridge, 1996.
Wilkinson, Sue and Celia Kitzinger (eds). *Heterosexuality*, Newbury Park, CA, 1993.

Homosexuality

Cant, Bob and Susan Hemmings. *Radical Records: Thirty Years of Lesbian and Gay History, 1957–87*, London, 1988.
Cook, Matt. *London and the Culture of Homosexuality, 1885–1914*, Cambridge, 2003.
Crisp, Quentin. *The Naked Civil Servant*, London, 1968.
Doan, Laura. *Fashioning Sapphism: The Origins of a Modern English Lesbian Subculture*, New York, 2001.
Ettorre, E.M. *Lesbians, Women and Society*, London, 1980.
Gardiner, Jill. *From The Closet To The Screen: Women at the Gateways Club, 1945–85*, London, 2003.
Gough, Jamie and Mike Macnair. *Gay Liberation in the Eighties*, London, 1985.
Grey, Antony. *Quest for Justice: Towards Homosexual Emancipation*, London, 1992.
Higgins, Patrick. *Heterosexual Dictatorship: Male Homosexuality in Postwar Britain*, London, 1996.
Houlbrook, Matt. *Queer London: Perils and Pleasures in the Sexual Metropolis, 1918–57*, Chicago, 2005.
Oram, Alison and Annmarie Turnbull. *The Lesbian History Sourcebook: Love and Sex between Women in Britain from 1780 to 1970*, London, 2001.
Power, Lisa. *No Bath but Plenty of Bubbles: An Oral History of the Gay Liberation Front, 1970–3*, London, 1995.
Smith, Patricia Juliana (ed.). *The Queer Sixties*, New York, 1999.
Walter, Aubrey (ed.). *Come Together: The Years of Gay Liberation, 1970–3*, London, 1980.
Weeks, Jeffrey. *Coming Out: Homosexual Politics from the Nineteenth Century to the Present* (rev. edn), London, 1990.
Wildeblood, Peter. *Against the Law*, London, 1955.

National Identity

Bracewell, Michael. *England Is Mine: Pop Life in Albion from Wilde to Goldie*, London, 1997.
Collins, Marcus. 'The Fall of the English Gentleman: The National Character in Decline, *c.*1918–1970', *Historical Research*, vol.75, no.187, 2002, pp.90–111.
Colls, Robert. *Identity of England*, Oxford, 2002.

Frost, David and Anthony Jay. *The English*, New York, 1967.
Koestler, Arthur (ed.). *Suicide of a Nation?*, London, 1963.
Ward, Stuart. '"No Nation Could Be Broker": The Satire Boom and the Demise of Britain's World Role', in Stuart Ward (ed.), *British Culture and the End of Empire*, Manchester, 2001.
Webster, Wendy. *Imagining Home: Gender, 'Race' and National Identity, 1945–64*, London, 1998.
Weight, Richard. *Patriots: National Identity in Britain, 1940–2000*, Basingstoke, 2002.

Immigration

Collins, Marcus. 'Pride and Prejudice: West Indian Men in Mid Twentieth-Century Britain', *Journal of British Studies*, vol.40, no.3, 2001, pp.391–418.
Gilroy, Paul. *There Ain't No Black in the Union Jack: The Cultural Politics of Race and Nation*, London, 1992.
Goulbourne, Harry. *Race Relations in Britain Since 1945*, Basingstoke, 1998.
Griffiths, Peter. *A Question of Colour?*, London, 1966.
Hall, Stuart, et al. *Policing the Crisis: Mugging, the State and Law and Order*, Basingstoke, 1978.
Paul, Kathleen. *Whitewashing Britain: Race and Citizenship in the Postwar Era*, Ithaca, NY, 1997.
Phillips, Mike and Trevor Phillips. *Windrush: The Irresistible Rise of Multiracial Britain*, London, 1998.
Waters, Chris. '"Dark Strangers in Our Midst": Discourses of Race and Nation in Britain, 1947–63', *Journal of British Studies*, vol.36, no.2, 1997, pp.207–38.

Swinging London

Dallas, Karl. *Swinging London: A Guide to Where the Action Is*, London, 1967.
Davies, Hunter (ed.). *The New London Spy*, London, 1967.
Fabian, Jenny and Johnny Byrne. *Groupie*, London, 1969.
Fountain, Nigel. *Underground: The London Alternative Press, 1966–74*, London, 1988.
Fryer, Jonathan. *Soho in the Fifties and Sixties*, London, 1998.
Levy, Shawn. *Ready, Steady, Go!: The Smashing Rise and Giddy Fall of Swinging London*, New York, 2002.
Rycroft, Simon. 'The Geographies of Swinging London', *Journal of Historical Geography*, vol.28, no.4, pp.566–88.
Saunders, Nicholas. *Alternative London*, London, 1970.

Youth Culture

Cohen, Stanley. *Folk Devils and Moral Panics: The Creation of the Mods and the Rockers*, London, 1972.

Eppel, E.M. and M. Eppel. *Adolescents and Morality*, London, 1966.

Fowler, David. *The First Teenagers: The Lifestyle of Young Wage-Earners in Interwar Britain*, London, 1995.

Hall, Stuart and Tony Jefferson (eds). *Resistance Through Rituals: Youth Subcultures in Postwar Britain*, London, 1975.

Hamblett, Charles and Jane Deverson. *Generation X*, London, 1964.

Hebdige, Dick. *Subculture: The Meaning of Style*, London, 1979.

Laurie, Peter. *The Teenage Revolution*, London, 1965.

Musgrove, Frank. *Youth and the Social Order*, London, 1964.

Osgerby, Bill. *Youth in Britain since 1945*, Oxford, 1998.

Pearson, Geoffrey. *Hooligan: A History of Respectable Fears*, London, 1983.

Thornton, Sarah. *Club Cultures: Music, Media and Subcultural Capital*, Cambridge, 1995.

Wilkinson, Helen and Geoff Mulgan. *Freedom's Children*, London, 1995.

Willis, Paul E. *Profane Culture*, London, 1978.

Willmott, Peter. *Adolescent Boys of East London*, London, 1966.

The Counterculture

Berke, Joseph (ed.). *Counter Culture: The Creation of an Alternative Society*, London, 1969.

Cooper, David (ed.). *The Dialectics of Liberation*, Harmondsworth, 1968.

Dunn, Nell. *Living Like I Do*, London, 1979.

Green, Jonathon. *All Dressed Up: The Sixties and the Counterculture*, London, 1999.

Green, Jonathon. *Days In The Life: Voices of the English Underground, 1961–71*, London, 1988.

Landry, Charles et al. *What A Way To Run A Railroad: An Analysis of Radical Failure*, London, 1985.

Marowitz, Charles. *Burnt Bridges: A Souvenir of the Swinging Sixties and Beyond*, London, 1990.

Martin, Chad. 'Paradise Now: Youth Politics and the British Counterculture, 1958–74', Stanford University PhD thesis, 2003.

McKay, George. *Senseless Acts of Beauty: Cultures of Resistance since the Sixties*, London, 1996.

Mills, Richard. *Young Outsiders: A Study of Alternative Communities*, London, 1973.

Musgrove, Frank. *Ecstasy and Holiness: Counter Culture and the Open Society*, London, 1974.

Neville, Richard. *Play Power*, London, 1970.

Nuttall, Jeff. *Bomb Culture*, London, 1968.
Rigby, Andrew. *Communes in Britain*, London, 1974.
Stansill, Peter and David Mairowitz (eds). *BAMN (By Any Means Necessary): Outlaw Manifestos and Ephemera, 1965–70*, Harmondsworth, 1971.

Consumerism

Abrams, Mark. *The Teenage Consumer*, London, 1959.
Benson, John. *The Rise of Consumer Society in Britain, 1880–1980*, London, 1994.
Black, Lawrence and Hugh Pemberton (eds). *An Affluent Society? Britain's Postwar 'Golden Age' Revisited*, Aldershot, 2004.
Campbell, Colin. *The Romantic Ethic and the Spirit of Modern Consumerism*, Oxford, 1987.
Mort, Frank. *Cultures of Consumption: Masculinities and Social Space in Late Twentieth-Century Britain*, London, 1996.
Nixon, Sean. *Hard Looks: Masculinities, Spectatorship and Contemporary Consumption*, London, 1996.

Drugs and Alcohol

Davenport-Hines, Richard. *The Pursuit of Oblivion: A History of Narcotics, 1500–2000*, London, 2001.
Hilton, Matthew. *Smoking in British Popular Culture, 1800–2000: Perfect Pleasures*, Manchester, 2000.
Marks, Howard. *Mr Nice*, London, 1996.
Mass-Observation. *The Pub and the People: A Worktown Study*, London, 1943.
Melechi, Antonio (ed.). *Psychedelia Britannica: Hallucinogenic Drugs in Britain*, London, 1997.
Vasey, Daniel E. *The Pub and English Social Change*, New York, 1990.
Young, Jock. *The Drug Takers: The Social Meaning of Drug Use*, London, 1971.

Morality

Davies, Christie. *The Strange Death of Moral Britain*, New Brunswick, NJ, 2004.
Hemming, James. *Individual Morality*, London, 1969.
Himmelfarb, Gertrude. *The De-Moralization of Society: From Victorian Virtues to Modern Values*, New York, 1995.
Hunt, Alan. *Governing Morals: A Social History of Moral Regulation*, Cambridge, 1999.
Inglis, Brian. *Public Conscience and Private Morality*, London, 1964.
Joad, C. E. M. *The Future of Morals* (rev. edn), London, 1946.
McKibbin, Ross. *Classes and Cultures: England, 1918–51*, Oxford, 1998.

Rose, Nikolas. *Governing the Soul: The Shaping of the Private Self*, London, 1990.
Smith, E. Parkinson and A. Graham Ikin. *Morality—Old and New*, Derby, 1964.
Whiteley, C.H. and Winifred M. Whiteley. *The Permissive Morality*, London, 1964.

Religion

Archbishop of Canterbury Group. *Putting Asunder: A Divorce Law for Contemporary Society*, London, 1966.
Barclay, William. *Ethics in a Permissive Society*, London, 1971.
Brown, Callum G. *The Death of Christian Britain: Understanding Secularisation, 1800–2000*, London, 2001.
Demant, V. A. *Christian Sex Ethics: An Exposition*, London, 1963.
Heron, Alastair (ed.). *Towards a Quaker View of Sex*, London, 1963.
Lewis, Jane and Patrick Wallis. 'Fault, Breakdown and the Church of England's Involvement in the 1969 Divorce Reform', *Twentieth-Century British History*, vol.11, no.3, 2000, pp.308–32.
Lunn, Arnold and Garth Lean. *Christian Counter-Attack*, London, 1969.
Machin, G.I.T. 'British Churches and Social Issues, 1945–60', *Twentieth Century British History*, vol.7, no.3, 1996, pp.345–70.
Newsom, G.E. *The New Morality*, London, 1932.
Potter, Harry. *Hanging in Judgement: Religion and the Death Penalty in England from the Bloody Code to Abolition*, London, 1993.
Rhymes, Douglas. *No New Morality: Christian Personal Values and Sexual Morality*, London, 1964.
Robinson, John A.T. *Honest to God*, London, 1963.

The Right

Brittain, Samuel. *Capitalism and the Permissive Society*, Basingstoke, 1973.
Douglas, Gillian. 'Family Law under the Thatcher Government', *Journal of Law and Society*, vol.17, no.4, 1990, pp.411–26.
Durham, Martin. *Sex and Politics: The Family and Morality in the Thatcher Years*, Basingstoke, 1991.
Gummer, John Selwyn. *The Permissive Society: Fact or Fantasy?*, London, 1971.
Smith, Anna Marie. *New Right Discourse on Race and Sexuality: Britain, 1968–90*, Cambridge, 1994.
Thatcher, Margaret. *The Downing Street Years*, London, 1993.
Thatcher, Margaret. *The Path to Power*, New York, 1995.

The Left

Ali, Tariq. *Street Fighting Years: An Autobiography of the Sixties*, London, 1987.

Archer, Robin et al. (eds). *Out of Apathy: Voices of the New Left, Thirty Years On*, London, 1989.

Black, Lawrence. *The Political Culture of the Left in Affluent Britain, 1951–64: Old Labour, New Britain?*, Basingstoke, 2002.

Jenkins, Roy. *A Life at the Centre*, London, 1991.

Jenkins, Roy. *The Labour Case*, Harmondsworth, 1959.

Stanford, Peter. *Lord Longford: A Life*, London, 1994.

Thompson, Peter. 'Labour's "Gannex Conscience"?: Politics and Popular Attitudes in the "Permissive Society"', in Richard Coopey, Steve Fielding and Nick Tiratsoo (eds), *The Wilson Governments, 1964–70*, London, 1993.

Vague, Tom. *Anarchy in the UK: The Angry Brigade*, Edinburgh, 1997.

Widgery, David. *The Left in Britain, 1956–68*, Harmondsworth, 1976.

Permissive Legislation

Abse, Leo. *Private Member*, London, 1973.

Department of Education and Science. *Youth and Community Work in the 1970s*, London, 1969.

Devlin, Patrick. *The Enforcement of Morals*, London, 1959.

Fisher, Trevor. 'Permissiveness and the Politics of Morality', *Contemporary Record*, vol.7, no.1, 1993, pp.149–65.

Grayson, Richard. 'Mods, Rockers and Juvenile Delinquency in 1964: The Government Response', *Contemporary British History*, vol.12, no.1, 1998, pp.19–47.

Hindell, Keith and Madeleine Simms. *Abortion Law Reformed*, London, 1971.

Home Office. *Report of the Committee on Homosexual Offences and Prostitution*, London, 1957.

Home Office. *Report of the Committee on Obscenity and Film Censorship*, London, 1979.

Jeffrey-Poulter, Stephen. *Peers, Queers and Commons: The Struggle for Gay Law Reform from 1950 to the Present*, London, 1991.

Law Commission. *Report of the Grounds of Divorce: The Field of Choice*, London, 1966.

Lees, B.H. *Divorce Law Reform in England*, London, 1971.

Lord Chancellor's Department. *Report of the Committee in the Age of Majority*, London, 1967.

National Deviancy Conference. *Permissiveness and Control: The Fate of the Sixties Legislation*, London, 1980.

Newburn, Tim. *Permission and Regulation: Law and Morals in Postwar Britain*, London, 1992.

Pym, Bridget. *Pressure Groups and the Permissive Society*, Newton Abbot, 1974.

Report of the Royal Commission on Marriage and Divorce, London, 1956.

Report of the Select Committee on Obscene Publications, London, 1958.

Stone, Lawrence. *Road to Divorce: England, 1530–1987*, Oxford, 1992.
Summerskill, Edith. *A Woman's World*, London, 1967.
Wolfenden, John. 'The Permissive Society', *Proceedings of the Royal Institution of Great Britain*, vol.46, 1973, pp.19–35.
Wootton, Barbara. 'Holiness or Happiness', *The Twentieth Century*, vol.158, 1955, pp.407–16.

Censorship

Aldgate, Anthony. *Censorship and the Permissive Society: British Cinema and Theatre, 1955–65*, Oxford, 1995.
Arts Council Working Party. *The Obscenity Laws*, London, 1969.
Barker, Martin. *A Haunt of Fears: The Strange History of the British Horror Comics Campaign*, London, 1984.
Bell, Clive. *On British Freedom*, London, 1923.
Cloonan, Martin. *Banned! Censorship of Popular Music in Britain, 1967–92*, Aldershot, 1996.
Johnston, John. *The Lord Chamberlain's Blue Pencil*, London, 1990.
Joynson-Hicks, William, Viscount Brentford. *Do We Need A Censor?*, London, 1929.
Lawrence, D.H. *Pornography and Obscenity*, London, 1929.
Palmer, Tony. *The Trials of Oz*, London, 1971.
Pornography: The Longford Report, London, 1972.
Robertson, Geoffrey. *Obscenity: An Account of Censorship Laws and Their Enforcement in England and Wales*, London, 1979.
Robertson, James C. *The Hidden Cinema: British Film Censorship in Action, 1913–75* (rev. edn), London, 1993.
Rolph, C.H. (ed.). *The Trial of Lady Chatterley*, Harmondsworth, 1961.
St John-Stevas, Norman. *Obscenity and the Law*, London, 1956.
Sutherland, John. *Offensive Literature: Decensorship in Britain, 1960–82*, London, 1982.
Thompson, Bill. *Soft Core: Moral Crusades against Pornography in Britain and America*, London, 1994.
Travis, Alan. *Bound and Gagged: A Secret History of Obscenity in Britain*, London, 2000.
Trevelyan, John. *What the Censor Saw*, London, 1973.

Anti-Permissiveness

Anderson, Digby (ed.). *The Loss of Virtue: Moral Confusion and Social Disorder in Britain and America*, London, 1992.
Bristow, Edward J. *Vice and Vigilance: Purity Movements in Britain since 1700*, Dublin,

1977.
Capon, John. *And There Was Light: The Story of the Nationwide Festival of Light*, London, 1972.
Hansford Johnson, Pamela. *On Iniquity: Some Personal Reflections Arising Out of the Moors Murder Trial*, London, 1967.
Hitchens, Peter. *The Abolition of Britain: The British Cultural Revolution from Lady Chatterley to Tony Blair* (rev. edn), London, 2000.
Holbrook, David. *The Pseudo-Revolution: A Critical Study of Extremist 'Liberation' in Sex*, London, 1972.
Johnson, Paul. *Wake Up Britain!*, London, 1994.
The Nation's Morals: Proceedings of the Public Morals Conference, London, 1910.
Tracey, Michael and David Morrison. *Whitehouse*, London, 1979.
Whitehouse, Mary. *Whatever Happened to Sex?*, Hove, 1977.
Whitehouse, Mary. *Who Does She Think She Is?*, London, 1971.

Protest Movements

McKay, George (ed.). *DIY Culture: Party and Protest in Nineties Britain*, London, 1998.
Stephens, Julie. *Anti-Disciplinary Protest: Sixties Radicalism and Postmodernism*, Cambridge, 1998.
Byrne, Paul. *Social Movements in Britain*, London, 1997.
Cockburn, Alexander and Robin Blackburn. *Student Power: Problems, Diagnosis, Action*, Harmondsworth, 1969.
Devlin, Bernadette. *The Price of My Soul*, New York, 1969.
Duff, Peggy. *Left, Left, Left*, London, 1971.
Hornsey College of Art Students and Staff. *The Hornsey Affair*, Harmondsworth, 1969.
Lent, Adam. *British Social Movements since 1945: Sex, Colour, Peace and Power*, Basingstoke, 2001.
Parkin, Frank. *Middle-Class Radicalism: The Social Bases of the British Campaign for Nuclear Disarmament*, Manchester, 1968.
Taylor, Richard and Colin Pritchard. *The Protest Makers: The British Nuclear Disarmament Movement of 1958–65, Twenty Years On*, Oxford, 1980.
Thomas, Nick. 'Challenging Myths of the 1960s: The Case of Student Protest in Britain', *Twentieth-Century British History*, vol.13, no.3, 2002, pp.277–97.

Women's Liberation

Allen, Sandra et al. (eds). *Conditions of Illusion: Papers from the Women's Movement*, Leeds, 1974.
Campaign for Homosexual Equality. *Women Together: Report of a Meeting of Women*

from the Gay Movement and from the Women's Movement, Manchester, 1973.

Feminist Anthology Collective. *No Turning Back: Writings for the Women's Liberation Movement, 1975–80*, London, 1981.

Greer, Germaine. *The Female Eunuch*, London, 1970.

Kappeler, Susanne. *The Pornography of Representation*, Cambridge, 1986.

Love Your Enemy?: The Debate between Heterosexual Feminism and Political Lesbianism, London, 1981.

Lovenduski, Joni and Vicky Randall. *Contemporary Feminist Politics: Women and Power in Britain*, Oxford, 1993.

Mitchell, Juliet. *Women's Estate*, Harmondsworth, 1971.

Oakley, Ann. *Sex, Gender and Society*, London, 1972.

Rhodes, Dusty and Sandra McNeill (eds). *Women Against Violence Against Women*, London, 1985.

Roseneil, Sasha. *Common Women, Uncommon Practices: The Queer Feminism of Greenham*, London, 2000.

Rowbotham, Sheila. *Promise of a Dream: Remembering the Sixties*, London, 2000.

Sebestyen, Amanda (ed.). *'68, '78, '88: From Women's Liberation to Feminism*, Bridport, 1988.

Segal, Lynne. *Straight Sex: The Politics of Pleasure*, London, 1994.

Setch, Eve. 'The Face of Metropolitan Feminism: The London Women's Liberation Workshop, 1969–79', *Twentieth-Century British History*, vol.13, no.2, 2002, pp.17–37.

Setch, Eve. 'The Women's Liberation Movement in Britain, 1969–79: Organisation, Creativity and Debate', University of London PhD thesis, 2001.

Six Point Group. *In Her Own Right*, London, 1968.

Wandor, Michelene (ed.). *The Body Politic: Writings from the Women's Liberation Movement in Britain, 1969–72*, London, 1972.

Comparative Works

Crow, Thomas. *The Rise of the Sixties: American and European Art in the Era of Dissent*, London, 1996.

Fraser, Ronald (ed.). *1968: A Student Generation in Revolt*, New York, 1988.

Inglehart, Ronald, Miguel Basañez and Alejandro Moreno. *Human Values and Beliefs: A Cross-Cultural Sourcebook*, Ann Arbor, MI, 1998.

Inglehart, Ronald. *The Silent Revolution: Changing Values and Political Styles among Western Publics*, Princeton, NJ, 1977.

Kern, Stephen. *The Culture of Love: Victorians and Moderns*, Cambridge, MA, 1992.

Kurlansky, Mark. *1968: The Year That Rocked the World*, New York, 2003.

Marwick, Arthur. *The Sixties: Cultural Revolution in Britain, France, Italy and the United States, c. 1958–74*, Oxford, 1998.

Mellor, David Alan and Laurent Gervereau (eds). *The Sixties: Britain and France, 1962–73*, London, 1997.
Roszak, Theodore. *The Making of a Counter Culture* (rev. edn), Berkeley, CA, 1995.

The United States

Anderson, Terry H. *The Movement and the Sixties*, New York, 1995.
Bailey, Beth. *Sex in the Heartland*, Cambridge, MA, 1999.
Braunstein, Peter and Michael William Doyle (eds). *Imagine Nation: The American Counterculture of the 1960s and 1970s*, New York, 2002.
Dickstein, Morris. *Gates of Eden: American Culture in the Sixties* (rev. edn), Cambridge, MA, 1997.
Ehrenreich, Barbara, Elizabeth Hess and Gloria Jacobs. *Re-Making Love: The Feminization of Sex*, London, 1986.
Farber, David (ed.). *The Sixties: From Memory to History*, Chapel Hill, NC, 1994.
Frank, Thomas. *The Conquest of Cool: Business Culture, Counterculture, and the Rise of Hip Consumerism*, Chicago, 1997.
Freeman, Jo (ed.). *Social Movements of the Sixties and Seventies*, New York, 1983.
Heidenry, John. *What Wild Ecstasy: The Rise and Fall of the Sexual Revolution*, New York, 1997.
Matusow, Allen J. *The Unraveling of America: A History of Liberalism in the 1960s*, New York, 1986.
Miller, Jim. *Democracy Is In The Streets*, New York, 1987.
Tischler, Barbara L. (ed.). *Sights on the Sixties*, New Brunswick, NJ, 1992.
Waugh, Thomas. *Hard to Imagine: Gay Male Eroticism in Photography and Film from the Beginnings to Stonewall*, New York, 1996.

Continental Europe

Herzog, Dagmar. *Sex After Fascism: Memory and Morality in Twentieth-Century Germany*, Princeton, NJ, 2005.
Lumley, Robert. *States of Emergency: Cultures of Revolt in Italy from 1968 to 1978*, London, 1990.
Mendras, Henri and Alistair Cole. *Social Change in Modern France: Towards a Cultural Anthropology of the Fifth Republic*, Cambridge, 1988.
Poiger, Uta G. *Jazz, Rock, and Rebels: Cold War Politics and American Culture in a Divided Germany*, Berkeley, CA, 2000.
von Dirke, Sabine. *'All Power to the Imagination': The West German Counterculture from the Student Movement to the Greens*, Lincoln, NE, 1997.

Index